Crossings and Encounters

The Carolina Lowcountry and the Atlantic World

Sponsored by the Program in the Carolina Lowcountry and the Atlantic World of the College of Charleston

Crossings and Encounters

Race, Gender, and Sexuality in the Atlantic World

EDITED BY

Laura R. Prieto and Stephen R. Berry

THE UNIVERSITY OF
SOUTH CAROLINA PRESS

Published by the University of South Carolina Press
Columbia, South Carolina 29208

www.uscpress.com

Manufactured in the United States of America

29 28 27 26 25 24 23 22 21 20
10 9 8 7 6 5 4 3 2

Library of Congress Cataloging-in-Publication Data
can be found at http://catalog.loc.gov/.

ISBN: 978-1-64336-084-3 (hardcover)
ISBN: 978-1-64336-085-0 (ebook)

Contents

Acknowledgments

Our thanks go first of all to Sandy Slater, who organized the annual conference on the Carolina Lowcountry and Atlantic World at the College of Charleston that brought many of us together. Sandy provided wise counsel, unflagging encouragement, and good humor every step of the way.

We are also grateful for the intellectual generosity of colleagues—especially Richard Godbeer, John W. White, and Terri Snyder—who made insightful recommendations on the shape that this essay collection might take. It was a delight working with the contributors to this project, and we feel fortunate that they were willing to share their research in a collaborative volume. At the University of South Carolina Press, Alex Moore, Linda Fogle, Jonathan Haupt, Simon Lewis, Richard Brown, and Ehren Foley have shown vast patience with our slow progress bringing the complete manuscript together. Our colleagues and students at Simmons University kept us motivated by asking about the book at appropriate junctures. Sarah Leonard, Zhigang Liu, Steve Ortega, Jess Parr, and Franny Sullivan make for the most genial, supportive History Department one could hope for. Laura Koch, our graduate assistant, provided scrupulous, sharp-eyed assistance at the formative stages, while Stephen Berry Jr. helped locate illustrations.

As with any scholarly publication, the research in this book depended on the assiduous work of librarians and archivists from institutions across the Atlantic. The essays within made substantial use of collections from the Archives Nationales d'Outre Mer in Aix-en-Provence, the Archivo General de la Nación of Mexico, the Arquivo da Cúria Metropolitana de São Paulo, the Arquivo do Estado de São Paulo, the British Library, the Massachusetts Historical Society, the Nationaal Archief of the Netherlands, the National Archives of the United States, the New Orleans Public Library, the New York State Archives, and the Notarial Archives Research Center in New Orleans. While we are unfortunately unable to name all of the individuals who contributed at each institution, the editors do want to single out some in particular. Amanda Strauss, Robin Wheelwright Ness, and Peter Harrington of the Brown University Libraries graciously gave us access to an elusive illustration; they truly embody the ethos of a research-centered institution. Sabina Beauchard at the Massachusetts Historical Society helped us secure permissions to materials there. We want to thank Mark Allan for sharing with us his lovely professional photographs from the Barbican's production of

Desdemona. Mark Cook not only provided the volume with two beautiful maps but was a joy to work with during the project's final stages.

As always, we deeply appreciate how our respective families and friends sustain and support us. For every time they may have distracted us from our allotted writing and editing time, they have rescued us tenfold with their love.

Foreword

In this collection of essays, a variety of presentations, by established as well as burgeoning scholars, creates a sustained dialogue. This leads to wonderfully dynamic and interesting conversations and debates.

The mission of the Carolina Lowcountry and the Atlantic World (CLAW) Program is "to promote scholarship and public engagement with the history and culture of the Lowcountry region, the Atlantic World, and the connections between the two." A reflection of this mission, this collection brings together not just a wealth of detailed scholarship but also the variety of ways in which race, gender, and sexuality intersect in the Atlantic world. These essays encompass a variety of geographies, peoples, and events, yet all speak to the incredible diversity of experience. The myriad cultures and communities that contested space, identities, and terrain reflect the continual exchange of ideas in the Atlantic world. The cross-cultural encounters dramatically altered conceptions of gender, sexuality, and the creation of racist and misogynistic regimes of power.

I am especially proud of the interdisciplinary nature of these essays. Though most of the scholars represented here would identify as historians, these essays also incorporate literature, geography, migration patterns, family dynamics, religion, and politics, not to mention studies of the multiplicities of identities. Yet through all the upheaval and exchange, the Atlantic Ocean remains omnipresent, touching shores, moving people, and undulating in the background as the mighty facilitator. The one constant is this body of water that serves as a canvas upon which these histories were painted, layer after layer, by the actors and events and then again by historians. One of the allures of studying the Atlantic is the paradox of its richness and depth viewed against its intangibility; the whole can never be grasped. However, these eight essays offer insight into that enigmatic history and call our attention to the complexities of these divergent lived experiences, bonded by water and change.

Sandra Slater

Stephen R. Berry

Introduction

Look at most world maps, and the Atlantic Ocean sits near the center, bordered on the left by the Americas and on the right by Africa, Europe, and Asia, with Oceania relegated to the margins. In this common depiction, the Atlantic Ocean stands as a carefully demarcated point of reference, an unchanging fact enduring through the centuries. This cartographic fixedness masks the process of discovery that "invented" the unified Atlantic from a mixture of locally known coastal seas and newly encountered places. In the fifteenth century, mapmakers preferred the label "the Western Ocean" for the body of water they placed on the edge of the known world. Rather than establishing a static point of reference, the evolution of world maps indicates how the Atlantic Ocean has moved quite literally from border to center. Furthermore, a modern map cannot convey the multitude of changes that have continually shaped this oceanic region in the five centuries since surveyors first started to sketch the full scope of its ever-shifting shorelines. In reality, the label Atlantic Ocean conveys an ongoing process as much as a stable place even before one considers the complicated human interactions with that geography.[1]

While evidence suggests that people occasionally traversed the Atlantic before Christopher Columbus's epochal expedition in 1492, the Spanish-sponsored mariner initiated an ongoing relationship between its disparate shores. The environmental consequences of this sustained transatlantic intercourse perhaps best illustrate the creation of this "New World." The "Columbian Exchange" reshaped the physical world as ships intentionally and unintentionally transported fauna, flora, and fungi across the oceanic barrier, which had previously facilitated the development of separate biospheres. Some species thrived in their new environments, while others struggled against new rivals and predators. Above all, this exchange involved the transfer of human beings. Millions of men and women, free and enslaved, traversed the Atlantic in the subsequent centuries. Their crossings

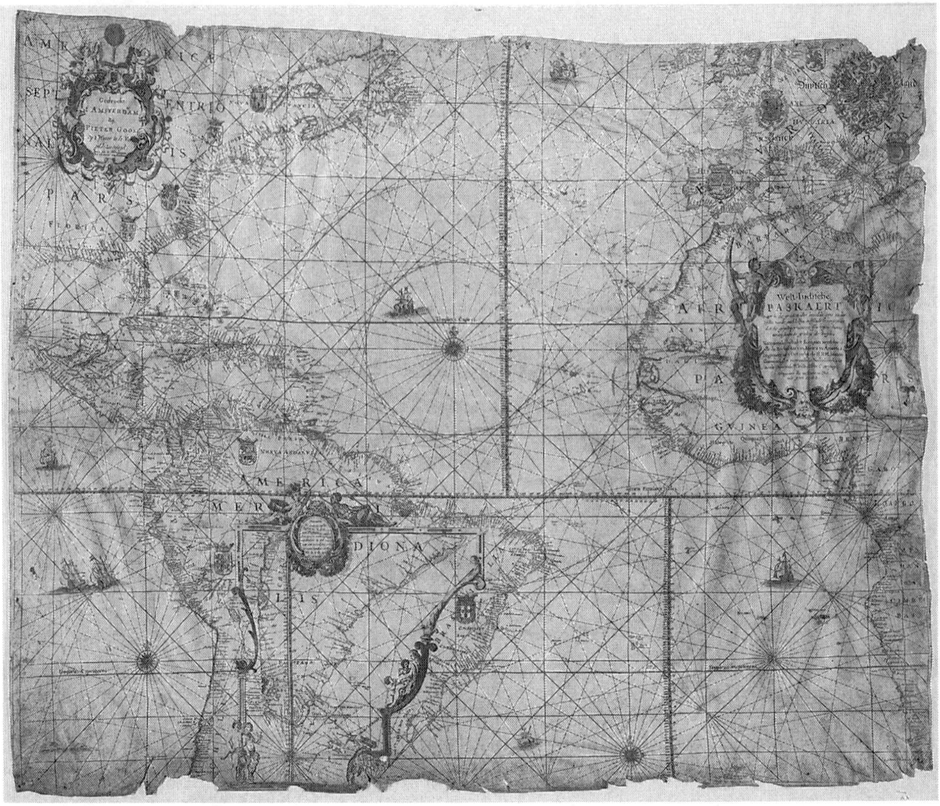

West Indische Paskaert (1650). Lionel Pincus and Princess Firyal Map Division, The New York Public Library. New York Public Library Digital Collections.

bore not only bodies and goods but also ideas and identities. Different views of the natural and spiritual worlds collided to remake further the physical landscape encountered by its inhabitants. These environmental "changes in the land" provided tangible markers of ideological processes. Cultural exchanges took place alongside the biological ones.[2]

For travelers and traders, refugees and indigenous peoples alike, the Atlantic context opened a new sense of self. The "discovery" of the New World unsettled how those on each continent subsisted and thought of themselves, exploding the boundaries of both lived experience and imagined possibilities. Studies of the encounters between the colonists and indigenous peoples of North America capture the cultural dynamism of this era, succinctly indicated in such titles as *The Indians' New World, The Middle Ground,* and *New Worlds for All.* Such encounters involved societal self-examination and adaptation, as well as cultural

Detail of African Cartouche from West Indische Paskaert (1650). Lionel Pincus and Princess Firyal Map Division, The New York Public Library. New York Public Library Digital Collections.

imposition and resistance. Newly encountered peoples had to be mapped, both geographically and conceptually. The cartographic depictions of a rapidly changing post-Columbus world frequently included visual depictions of representative peoples as well as newly denominated places. Their coloring, clothing (or lack of it), and accompanying commodities signified both these peoples' physical locations and their symbolic places in a developing hierarchy of humanity.[3]

As peoples moved around and through the Atlantic, their encounters with others forced new categorizations of human differences. For example, the maritime historian Marcus Rediker identified the slave ship as the instrument that forged ideas of racial difference: "In producing workers for the plantation, the ship factory also produced 'race.'" Aboard ship, the ethnically and nationally diverse "motley crew" became "white men," and the equally diverse peoples of the African continent swept into transatlantic slavery became "black." The interaction produced new internal and external definitions of self. As a recent handbook of Atlantic history defined this process, "The concept of ethnogenesis, or the invention and reproduction of a sense of collective self, has emerged as a powerful tool for describing the building and rebuilding of cultures in response to the movements of people and inventions of new institutions that marked the Atlantic World." The varied and changing myriad cultures occupying each of the continents sought new explanations or hardened old ones when they encountered an abundance of new peoples.[4]

Just as with maps of the Atlantic, previously fluid and flexible markers of identity assumed the appearance of fixedness in the centuries after first contact. While European overseas conquests primarily sought political and economic expansion, they also involved legal and intellectual shifts in the understanding of sexual and racial difference. Atlantic societies attached these culturally contrived meanings to perceived biological differences. In terms of race, multiple scholars have argued that the concept itself was a distinct product of the Columbian Exchange. In the words of the historian Joyce Chaplin, "perhaps more than any other set of ideas, race was Atlantic."[5] Although, as a means of stratifying society, race permeated the Atlantic world, the variety of classification systems circulating in that world aptly illustrates the mercurial nature of racial distinctions. Peoples' racial identifications could change both over time and as they moved between places.

An episode recorded in the logbook of the Rhode Island privateer *Revenge* dramatically depicts the fragile and flexible status of an Atlantic creole amid the religious and political conflicts of the eighteenth century. In 1741, the privateer recaptured a Boston sloop, which the "proud Dons" had seized in the previous days. The *Revenge*'s crew interrogated a black militiaman from Saint Augustine named Francisco Menéndez, who commanded the Spanish prize crew. Menéndez hailed from a thriving free black community outside Saint Augustine, Mose (or Fort Mose as the British termed it), which included numerous men and women who had escaped enslavement in South Carolina. During the first years of the War of Jenkins' Ear, General James Oglethorpe led a failed expedition against Saint Augustine, during which a combined force of Spanish, free black, and Native American militias attacked Oglethorpe's force at Mose, killing seventy-five of the invaders in an event that the British Atlantic remembered as "Bloody Mose" or "Fatal Mose." The men aboard the *Revenge* accused Menéndez of leading the "Comp[an]y that had gived the English so barborously when taken att the Fort." Menéndez initially denied the accusation but later confessed after extensive flogging and threat of castration. Before the admiralty court in New Providence, Bahamas, the *Revenge* requested that Menéndez be sold into slavery and the proceeds distributed along with the other shares of the privateer's profits. Using a mixture of torture-derived hearsay and theological rationale, the *Revenge*'s representative contended that the barbarities of this supposedly free, supposedly Catholic Spaniard proved that he did not have "the least drop of blood either of liberty or Christianity." The court sided with the Rhode Islanders. Francisco Menéndez was sold alongside the ship he had once commanded.[6]

Studies of the Atlantic world often emphasize the possibilities for change that the intersections of the multiple cultures inhabiting the Atlantic basin offered people. Individuals from colonized or disempowered groups demonstrated the hybridity and fluidity of status through their active negotiation of the space created in the margins and meetings of empires. Like others of African descent, Menéndez demonstrated how, in the marchland between Spanish and British colonies, an Atlantic creole successfully used imperial needs for personal advancement. Yet, Menéndez's case also illustrates that fluidity of status had negative consequences. The British binary of race placed him in the role of slave, not leader. The Roman Catholic identity that gained him greater acceptance in Florida became a liability when he was in British hands. The advantages that free blacks enjoyed in one part of the Atlantic could quickly turn into liabilities elsewhere.

Racial concepts emerged within particular Atlantic contexts that shifted according to the political and economic needs of distinct locations. Closely tied to the economic exploitation of chattel slavery and the uses of political power, the concept of racial difference outlived many of the institutions from which it originated while not losing its power to define. Perceived distinctions of culture, religion, and ethnicity gradually calcified into modern concepts of race, but with tremendous mutability and contextual differences.[7]

At the same time that racial categories developed, profoundly different definitions of masculinity and femininity, of marriage and family, and of legitimate sexual expression clashed from the first contacts on. While not products of the Columbian Exchange, the meanings attached to sexuality and sexual difference played an integral role in the development of the Atlantic world while themselves being shaped by the cultures they had helped to produce. European notions of gender played a crucial role in the narration and justification of the discovery of previously unknown virgin lands. This gendering of previously unknown spaces symbolically justified the subsequent physical invasions of the various European powers that sought to reproduce their cultures in a fertile (and, in their depictions, not yet inseminated) space. This rhetorical employment of gender accompanied other symbols that established rightful and legal possession of previously inhabited and cultivated spaces.[8]

The exporting of traditional "gender roles and household structures to the new colonies was a critical part of achieving colonial success," while the maintenance of indigenous peoples' own gender-defined practices proved a vital part of resistance to cultural outsiders.[9] For example, in colonial Virginia, Algonquian males derided attempts to induce them to adopt settled farming, simultaneously mocking Englishmen who performed what in their eyes was women's work. For the English, Algonquian women's "drudgery" and the men's "indolent" hunting clearly marked the natives as cultural inferiors.[10]

As with racial conceptions, gendered expectations varied between places and changed over time. The prior Iberian encounter with Islam led to an emphasis on containing female sexuality in order to maintain familial honor while allowing males to demonstrate their masculinity through their sexual exploits. The picaresque tale of Catalina de Erauso readily illustrates the gendered aspects of Iberian familial expectations and how exploitation of the New World could challenge performance of those sexually defined roles. A Basque woman who fled the cloistered life a Dominican convent in San Sebastián, Spain, de Erauso remade herself as a man, crossed the Atlantic, and participated in the ongoing seventeenth-century Spanish process of conquering Chile. In a journey filled with petty disputes that quickly escalated into violent conflicts, de Erauso traversed South America with a hyper display of Spanish masculinity, wooing women and crossing swords with men (including a duel in which she killed her own brother). When she finally revealed her biological sex in confession to a bishop, the story of her adventures spread across the Atlantic, leading to a military pension for La Monja Alférez (the Lieutenant Nun) from the Spanish Crown and a papal dispensation from Pope Urban VIII that allowed her to continue dressing in men's clothing. Exchanging her habit for a sword opened new worlds for de Erauso; crossing the Atlantic allowed her to reinvent herself in ways that both challenged and conformed to societal norms.[11]

Rather than evolving as separate discussions, concerns about race and gender intertwined throughout the Atlantic. Communities looked to fixed roles for a sense of order, yet the fluid, contingent nature of the Atlantic world enabled some individuals to transcend their assigned roles and remake themselves. As Eliga Gould noted in his response to Jorge Cañizares-Esguerra regarding the cross-pollination possible in borderland spaces, "The peripheries of the Spanish- and English-speaking Atlantic empires produced a disproportionate number of non-European intermediaries and go-betweens, some of whom wielded influence that reached to the highest levels of national power."[12] These dynamic relationships among gender, sexualities, and race have captivated a generation of Atlantic Studies researchers since the 1970s. *Crossings and Encounters: Race, Gender, and Sexuality in the Atlantic World* gathers innovative work on these three key themes that have come to dominate current historical scholarship. The essays include contributions by both senior and emerging young scholars. The essay topics range broadly from contact zones in the seventeenth-century Americas to the postcolonial present, and they cover the full range of the Atlantic world, with a focus on the Caribbean, North America, and Latin America. Collectively, the essays reveal the Atlantic as a fertile site for the construction of identities and communities. They offer fresh analytical insights and rethink traditional narratives, with significant implications beyond each essay's particular focus.[13]

In the past two decades, Atlantic history has become the principle medium for scholars studying the colonial era. One visible way to trace this trend is to review article titles that have appeared in the major outlets for the study of early American history and culture. In April 1999, the *William and Mary Quarterly* published a theme issue on the "African and American Atlantic Worlds." Prior to this issue, the word "Atlantic" had appeared in only four article titles published by the journal. Since its appearance, the quarterly has published four dozen articles whose titles include this oceanic descriptor and other theme issues devoted to "Slaveries in the Atlantic World" and "Centering Families in Atlantic Histories." No wonder David Armitage could declare, in a 2002 essay, "we are all Atlanticists now—or so it would seem." While a relatively recent and still expanding field, the label "Atlantic" has quickly become the discursive norm in historical study. The author of a twenty-year retrospective on Marcus Rediker's *Between the Devil and the Deep Blue Sea* opined that "today, a book on this topic would undoubtedly have 'Atlantic' somewhere in the title." The Atlantic approach "has often been reduced to little more than buzzword, badge of cultural capital, or useful signaling shorthand in grant proposals," as Peter Coclanis has repeatedly cautioned. This universal but maddeningly indefinite use of the Atlantic as an organizing device has "sucked up a lot of scholarly air and seized a lot of scholarly space," perhaps to the detriment of other possible historical explanations or perspectives.[14]

The broad temporal and geographical scope represented by the essays in this volume illustrates both the possibilities and the difficulties involved in Atlantic history. Taken together, the following essays develop Paul Gilroy's suggestion that "cultural historians could take the Atlantic as one single, complex unit of analysis in their discussions of the modern world and use it to produce an explicitly transnational and intercultural perspective." While often focusing on particular national settings, the following essays see borders as entangled and permeable while emphasizing the hybrid nature of post-Columbian societies in the Americas and Caribbean. Rather than suggesting a unified Atlantic revolving around a central hub, however, the essays demonstrate the complex range of responses to similar processes of cultural engagement.[15]

In order to provide interpretive clarity as to what the term "Atlantic" means in terms of distinct historical analysis, David Armitage has crafted a trichotomous classification of Atlantic approaches that helpfully explains this volume's particular contributions to the field. The first, and least investigated, conceptualization of this oceanic space Armitage labels "circum-Atlantic," referring to "the history of the Atlantic as a particular zone of exchange and interchange, circulation and transmission." In other words, circum-Atlantic history seeks to understand the oceanic unit as a whole and not merely as the summation of its various regions. A second approach, which Armitage identified as "trans-Atlantic," emphasizes

Map of the Atlantic World by Mark Cook (2019).

comparison. The interconnections within the common oceanic zone allow for the side-by-side examination of processes in different regions. Because of the linguistic range and historiographical breadth that these approaches require, they might be best undertaken by a collection of scholars rather than just a single individual. Collectively, the essays in this volume understand the phenomena of race, gender, and sexuality as proceeding in a common Atlantic *mentalité* variously manifested in each particular context. While no single essay examines race, gender, and sexuality in the Atlantic world as a whole and while the coverage is far from comprehensive, taken together the essays produce a bricolage portrait of these topics that allows meaningful comparisons of the different situations. Or, to use the metaphor of Patrick Griffin, rather than a map of the overall Atlantic experience, the stories that follow represent a type of sea chart tracing the movements and interactions of people.[16]

Most of the published historical scholarship that bears the appellation "Atlantic" falls into Armitage's third category, "cis-Atlantic," which describes works that focus on the broader cultural connections of a particular place. The essays in this volume exemplify this approach in their investigations of distinct and distinctly different communities within Spanish, Portuguese, English, or Dutch contexts. Such studies utilize the specificity that comes with a local study while maintaining the outward ties and comparative milieus that link diverse oceanic regions. Unlike circum-Atlantic approaches that summarize a broad range of existing scholarship, these works focus on unfolding new sources or interpreting particular phenomena within the contextual web of Atlantic connections. The inherent weakness of such approaches is that they can continue narrow national narratives rather than breaking the boundaries of traditional imperial storylines. Jorge Cañizares-Esguerra and Benjamin Breen succinctly warned of this inherent problem: "Works of Atlantic history have repeatedly emphasized themes of interconnection, circulation, encounter, and exchange. Yet, national or linguistic boundaries often limit the underlying research behind these studies. Scholarship on British, Dutch, French, Spanish, and Portuguese Atlantics follows separate trajectories."[17]

This work attempts to avoid the obstacles of traditional national boundaries by placing a diverse range of scholarship within a single Atlantic context, creating comparative parallels between the various discourses of race, gender and sexuality. The specific processes of defining cultural identity varied from locale to locale, but when these discourses are viewed alongside one another, common themes emerge. For example, the role that religion played in creating and defining difference emerges in several of the essays. As Deborah Hamer argues within her essay on Dutch-Indian marital and sexual relationships in the seventeenth century, conversion to Christianity proved useful in overcoming strictures that prohibited illicit sexual encounters, because the foundation of these prohibitions was religious, not racial. Policing of these marital relationships represented attempts to use sexual mores to establish cultural identities. Michele Mericle's study of Inquisitorial persecutions of the Portuguese community of Mexico City discovered not just that authorities confronted a supposed "judaizing" conspiracy that undermined religious conformity but that this particular auto-de-fé focused on a commercial network of women. The persecution of "rabinas" not only sought ends of religious conformity but also pursued unstated gender goals by limiting the cultural power of ambitious Portuguese women within Spanish Mexico.

Religious beliefs or organizations not only enforced boundaries but also created discursive and institutional spaces that allowed independent thought and cultural identity to thrive. Other scholars have noted the role of religious communities in fostering alternate power dynamics for women and for people of color in the Atlantic world, but Alicia Monroe unfolds the role of secular organizations in creating a new sense of masculinity for Afro-Brazilian men after emancipation. Alternatives to religious orders and confraternities, organizations such as the Masons and the Beneficent Society of Men of Color served the purposes of both advocacy and mutual aid. Beyond the temporal aid that they provided for members, these organizations functioned to instill a distinct sense of black masculinity in the face of continued racial inequality after emancipation.[18]

Another comparative theme that collectively emerges from these essays is the power of writing both to establish and to undermine cultural boundaries. Few people ever experienced the Atlantic world in its physical totality, so other forms of communication created powerful imaginings of the people and cultures on disparate shores. Travel narratives profoundly shaped people's perceptions of places that they would never visit, even Ned Ward's ineloquent, satirical account of *A Trip to Jamaica,* which Erika Gasser places in the context of late seventeenth-century London's misogynistic pamphlet literature. As Gasser notes, understanding Ward's work is valuable not because of its accuracy or detail of colonial societies but for showing how a vituperative portrait of colonial women—English, Native, or African—shaped English views of the colonies. Gasser argues that Ward employed the familiar satirical paradoxical portrait of the frail yet dominating female to represent colonial spaces to such an extent that the misogyny overwhelms the colonial description. Similarly, the Dutch literature promoting gender and sexual norms that Deborah Hamer examines created the conditions for sexual encounters in the New Netherlands.

Writing about colonial spaces and subjects offered a mechanism for defining oneself, and texts could reveal variations between cultural interpretations. Laura R. Prieto describes the role of groundbreaking historical research and writing about the "tripulantes"—members of Christopher Columbus's crew—in the life and transformation of Alice Bache Gould. Gould's intellectual immersion in the Atlantic world and her exploration of common sailors manifested the ability of Atlantic crossings to open new worlds even for a Massachusetts-born woman in the age of steam at the beginning of the twentieth century. Writing had the power to transform, but texts themselves could be transformed through specific cultural interpretations, particularly in terms of dramatic performance. In her essay, Tessa Roynon explores how the performance piece *Desdemona* resonates differently depending on where it is displayed. A response to issues of race and gender raised in William Shakespeare's *Othello, Desdemona* demonstrates the fluidity of these historical categories as reimagined in various postcolonial sites around the Atlantic.

Another salient aspect that emerges from this volume's explorations of race, gender, and sexuality in the Atlantic world is the role of mobility in reshaping power dynamics and opportunities. Physical relocation as well as writing stimulated Alice Bache Gould's transformation. As Prieto aptly notes, Gould's extended sojourn in Puerto Rico enabled her to escape the hold of domesticity and the affliction of neurasthenia and opened doors into other academic fields. Mobility facilitated change not just for individuals but also for groups, as Elizabeth Neidenbach argues regarding female Haitian migrants in the Revolutionary era. Neidenbach uses notary documents recorded in Cuba, New Orleans, and Charleston to reconstruct the movement of free women of color between 1791 and 1810, showing their successful re-creation of their livelihoods and lifestyles despite the barriers of race, gender, and dislocation.

Neidenbach's account also shows how otherwise marginalized figures skillfully used legal systems and documents to secure personal and familial legacies. While other scholars have noted the power discrepancies that resulted from the European imposition of printed legal documents to deprive native peoples of land and sovereignty, those same notary processes could be utilized to establish and secure ownership of oneself and one's property. For free women of color, Neidenbach argues, arrival at a new port city required securing necessary paperwork, which then served as a bulwark against future challenges to status. Similarly, Joshua Bearden explores two court cases involving Native women from interracial backgrounds who attempted to protect their property and status amid the turmoil of Indian removal in the 1830s. Western legal traditions of coverture conflicted with Native traditions regarding matrilineal property and divorce, and the courts in Mississippi and Alabama rendered decisions that acknowledged the hybrid situation that emerged from the entangled cultures of the colonial frontier. As Bearden notes, "Native women of interracial heritage attempted to wrap themselves in the mantle of white womanhood in efforts to maintain their traditional property rights in Native society." Western expansion in the late eighteenth and early nineteenth centuries required the developing nation-state to address the racial aspects of citizenship and the role of women in the body politic.[19]

Collectively, these essays demonstrate the complicated interactions of multiple cultures within an Atlantic context, suggesting that many of the modern world's continuing struggles with issues of race, gender, and human sexuality evolved out of these particular interactions. Indeed, a principal contribution of this volume is the manner in which it extends the device of Atlantic history into the present. While 1492 provides a seemingly unambiguous beginning to Atlantic history, no scholarly consensus establishes a definitive end to the era. Some scholars bring the era of the Atlantic world to a close at the beginning of the nineteenth century, as waves of revolution significantly diminished the role of transatlantic empires in the Americas, and Europe increasingly dedicated itself to the projects of colonizing

Africa and Asia. In this telling, the Atlantic world was succeeded by a Pacific one, which presents a troubling chronology that, as Peter Coclanis notes, misses the crucial role that Asia played in the earlier period.[20] This timeline also neglects the continuing importance and distinct development of Atlantic constructs into the twentieth century. Other historians track the Atlantic story through the end of African slavery in the Americas, as Brazil's "Golden Act" of 1888 brought the institution to a close.[21] Yet this narration, too, has its problems, particularly in the way it diminishes the broader complications of the continued racial and political struggles that followed colonialism and slavery in the Americas.

As Monroe's, Prieto's, and Roynon's essays in this volume show, salient connections exist between the Atlantic worlds of the sixteenth and seventeenth centuries and those of the twentieth and twenty-first. The entanglements created by the intermingling of peoples and cultures from the Americas, Africa, and Europe continue, and not just in terms of political organizations like NATO. As Deborah Hamer demonstrates regarding Dutch attitudes toward mixed marriages in seventeenth-century Brazil, people adapted laws and customs created previously in a different context to regulate and understand their own. The hybrid entanglements of the Atlantic colonial era produced distinct cultural formulations regarding race and gender. The political and legal changes of independence and emancipation further complicated understandings of sexual and racial identity as people sought to define themselves in new ways.

Deborah Hamer

"Our Dutchmen run after them very much"

Cross-Cultural Sex in New Netherland and the Dutch Global Empire

Writing in 1960, Allen Trelease argued that, as a "frontier," New Netherland was characterized by the "opportunity" for cross-cultural sex. Lacking in sources that would offer quantitative evidence as to the prevalence of this cross-cultural sex, Trelease resorted instead to comparison: cross-cultural sex was more common in New Netherland than in New England but less common in the Dutch colony than in French and Spanish colonies.[1] In the absence of a significant body of sources to draw on in writing about cross-cultural sex and marriage in New Netherland, thinking comparatively has proven attractive to a number of historians. Tom Midtrød situates his discussion of mixed-race people in New Netherland in the context of the developing *métis* identity in New France, and Nan A. Rothschild compares Dutch–Mohawk interactions in the upper Hudson Valley with Spanish–Pueblo interactions in the Southwest to throw into relief the minimal nature of the Dutch–Mohawk connection when measured against the Spanish–Pueblo one.[2] Other historians have simply thrown their hands up in despair at the idea of investigating cross-cultural sex, offering the few surviving references as evidence that this sex was "regular" in New Netherland, but not particularly significant.[3]

While comparison has been a key part of the arsenal that historians have used to understand cross-cultural sex in New Netherland, its use has focused on relating Dutch practices to those of other European empires in the Americas. But comparisons between the Dutch in New Netherland and the Dutch in other parts of their seventeenth-century global empire remain underdeveloped.[4] By situating

New Netherland within a larger context, it becomes clear just how much of an outlier New Netherland was on the Dutch global scene. Christian marriages and alternative ways of organizing long-term, cross-cultural relationships were common across the Dutch world, but in New Netherland cross-cultural sex remained episodic, producing few lasting relationships and no formal Dutch marriages. This suggests that something particular to the situation in New Netherland is the key to explaining the aversion to long-term, cross-cultural unions—both on the part of authorities and on the part of the vast majority of colonists—whether within or outside of marriage.

In Dutch historiography, the Atlantic world and the West India Company on one side and the Indian Ocean world and the East India Company on the other side are cast as separate fields of study, and the latter has received a great deal more attention than the former. In part, this follows from the fact that these two separate companies naturally maintained two independent archives in the early modern period, and this archival structure encourages fragmentation in studying the Dutch global empire. It also comes out of the fact that, in the Netherlands, the East Indies are more fondly remembered as a "successful" colonial venture. Dutch power in the Atlantic world reached its apogee in the middle of the seventeenth century before going into steep decline, at least in territorial terms, with the losses first of Brazil, in 1654, and then of New Netherland, in 1664.[5] Therefore for a long time there was a great deal more appetite for studies of the Dutch East Indies than for investigation of the Dutch Atlantic world. By taking what is undoubtedly an imperfect and certainly not comprehensive comparative leap here, this work makes a larger case that such east–west comparisons have much to add to the histories of individual Dutch colonies and the larger early modern Dutch empire. Because of the focus on situating New Netherland, which the English took from the Dutch in 1664, in the wider world, attention here will largely be on Dutch colonial activities in the first two thirds of the seventeenth century, including in Batavia, Elmina, and Brazil but not in Suriname, Curaçao, and the Cape Colony in South Africa, which flourished in the late seventeenth and eighteenth centuries.

The comparisons should not be understood as an attempt to create some kind of argument about specifically Dutch proclivities or character. Indeed, it is precisely the opposite intention that animates this inquiry. This is partially because it is not clear how formally Dutch any of the Dutch colonies actually were. Both trading companies desperately needed recruits and took volunteers from England, France, the German states, and Scandinavia, and soldiers, in particular, tended to be foreign.[6] More important, as recent research on the Atlantic world makes clear, there was no singular English or French approach to cross-cultural sex and marriage. Instead, local circumstances in individual colonies made all the difference.[7] A look at how the Dutch approached unions with indigenous women in a variety of places across the globe suggests how much local circumstances and local people affected Dutch policies and activities in every place the Dutch settled. As the diversity of policies related to cross-cultural sex and the variety of on-the-ground sexual arrangements in the Americas as a whole become clearer, knowing about the Dutch adds to this picture of variation as the rule throughout Atlantic empires and suggests the power of comparing North America with the rest of the world.[8]

Although the Dutch were particularly global in the early modern period, sending more people to Asia than all other European powers combined before 1800, other European nations were similarly globally oriented in this period, and a major critique of Atlantic history has been that it ignores this global orientation by artificially cordoning off the Atlantic basin from the rest of the world.[9] While some major recent work has tried to bridge this divide and think globally, much of it has focused on trade and the circulation of goods rather than on social and gender history. But, as Natalie Zemon Davis argues, social history and gender history are actually very much part of the same project as global history in that all three approaches work toward a "decentering" of Europe and its elites.[10] Because of the high level of Dutch activity in both the Atlantic world and Asia in the seventeenth century, the Dutch case offers an unparalleled opportunity to look at cross-cultural sex in a global context. Dutch expectations about how women ought to comport themselves shaped Dutch perceptions about the extent to which non-European women met these standards. Gender emerges as central to explaining the unique situation of New Netherland.

Henry Hudson explored the river that bears his name in 1609, and his explorations formed the basis for the Dutch claim to New Netherland. Between 1609 and 1621, various Dutch merchants traded for furs, both independently and, from 1614 to 1617, under the auspices of the New Netherland Company. When the States General chartered the Dutch West India Company (WIC) in 1621, colonization for the first time became a goal, alongside the continuation of the fur trade. The WIC sent its first colonists to New Netherland in 1623 or 1624.[11] In the late 1620s, there were probably only between three hundred and five hundred colonists, though the number would grow in the 1630s to between 1,500 and 2,000 settlers, with particular increases in the area of Rensselaerswyck (the upper Hudson River Valley) rather than Manhattan. After 1640, New Netherland's population stagnated, perhaps even decreasing, until 1650, when growth picked up again. By 1664, when the Dutch surrendered the colony to the English, there were between 7,000 and 9,000 colonists concentrated in the colony's two cities: Beverwijck (now Albany), which had slightly more than 1,000 people, and New Amsterdam, which was populated by 2,500 people.[12]

The West India Company documents that would elucidate the situation in the colony's early years do not, unfortunately, survive. This is particularly problematic because the gender imbalance in the colony was highest in its earliest years, and a number of historians point to this factor as a primary reason for cross-cultural relationships; it is also problematic because patterns for the later period may have been set by actions in the earlier one. In any case, an extensive documentary record for New Netherland begins only in 1638, with the arrival of the new director, General Willem Kieft. Perhaps as part of his more general interest in transforming New Amsterdam into a town with "Holland style rules and regulations" and creating a more orderly society, he issued a new ordinance against "adulterous intercourse with heathens, blacks, or other persons."[13] Apparently in response to the ordinance, the *fiscael* (sheriff and prosecutor) immediately prosecuted two soldiers for having sex with Indian women in New Amsterdam. The surviving records provide no information about the women, but they were most likely Munsee-speaking Algonquians, as the Munsee lived in the closest proximity to the town.[14]

There is one final reference to cross-cultural sex in New Amsterdam, in 1641, a complaint marking the final mention of cross-cultural sex in the city of New Amsterdam, though not the colony as a whole. In that year, Jan Damen, a colonist, tried to have a Company soldier, Jan Platneus, disqualified from testifying against him in court on the grounds that Platneus was "a perjurer and incompetent to give any testimony, because he has committed adultery with Indian women."[15] Kieft's prosecutions in 1638 and 1639 likely led to the decline of cross-cultural sex, but it is also important to note that Kieft quickly embarked upon an extraordinarily violent war that lasted from 1643 to 1645, and this war surely made Indigenous people wary of having too much contact with the Dutch in New Amsterdam. After the second Dutch–Munsee War, called the Peach War, which concluded in 1656, it seems even less likely that Munsee people would have visited the city. Many had stopped living near the city, and this lack of geographical closeness must have affected the opportunities for physical intimacy.[16]

In the area surrounding the upper Hudson River Valley, much more evidence for cross-cultural sex survives, as do indications that these relationships continued until the end of the Dutch period. At about the same time that Kieft arrived and began his crackdown on cross-cultural sex, Kiliaen van Rensselaer, the owner of the patroonship, or private colony, of Rensselaerswyck, near what would later become Albany, also turned his attention to cross-cultural sex. Given the location of the patroonship, the cross-cultural sex could have been with either Mohawk (Haudenosaunee) or Mahican (Algonquian) women. In 1639, van Rensselaer wrote to Arent van Curler, his representative in the colony, to order him to have the governing council introduce an ordinance against such sex.[17] Perhaps unsatisfied with the resulting ordinance, the text of which does not survive, van Rensselaer himself composed a more detailed ordinance in 1643, specifying a fine for first-time offenders of twenty-five guilders and increasing the fines to fifty guilders if the woman became pregnant and to one hundred guilders if she actually bore a child. He also mandated a yearly fine of fifty guilders with an option for banishment for repeat offenders.[18] Johannes Megapolensis, the Reformed minister whom van Rensselaer employed in his colony, wrote in 1644 that the Mohawk women "are exceedingly addicted to whoring; they will lie with a man for the value of one, two or three *schillings,* and our Dutchmen run after them very much."[19] Johan van Rensselaer, Kiliaen's son, who followed him as administrator of the colony, ordered his appointed *schout* (sheriff) to prosecute offenders of the previous ordinances because "it is a scandal that the Christians should mingle themselves unlawfully with the wives or daughters of Heathens."[20] There is no evidence to suggest that anyone was ever ensnared in prosecution as a result of any of the van Rensselaer family's ordinances, but court records for the area survive only for the four-year period from 1648 to 1652. In September 1659, a number of Mohawk chiefs presented proposals to Dutch authorities in Albany for ways to maintain and strengthen the relationship between the two groups. One of their requests was "that when any one of their people dies and one of the Dutch is her mate, he ought to give to the relatives of the deceased one or two suits of cloth."[21]

For all of the urgency in the legal code and the discussion surrounding cross-cultural sex, it is difficult to find evidence of any specific individuals who were actually engaged in cross-cultural unions. In 1653, Pierre Esprit Radisson, a Frenchmen captured by Mohawks, reported that he met a woman in the Mohawk camp where he was imprisoned who was reportedly the child of an Indian woman and a Dutch man.[22] There was also a Mohawk woman whom Dutch colonists referred to as "Corlaer's daughter," likely the daughter of Arent van Curler, Kiliaen van Rensselaer's aforementioned official in Rensselaerswyck.[23]

There seem to have been very few long-term relationships; the most well known was that between Cornelis Teunisz van Slijck and an unknown Mohawk woman. Van Slijck arrived in Rensselaerswyck in 1634 to take up a position as carpenter. He ultimately had three or possibly four children with his partner, and he seems to have parlayed the connection into a land grant from the Mohawk.[24] In the Delaware River Valley, there was also a man known as Jacob *mijn vrient* (my friend) who had a union with a Susquehannock woman. Stuyvesant described Jacob as having "lived for years among the Mincquaase Indians [*wilden*], acted like an Indian [*wilt*], he married an Indian, or used her as a concubine, and procreated various children with her."[25] It is only in the discussion of Jacob *mijn vrient* that the word "marriage" arises, and here it seems to stand in for a serious attachment in that Stuyvesant himself seems to have been unsure how to describe a long-term commitment that occurred outside the sanction of Dutch civil marriage or Christian marriage.

When Dutch authors of the 1650s, the period of New Netherland's greatest population growth, described cross-cultural sex, they often located it in an unspecified earlier period. In Adriaen van der Donck's 1651 *Description of New Netherland,* he explained that the Native women "have an attractive grace about them, for several Dutchmen, before many Dutch women were to be had there, became infatuated with them."[26] David Pietersz de Vries's 1655 account of his negotiations with an Algonquian sachem on Staten Island in 1643 presented the sachem as complaining about Dutch attacks on his people because

> at the beginning of our [Dutch] voyaging there, we left our people behind with the goods to trade, until the ships should come back; they had preserved these people like the apple of their eye; yeah, they had given them their daughters to sleep with, by whom they had begotten children, and there roved many an Indian who was begotten by a *Swanneken* [Dutch], but our people had become so villainous as to kill their own blood.[27]

Both van der Donck and de Vries were promoters, trying to attract additional colonists to New Netherland, and their descriptions of cross-cultural sex may have been intended to show potential colonists who were well aware of the cross-cultural violence in the colony that, in fact, there was nothing to fear from Indigenous peoples. Indeed, the two men may have been using such unions as a shorthand to express the argument that the Dutch had much in common with Indigenous peoples and that the two groups had mutually legible cultures and practices, while also situating that friendliness in the past. They could create the impression for potential colonists that, as of the moment in which they were writing, Indigenous peoples had historically been friendly but were currently more geographically distant and also less significant than they had been in the preceding period.[28] Such an impression of commonality but also increasing distance would have been key to attracting colonists who would have associated New Netherland more with intercultural violence, such as Kieft's War (1640–1645), than with intercultural peace.

Given the impressionistic nature of much of the evidence for cross-cultural sex, it is difficult to interpret. The evidence could be read to argue that cross-cultural sex was extremely common in New Netherland but that it is generally absent from legal records. Perhaps this absence could be explained by the traditional Dutch practice of *compositie,* paying off the sheriff to forget a legal case, which was often used in prostitution cases in the Dutch Republic.[29] Or the evidence could be read to suggest extremely high anxiety over the possibility of cross-cultural sex and mixed-race children, an anxiety that was widely shared by New Netherland's elites and many ordinary colonists and that made cross-cultural sex relatively uncommon. If we turn from New Netherland outward to the Dutch Republic and the larger Dutch global empire, we see how strange New Netherland was in comparison to other parts of the Dutch world. Whether we interpret New Netherland's evidence as suggesting the ubiquity of cross-cultural sex or its rarity, the minimal and relatively oblique evidence becomes clearer when it is paired with more open behavior and discussion elsewhere.

As the Dutch first turned to overseas trade in the last decades of the sixteenth century and the first decades of the seventeenth century, there were some ongoing but generally unsuccessful efforts in the Dutch Republic to create the concept of illegal boundary-crossing marriages. Obviously, there had long been certain marriages that were considered illegal to perform and invalid if solemnized, such as those between family members or between partners when one or both was already engaged or married to another party. But with the increase in religious diversity, new ideas percolated, particularly within the hierarchy of the Dutch Reformed Church, about creating religious boundaries that would mark off unacceptable marriage partners. For example, the provincial synods of Holland refused to marry anyone who was baptized to anyone unbaptized, likely intending to exclude marriages between Anabaptists and the other Christians in the Dutch Republic.[30] Yet even as the Dutch Reformed Church lobbied city governments in the Dutch Republic or the States General at the national level to enact new laws against baptized/unbaptized pairs, governments did not take steps to augment the existing marriage legislation.[31]

Indeed, some of the city of Amsterdam's marriage laws (to be sure, the most liberal in the Dutch Republic) seem to have had the effect—whether intentional or not—of breaking down boundaries between people and encouraging marriages that crossed the lines that the Reformed Church was struggling to bring into existence. While the Reformed Church tried to stop its own members from marrying Catholics, Anabaptists, or Lutherans by exerting pressure on those who declared such an intention, the city required the Reformed Church to solemnize these marriages if they were asked to do so, and it also offered a civil marriage ceremony before city magistrates. Before 1604, there was also the option of marrying before a notary, again a nonreligious option that mitigated the Reformed Church's position.[32] These policies were likely designed with a view toward ensuring that the city could monitor and record all marriages within its jurisdictions and were also supposed to bring couples into contact with the Reformed Church for the purpose of convincing them of the superiority of that church. In practice, however, they also left mixed couples with a great deal of room to maneuver if they felt pressure from either the Reformed Church or other religious communities to abandon their marriage plans.

Even in cases, such as Jewish–Christian marriage, where the government did express concern about maintaining boundaries and being exclusionary, this concern resided—as is to be expected in an era before racial thinking had become well entrenched—in religion, not in any notion of physical or bodily character.[33] A Christian could marry a Jew in Amsterdam so long as the latter converted to Christianity.[34] Perhaps more telling is the fact that prostitution and also more stable nonmarital unions that united Jewish men with Christian women were prohibited in legal codes but generally continued apace.[35] As the Dutch began to encounter "new" peoples overseas in forts, trading posts, and settlements, many held flexible views about who could be constituted a permissible partner for marriage or long-term union.

Sustained Dutch attention turned first to Asia and then, only a couple of decades later, to the Atlantic world. The States General chartered the Dutch East India Company (Vereenigde Oost-Indische Compagnie or VOC) in 1602, whereas the West India Company (WIC) would receive its first charter only in 1621. There was a great deal of variability in the VOC's position in different parts of Asia, with the VOC making its greatest inroads in the first half of the seventeenth century—often, though not always, through horrifying acts of violence—in Batavia, Ambon, Banda, the Moluccas, the Coromandel coast of India, Malacca, and Formosa. In other parts of Asia, particularly Japan and China, the Dutch were very clearly dependent on the goodwill of their hosts to continue trading. Central Dutch administration was located in Batavia (Jakarta) after 1619, and it was here that the greatest population of Dutch people resided. Batavia also had the most well-developed Reformed Church institutions.

Femme Gaastra has estimated that, in 1625, there were a total of 7,700 VOC employees in all of Asia, including both low-level personnel such as soldiers and sailors and higher-level personnel including clerks and administrators, a total that suggests that the Dutch would have been a tiny minority in any area in which they settled or traded.[36] By 1700, the total Dutch population in Asia would rise to 25,000 VOC employees, including all outposts and shipping, but again, the Dutch would have constituted only a small part of the population.[37]

The idea that all were presumed to be acceptable marriage partners in the early decades of Dutch expansion seems to be borne out by the initial discussions of marriage and marriage policy within the VOC's upper echelons. In 1612, Governor General Pieter Both wrote from Fort Orange in Ternate (one of the Moluccas) with a classical allusion: "in order to plant this country with our nation, it would be better to do as Romulus did and to make the local women marry our people he advocated for the Dutch to follow the policy of Romulus and marry with the local women."[38] Both was incensed a few months later that the government on the island of Makian, another of the Moluccas, refused to let VOC personnel marry local Muslim women. He then proposed that they acquire "heathen women" who would marry the men and produce children with them.[39] Both, thus, seems to have envisioned marriages that were rooted in violence, as the Romans under Romulus had captured and raped the Sabine women before taking them as wives. He offered no thoughts on the religious terms under which these marriages would take place.[40] Although Both seemed unbothered by the prospect of his men marrying women who were obviously not Christian, others within the VOC government were more troubled. In instructions for the Governor and Council of the Indies in 1617, the Company's directors did permit marriage between Dutch colonists and *Indiaansche* women who had been baptized and required them to bring up any children such unions produced as Christian.[41]

As the Dutch presence in Asia became more formalized, particularly with the establishment of the city of Batavia as the VOC's administrative and political capital, there arose still greater interest in cross-cultural marriage, which was understood as a way to populate the new city and root Dutch people in it. The Reformed Church's consistory court in Batavia took an interest in regulating these cross-cultural marriages, and although it initially seems to have adopted a stance that required Christian unity to make a marriage, the court ultimately wavered and suggested that it could envision marriages that might unite a Christian with a non-Christian. In 1621, the consistory declared that it would marry only Christians with other Christians, but it also allowed for a prospective partner who did not speak a language in which she could receive Christian instruction to take on godparents instead of converting. These godparents were to ensure that the new partner received Christian education and then baptism at some later point. The acceptance of godparents allowed for marriage even in the absence of baptism for, as the consistory explained, it was better to avoid concubinage and sin than to delay marriage. The only people that the consistory firmly rejected as prospective marriage partners were those who refused godparents or explicitly stated that they would not abandon their faiths.[42] Similar plans for conversion and marriage were suggested for Banda, where local women were to attend a VOC-sponsored school, become Christian, and then marry Dutch men.[43]

Unsurprisingly, in some cases, these marriages were characterized by a lack of sincere interest in Christianity on the part of the bride. There may also have been a lack of linguistic overlap between some couples, making communication difficult. For example, in 1625, the consistory proposed, though it ultimately rejected, a plan to entice women who were married to Dutch men to come to preaching and prayer offered in Malay through the promise of free rice.[44] And a 1641 ordinance declared that *Inlandsche* women who were not proficient in Dutch were prohibited from marrying Dutch men.[45] For some, like the minister George Candidius in Formosa, lack of religious unity was part of the attraction of a marriage. Candidius wanted to marry a Sinkan woman on the island because he believed that this might be a key way to advance the Reformed Church's missionary goals. Women were the primary holders of religious power in Formosan society, so only from a woman could he learn more about local religious culture and successfully uproot it.[46]

Despite the concerns about religion and language, there was a great deal of interest in encouraging these cross-cultural, though preferably still Christian, marriages. Men who married in Batavia received their full wages every month, a rule explicitly crafted to encourage men to marry in Batavia and remain there rather than return to the Dutch Republic. Those who were unmarried or were married to women in Europe could get only a portion of their monthly wages in Batavia and had to wait until they returned to the Dutch Republic for the balance.[47] Before 1621, even high-ranking VOC officials were entering marriages with either mixed-race (Portuguese) women or local Asian women. Between 1622 and 1631, at least in Batavia, there was a decline in the number of cross-cultural marriages because the VOC sponsored a program of female migration from the Dutch Republic. Thereafter, cross-cultural marriages became more characteristic of the lower ranks in the VOC, so mixed-race status came to carry class as well as racial implications.[48] Still, as Jean Gelman Taylor has argued, the original cohort of VOC elites before 1621 created a system in which their mixed-race children were highly sought-after marriage partners whose marriages to other members of the VOC's elite helped bind this group together.[49] For example, Cornelis van Nijenroode, the head of the Dutch factor in Hirado in Japan, had two daughters with his concubines there. In 1637, after van Nijenroode's death and protracted negotiations with the Japanese government, the two girls arrived in Batavia, where they were apparently brought up in the VOC's orphanage. In 1652, at the age of twenty-three, Cornelia, one of the daughters, married Pieter Cnoll, the head merchant in Batavia, and after his death she entered an ultimately extremely unhappy marriage with Johan Bitter, a member of Batavia's court of justice, a position that put him only one rung below the handful of men who were part of Batavia's high government.[50]

Long-term relationships outside marriage were also common in parts of Dutch Asia and included both people who professed Christianity and those who did not. The VOC government in Batavia did prohibit its employees from engaging in concubinage with their enslaved domestic laborers in 1620.[51] The repeated revisions to this law suggest that there were difficulties in securing compliance, which, in turn, suggests that there was a great deal of sex happening.[52] It is likely that, as historians of slavery in the Atlantic world have shown, much of this sex was violent and coercive, but it is difficult to find any accounts of these relationships in domestic settings. There may have been some preference in general for having a concubine rather than marrying, because marriage bound a man to stay in Asia until his wife's death, whereas concubinage allowed for the possibility of returning home.[53]

In parts of Southeast Asia, though not generally in Batavia, where men were either marrying enslaved and dislocated women or elite women who already identified as Dutch, entering a long-term union (generally not solemnized with Christian or Dutch rites) could also help a VOC employee enrich the Company and, perhaps, himself. An elite woman could marry various European men successively without dishonor as a way to incorporate new people into a preexisting trading network.[54] For example, in Ayutthaya, in Siam, Osoet Pegua at first became a concubine to a VOC merchant in the 1620s and then, after the merchant's departure, became the concubine to two successive VOC merchants.[55] A 1655 report about Ayutthaya suggests that all forty of the Dutch men at the trading post had concubines. As justifications for their actions, the men claimed that it was simply impossible to live in a constant state of abstinence and that it was preferable to have concubines than to turn to prostitution.[56]

Though less prevalent than in VOC Asia, there were also significant numbers of stable, long-term sexual relationships, both within and outside marriage, in the Dutch Atlantic world. In Africa, the major lasting site of Dutch activity was Elmina, on the Gold Coast, which the Dutch took from the Portuguese in 1637 as part of a project to ensure a steady supply of enslaved people to the Dutch sugar colony in Brazil in order to access the valuable trade in gold and ivory.[57] At Elmina, the Dutch continued a preexisting Portuguese–Akan practice of *calisaren,* unions concluded under joint Dutch and Akan auspices. These unions occurred outside traditional Dutch marriage law, which required solemnization either in the Reformed Church or before civil authorities, but they were officially recognized by both Dutch and Akan authorities on the Gold Coast as creating mutual obligations between the partners. Among other Dutch–Akan agreements, the WIC's governor in Elmina and his councilors would swear on the Bible while Elmina's Akan leaders would swear on their ancestors to maintain the laws that mediated interactions between the two groups, including the practice of *calisaren* (marriage from the Portuguese *casar,* to marry).[58] The Akan favored *calisaren* as means to incorporate Dutch men and mixed-race children into their *abusuas,* lineage groups, which were organized matrilineally. *Calisaren* also worked to the advantage of the *abusuas,* because Dutch men tended to leave property, of which the head of the lineage could then take control, to their partners and children when they died or departed Elmina. The Akan women in these long-term unions were not generally Christian.

In Pernille Ipsen's study of the Danish West India Company on the Gold Coast, she suggests that a primary purpose for *calisaren* for both the Danish and the Ga was to protect the trade relationship between the two groups. If anything divisive happened within a particular marriage, the prior agreements between the Danish and the Ga for how to manage *calisaren* could be put into effect and prevent a household dispute from rending the larger trading ties between the two communities.[59] For Danish and Dutch men, the advantage of the system, in addition to its ensuring good relations between the two groups, was likely access to nursing, care, and food. In a disease environment that often felled Europeans, such support might promote survival.

Rape and sexual violence were central elements of the European system of enslaving Africans, but *calisaren* need to be understood in a completely different light.[60] Dutch men in Elmina certainly had many opportunities to rape and terrorize the enslaved women who were waiting in the dungeons below the fort to be shipped to the Americas, and this violence was possible because Europeans had taken the women from the protection that family and community offered. The women with whom Dutch men had long-term relationships were still embedded within their communities. While they might have varying statuses within an *abusua,* they—and their Dutch partners—could expect members of their lineage to protect them in the event of disputes and, indeed, could expect Akan authorities to protect them. In this matrilineal society, the children produced in these relationships generally stayed with the mother or her relations after the death or departure of the WIC employee. Highly placed WIC merchants were, however, occasionally able to bring their children back to the Dutch Republic with them, where they seem to have integrated into Dutch society.[61]

Elmina also had a population of mixed-race people with Portuguese origins, and Dutch men could enter relationships with these women as well. The Portuguese had built Elmina in 1482, and by the late sixteenth century Euro-Africans were a significant part of the city's population; these people spoke Portuguese and wore European clothes.[62] For example, in 1646, the WIC soldier Lourens Fidelerius died and left a significant bequest to his female partner, described in records as having a Portuguese father and a "mulatto" mother, and their one-year-old child.[63] Jacob Ruijchaver, the WIC's director on the Gold Coast, was to be the child's guardian.

While Elmina would loom particularly large in Dutch activities in the eighteenth century, the focus of Dutch Atlantic activities in the seventeenth century was northeastern Brazil. Wrested from Portugal in 1630 and lasting as a Dutch colony only until 1654, Brazil received the lion's share of the WIC's attention, and alliances with Indigenous populations in the colony proved central during the colony's brief incarnation. The Tupi-speaking people of Brazil's coast had long had contact with the Portuguese in Brazil, sometimes as key allies, sometimes as opponents, and ultimately as enslaved plantation workers. Before the Dutch arrived, many took refuge in Jesuit-run *aldieas* (villages), where they were exposed to the missionary activity of Jesuits but protected in some measure from greedy planters. While likely maintaining syncretic religious practices, the Tupi did seek out baptism and Catholic ritual objects, bringing them religiously closer to the Protestant Dutch than either the Akan or the Mohawk, who were not Christian. In Dutch-controlled territory, the Tupi-speaking population, who were mostly Potiguars, was in steep decline. In 1635, the population was close to 8,000, but in 1645, it would stand at only 3,500 as a result of both epidemic diseases and war with the Luso-Brazilian colonists.[64]

Evidence for long-term relationships is thinner for Brazil than for Batavia and Elmina. But, unlike New Netherland sources, the records do make some specific relationships visible. The most well known is that of Jacob Rabe and Dominga, a Tupi woman. Rabe served as the intermediary for the Dutch with the Tairariu, a different group of Indigenous allies, in the province of Rio Grande. He and Dominga lived on a plantation in Rio Grande, complete with both slaves and servants, but the Dutch commander there, George Garstman, disapproved of Rabe and his activities. In April 1646, Rabe was murdered, and evidence pointed to Garstman as the culprit, perhaps acting out of anger that Rabe had participated in a Tairariu attack on Luso-Brazilian colonists who killed Garstman's father-in-law or perhaps out of greed. Garstman had apparently tortured one of Rabe's servants to ascertain the location of some gold that he believed Rabe had hidden.[65]

Throughout the investigation and legal proceedings that followed, the High Council in Recife acknowledged that Dominga had the status of wife, and they referred to her exclusively as Rabe's *vrouw* (wife).[66] In the absence of a marriage register for the colony, it is difficult to know whether the pair had married according to Dutch ceremonies, but it is clear that they were widely acknowledged as a couple. Jacob Kint, the commander of the Tapuyas and Tupi in the Gojana, is also referred to in Dutch records as having a *Tupi brasiliaense* (Tupi) wife.[67] In November 1650, Jan Castiliaen requested permission to return to the Dutch Republic after sixteen years in Brazil, and he was told that he could go as long as he made provision for the care of his "Brazilian" *brasiliaensche* (Tupi) wife and child.[68] The High Council was, in this case, clear about the fact that such marriages were legitimate and that Brazilian wives and children could not simply be abandoned when they were no longer convenient. In December, Castiliaen requested permission to bring his wife and child back with him to the Dutch Republic; this permission was granted as long as he paid for their passage, again indicating that these pairings were recognized.[69]

There is also evidence of more widespread interest among Dutch soldiers in what was explicitly marriage. In March 1651, three Company soldiers requested permission to marry Tupi women from the *aldeia* of Paranguba in the province of Ceará. Thomas Kemp, the minister of the *aldeia,* explained that he opposed the requests for marriage because the "*brasiliaensche* nation Tupi were not appropriate for mixing with the Dutch." Kemp also reported that he thought the men might keep their wives as slaves, which would create hatred between the Dutch and their Indigenous allies.[70] Because of Kemp's opposition, Matthias Beck, the director of the province, wrote to the High Council in Recife asking whether he should allow the marriages. According to Kemp, in addition to these three, there were also a number of other soldiers living at the Dutch fort and at the silver mine who wanted to marry Indian women.[71] The High Council in Recife was troubled by the marriage requests from Ceará, because they feared that mixed relationships would anger the Tupi men. The Company's hopes for righting its financial situation were pinned on Ceará, because there had long been rumors that a rich silver mine existed there, which could help the Company pay off its crippling debts. The Tupi in Ceará had also massacred a Dutch garrison there in 1644, so their potential dissatisfaction was a legitimate concern. The High Council wrote back to Beck that it felt that it was a "very difficult thing to refuse someone the right to marry," but it was also clearly nervous about angering the Tupi men and endangering access to the mine.[72] The Council advised Beck to oppose the marriages as gently as possible but not forbid them outright.[73] Local circumstances might have dictated that these particular marriages be prevented, but the soldiers involved displayed a clear interest in marriage, and the High Council, though not the minister, demonstrated itself to be generally amenable to them.

In many places in which the Dutch built forts or settlements, they did enter into marriage or stable unions with women from the local populations. While there was certainly variability, with relationships most common in Asia and in Elmina and somewhat less common in Brazil, New Netherland emerges as an outlier in this comparative analysis, with abundant evidence of short-term, or perhaps even one-time, encounters, but little evidence for more lasting relationships. While what follows is speculative, it seems that ideas about gender were crucial to creating this difference. In a well-known letter to a friend describing his interactions with the Mohawk, Johannes Megapolensis explained, "they sleep by us, too, in our chambers before our beds. I have had eight at once lying and sleeping upon the floor near my bed."[74] This is often read as a sign of the closeness between the two groups, but it is also possible to read this comment as a sign of distance. The Mohawk either chose not to or were not welcomed by the Dutch to live in their city on a permanent basis. Instead, they required temporary places to stay while they conducted their trade. To be sure, the two groups still had close contact with each other during trading visits, but this was different from the situation in Batavia and Elmina, in which forts were surrounded by cities, and these cities explicitly included non-European peoples within their boundaries. In the eighteenth century, the fort at Elmina housed about 250 men, while the surrounding city had as many as 12,000 people.[75] While the numbers would have perhaps been smaller in the seventeenth century, the geography would have been similar. Batavia, too, was a city with the cross-cultural mixing that this implied.[76]

Whether a cause or merely an additional symptom of the lack of closeness between the Dutch and the Mohawk, this lack of close geographic proximity prevented long-term relationships. In addition, the Mohawk were a matrilineal and matrilocal society, so a long-term relationship would have required a Dutch man to leave the city of Beverwijck and move to the home of his new partner, indicating a partial withdrawal from Dutch society. Such a withdrawal would not have been part and parcel of marrying or having a long-term relationship with a local woman in Batavia or in Elmina. Similarly, in Brazil, the Dutch–Potiguar relationships that appear in the record suggest cohabitation and also that the women in these relationships were willing to relocate with their Dutch partners, even to the Dutch Republic itself.

The Dutch found the women they encountered in all parts of the Atlantic world strange and foreign, but the gender roles in the Mohawk community may have horrified them most. When describing the Gold Coast, Dutch authors clearly described women as "lascivious," but they also noted the harsh punishments for adultery in that society and observed that fathers and husbands still had a great deal of patriarchal authority.[77] For example, in early seventeenth-century voyages, both Andreas Ulsheimer and Samuel Brun noted that a husband could drive away a wife who was suspected of adultery.[78] This is not to suggest that these authors meant to create an equivalence between European and African practices; rather, they often positioned the husbands' acts as excessively cruel and thus not up to the standards of "civilized" society. Akan customary law also criminalized female adultery, and a Dutch partner could use this law to reject his partner.[79] Still, in this rejection of adultery the Dutch could see something similar to their own society in that men remained the clear heads of household. And while consistently describing women on the Gold Coast as sex-crazed in general terms, when authors actually described marriage practices, they made it clear that men actually took the lead in negotiating marriages for their daughters.[80] Pieter de Marees even noted the good character of the Gold Coast's women, saying that they often stayed near home rather than going out to gossip with neighbors.[81] Patriarchal authority was, therefore, clearly visible in Elmina; in addition, political authority more closely resembled that in Dutch society, with a male monarch at its head.

In Batavia, the Dutch controlled the city and its laws. While certainly not always enforced—either by choice or because authorities lacked the ability to do so—Dutch notions of patriarchal authority, sexual discipline, and punishment for adultery were officially the law, and Dutch men could count on Batavia's institutions—the Reformed Church, the local court, and the VOC government—to teach and uphold them. While prostitution certainly existed in Batavia, and some VOC officials and Dutch colonists were profiting from it, the situation was more akin to that found in cities in the Dutch Republic, where there was a distinct separation of honorable women from dishonorable ones and where definitions of female honor and dishonor were widely agreed upon. Many of the mixed-race people who had achieved Dutch status felt bound to uphold Dutch morality because this secured their place within Dutch society. And the women lower-status men tended to marry were dependent women, enslaved or formerly enslaved, who had been brought to Batavia from some other part of the Dutch East Indies. Such women were hardly in a position to act independently.[82]

New Netherland was different. Like the Akan people in Elmina, the Mohawk were an independent people who were not subject to the Dutch. But Mohawk and Dutch notions of proper sexuality and gender roles could not have differed more. The Haudenosaunee people were not patriarchal, and women had high status, though not necessarily equal status with men. While not direct participants in political debates, matrons played an important role in choosing Mohawk leadership and in deciding whether to go to war or make peace. Women were the farmers of Mohawk society, producing as much as three quarters of the food that people ate, and they held the plots of land.[83] Women were also able to consolidate power because of the matrilocal nature of society and their close relations with one another.[84] Women participated in extensive long-distance trade on their own, and this, combined with their access to the means of food production, meant that they did not need to marry.[85]

In terms of sexuality, Mohawk women were free to have sex before marriage and free to end marriages with divorce at their pleasure, without what the Dutch would have considered appropriate reasons. Although Dutch commentators did acknowledge that, within marriage, the custom was to remain faithful, they placed much more emphasis on what they considered to be the "whorelike" nature of the women and their ability to make their own personal choices about sexual partners.[86] For the Dutch, patriarchal authority and proper household order were lacking in this system in which women decided how to dispose of themselves and their resources.

New Netherland also had a small number of soldiers, and soldiers represented a smaller portion of the Dutch population in the colony than in other Dutch colonial situations, in which soldiers would be more numerous and were often the majority of the Dutch population. In New Amsterdam, the garrison had only about 50 soldiers in 1643, a number that would grow to 250 in the 1650s and then decline again to 180 in 1664. By comparison, Brazil had 6,000 soldiers in 1648.[87] Soldiers in the Dutch Republic sometimes married prostitutes and seem to have had more generally lax notions and less attachment to a burgher-like view of domestic order and female honor.[88] Perhaps, then, the presence of soldiers determined the extent of cross-cultural sex, as these men were more willing to take on partners ordinary Dutch men would reject, particularly those who had proven to be sexually available. It was not just Dutch definitions of proper femininity that prevented Dutch men from entering cross-cultural relations with Indigenous women; it was also definitions of proper masculinity. While a proper patriarch controlled the sexuality of his female dependents, and his honor depended upon this, alternative masculinities flourished for those, like soldiers, whose life situations did not allow them to articulate claims to honor on this basis. Instead, many soldiers participated in an alternative form of masculinity in which they placed less emphasis on sexual honor and instead might focus specifically on a propensity for disorderliness and drunkenness.[89]

The Christian status of a prospective bride or long-term partner cannot definitively explain whether a cross-cultural relationship could go forward, though conversion certainly helped. In 1640, the directors of the Amsterdam office of the WIC wrote to the government of the colony of Curaçao, ordering the colonists to prohibit anyone from treating "the Black and Indian women dishonestly." They were not to "associate with them lasciviously, whether voluntarily or by force," or they would lose all of their earned wages and suffer banishment. But the same law suggested that Dutch people could "marry Indian or Black women" if they had "been baptized . . . and incorporated into the community of Christ."[90] While there was never any direct discussion of cross-cultural marriage in New Netherland, in Curaçao this kind of marriage was made contingent on conversion. This resembles the situation in Batavia, where conversion, if relevant, was ideally supposed to precede cross-cultural marriage. Yet religion did not always make all the difference. In the VOC's early years, it was not assumed that Dutch men would marry Christian women, though it was, perhaps, assumed that, as heads of household, such men could ultimately convince their wives to become Christian. But in long-term concubinage situations like those found in Elmina, there was little thought given to conversion and little possibility of it, given the lack of church personnel to provide Christian instruction.

Gender and sexuality emerge, then, as central, as Dutch men preferred to enter marriage or union with women who would conform to the Dutch ideals of sexual honor and care for the household. They preferred partners who would be likely to stay indoors and who would remain faithful for the duration of a relationship.[91] And perhaps Mohawk women, too, were looking for things other than what Dutch men could offer them, preferring to remain in their matrilocal communities rather than subject themselves to patriarchal society and knowing that they could get the trade goods they wanted through their own efforts.

Although historians tend to think of the fur trade as a site that encouraged cross-cultural marriage and sex in the service of creating the kinship connections that would ensure profit, and the Dutch in New Netherland were at the forefront of that trade in the first half of the seventeenth century, cross-cultural sex was not, apparently, central to their conduct of that trade.[92] It is only through combining gender history with a global, comparative approach that this becomes clear, however. This raises questions about the way that the history of North America is investigated and suggests that situating colonial America in a global context may be useful for more than studies of circulation of people and goods.

Michele Mericle

Las Casas de las Rabinas

Three Generations of Women in a Crypto-Jewish Family in Seventeenth-Century New Spain

Historians of New Spain have identified the decade between 1640 and 1650 as one of the viceroyalty's most tumultuous, when contests over power led to profound shifts in the life of the colony.[1] Scholars have explored many of the changes that occurred in economic, political, religious, and social realms, but less attention has been paid to how the decade's events affected gender relations. One avenue for exploration of gender is through a consideration of the persecution by the Inquisition of New Spain's Portuguese community, in which women figured prominently as victims. The 1649 auto-de-fé, or "act of faith," had the highest percentage of female penitents of any in Mexico between 1521 and 1700.[2] In this persecution, women constituted fully one third of the accused.

Why were women so heavily targeted at this time? In order to explore this question, it is important first to consider the position of women in Spanish America during the seventeenth century. A small but growing body of work describes the various forms of female power in colonial society.[3] While this scholarship recognizes the real limitations placed on women in colonial Spanish America, it also points to the myriad ways in which women held considerable power in the home, in the marketplace, in convents, and in native and Spanish communities. This scholarship also emphasizes the protection of women's dowry wealth and partible inheritance rights by the Spanish legal system, which contrasts, for example, with the paucity of rights granted English women of the same era. The experience of *conversa* (convert) women bolsters the emerging view that women in Spanish America found significant room to maneuver. The elite *conversas* who compose the subject of this study tended to be wealthy and literate and wielded considerable influence in their homes and communities through the performance and maintenance of crypto-Jewish religious rituals. However, this comparative freedom was short lived, and the Inquisition was the primary institution that truncated this elite female *conversa* power.

I begin with a brief overview of the methodological and theoretical orientation of my argument, followed by a discussion of the political and economic contexts of the Inquisitorial persecutions of the Portuguese community during the 1640s in New Spain. Next, I focus on a recounting of the 1649 auto-de-fé, written by the Jesuit Matías de Bocanegra, in particular, his description of women representing three generations of the Váez-Enríquez family. I analyze the descriptions of these three women for insights regarding the activities and popular perceptions of *conversa* women. This analysis is augmented by consideration of sources derived from Inquisition interrogations, along with part of Gregorio M. de Guijo's diary of major events from the time period.

Theoretical Orientation

Cultural historians have charted a path for the use of sources such as Inquisition documents, official accounts, and diaries to examine the everyday lives of average people.[4] In this work, I follow the lead of Natalie Zemon Davis, who calls our attention to the root word of "fictional," *fingere,* which means "to form or to shape," in order to get at a broader understanding of storytelling. By focusing on the root meaning of fiction, Davis emphasizes the "forming, shaping, and molding elements" involved in the crafting of a narrative, rather than on whether those elements are "feigned" or untrue.[5] Thus, my emphasis is not upon what "actually happened" but rather upon what narrators *thought* would be "true, real, meaningful, and/or explanatory."[6]

Furthermore, when considering the religious praxis of crypto-Jews, I have drawn upon scholarship that provides insight into the definitional, historical, and experiential aspects of religion more generally. This scholarship contributes four key points that undergird my argument. First, "domestic" religion or "lived" religion, terms I use interchangeably, constitutes the bulk of religious experience for individuals, in that religion occurs in the private spaces of one's mind and one's home. Historians have tended to conflate institutional forms of religion with "orthodox" religion and have generally devoted scant energies to the investigation of domestic religion.[7] As women have not figured prominently in most institutional religious hierarchies, this has meant that the female religious experience, in particular, has been underinvestigated. The experience of laymen, however, has been similarly neglected.[8] Furthermore, sources such as Inquisition documents are especially well suited to an investigation of domestic religion, for the Inquisitors queried keenly into precisely these "lived" aspects of religious experience.

Second, "orthodoxy" tends to be more about power and institutions than about any absolute purity or adherence to an ideal religious form. All cultural forms—including religion—are fundamentally hybrid or syncretic, because this is the "predicament of culture."[9] Thus, *all* religious forms are contested, malleable, and contingent, even at the institutional level.[10] Therefore, in this study, the religious practices of the crypto-Jews are accepted as fully Jewish, even as they may have diverged from other forms common in other times and places.[11] Furthermore, as religion is naturally hybrid and in flux, what requires explanation is not syncretism but rather *anti*-syncretism. The scholar Meredith McGuire explains:

> All cultural traditions—including religious traditions—are based on this kind of interpenetration and interaction with external influences. Indeed, such hybridity is part of the dynamism, strength, richness, and appeal of the resulting synthesis. Since "syncretic processes are considered basic, not only to religion and ritual but to 'the predicament of culture' in general," Shaw and Stewart argue that what we should be analyzing is "*anti*-syncretism." In other words, all cultural groups are fundamentally syncretic, but not all have attitudes or social movements against the syncretism of others.[12]

Clearly, the Inquisition was an anti-syncretic institution, in that its raison d'être was to root out heresy. That it devoted so much time and energy to policing the inner lives of human beings suggests how quixotic the enterprise was at its foundation—even though in many ways it was remarkably successful. This study, therefore, is an exploration of one example of the exercise of, and resistance to, anti-syncretic institutional power, in which gender played an important part, within the historical context of seventeenth-century Mexico City.

Third, the clandestine nature of crypto-religions allows practitioners to create a world outside normative or dominant social mores. The historian Eliza Kent highlights Georg Simmel's observation that secrecy has the "ability to enlarge the realm of the possible by conjuring up counter-realities in tension with manifest, ordinary, or widely accepted reality."[13] The crypto-religious space can therefore function as a site of experimentation and/or resistance.[14] Kent elaborates upon some of the implications this "realm of the possible" has for the practice of crypto-religion: "The secret societies created among the crypto-religious are not only places where a new, perhaps radical vision of the world can be created and sustained, but they are also sociologically important in providing an arena for the exercise of leadership and autonomy especially important to those denied such arenas in the public world they share with non-converts."[15]

Not surprisingly, this enlarged realm of the possible has historically allowed women, especially, greater agency and power within the context of patriarchal societies, as they assumed positions of leadership in shadow worlds of their own creation.

In sum, the women under consideration here are viewed as practitioners of a domestic religion, which arguably constitutes the bulk of religious experience for all persons, that demonstrated integrity and adherence to Jewish forms on its own terms. The primary institution that truncated this practice was the Inquisition. The mission of the Inquisition was an intertwining of worldly and anti-syncretic concerns in that it helped to maintain colonial power structures through its insistence upon an "orthodox" form of Catholicism. Deviance from this orthodoxy made one vulnerable to charges of heresy and thus to the exercise of this variant of colonial power. Nonetheless, the inner, secret, and hidden aspects of this domestic religious practice provided women in particular, but men as well, with an alternate space in which to construct meaning, navigate social relationships, and redefine and re-create aspects of their world.

The 1649 Auto-de-fé in Context: The Rise and Fall of the Portuguese Nation

On April 11, 1649, the Mexican Inquisition staged a "great" auto-de-fé in the central plaza of Mexico City. The lavish and highly theatrical auto occurred after months of preparation and ritualized public announcements. Tens of thousands of people, including members of the religious orders, the nobility, university men, and royal officials, came from near and far to witness the spectacle of the sentencing and punishment of the accused. Of the 109 penitents in the auto, all but one, a Lutheran, were accused of Judaizing. Fifty-seven persons had already died, many in the deplorable conditions of the Inquisition prisons, leaving fifty-two to participate in the procession. Of these fifty-two, thirteen were "relaxed," or turned over by the Inquisition to secular authorities to be burned at the stake.

The auto-de-fé of 1649 culminated nearly a decade of Inquisitorial persecutions against Mexico City's Portuguese population, as well as against the Portuguese in the Spanish colonies more widely. Notably, in 1640s New Spain, the term "Portuguese" was virtually synonymous with the term "Jew." This suggests just how pervasive the conflation between the two had become. The Inquisition pursued communities of Portuguese crypto-Jews first in Cartagena in 1632, then in Lima in 1635, and finally in New Spain in 1641. These events have come to be known as the *complicidad grande,* or the "great conspiracy," whose proponents alleged that Portuguese residents of the Spanish colonies were scheming to ally with the Dutch to overthrow Spanish rule in the Americas. Scholars tend to see the actual evidence for any such conspiracy as quite thin for all three regions, but especially so for Mexico.[16]

Surprisingly, these attacks represented a sharp break in Inquisitorial policy toward the crypto-Jews, especially in Mexico City. For roughly the first third of the seventeenth century, the Mexican Inquisition had investigated only a handful of cases related to Judaizing and had ignored several complaints by persons who had reported suspicious behavior. For example, according to one document that was filed away in the Inquisition archives, a "synagogue" was operating just two doors down from the Inquisition offices on Calle Santo Domingo. Apparently passersby could hear the sounds of praying inside on Saturdays. It appears the Inquisition never investigated this charge.[17] There is even evidence of what might be considered a certain coziness between crypto-Jews and the Inquisitors, such as reports in Inquisition files that daughters of prominent crypto-Jewish families dated men who held high offices within the Inquisition.[18] Solange Alberro explains this coziness between crypto-Jews and Inquisitors as the result of class solidarity in the Americas. As elite Iberians were a tiny demographic minority in the New World, *peninsulares* in particular and elites more generally tended to privilege wealth and place of birth over religion in determining group identity.[19]

However, it is clear that during the 1640s this sense of elite group solidarity broke down in a number of ways, not least of which was a rift between Old and New Christians.[20] Three primary political and economic factors contributed to this breakdown of relations. First, Portugal had successfully broken away from Spain in 1640, thereby ending sixty years of unification between the two kingdoms. When this happened, Portuguese-born denizens throughout the Spanish Empire became suspect as potential traitors. Second, the Mexican Inquisition had declared in 1639 that, unless it received an influx of funds from the Crown or elsewhere, it would have to close its doors, for it was essentially bankrupt. And third, the arrival of Juan de Palafox y Mendoza to fill the post of Bishop of Puebla in 1640 radically altered the political landscape to such a degree that alliances among elites were reconfigured. Of particular relevance for the Portuguese, Palafox removed the Duke of Escalona from the position of viceroy. The Duke of Escalona had been seen as a special protector of the Portuguese community. Not surprisingly, persecutions commenced rapidly once the Duke was out of office.

The most critical factor may have been not political or economic but social: the increasingly strong sense of resentment and jealousy among Old Christian elites toward the extraordinarily successful *converso* merchant community.[21] It is important to get a sense of just how exceptional this community was in order to understand its significance. Daviken Studnicki-Gizbert describes this global community, also known as the "Portuguese Nation," as one of the most dynamic capitalist actors in the early modern Atlantic world.[22] Most of the more than four hundred suspected Judaizers brought before the Mexican Tribunal in the 1640s were humble shopkeepers, shop assistants, craftsmen, or peddlers. In contrast, the wealthy merchants of the community were comparatively few.[23] But these few merchants were fabulously wealthy. Most had risen from humble beginnings to oversee commercial networks that stretched across the Pacific through Manila and on to China. They extended domestically throughout the Spanish colonies. Many made incursions into Dutch and Portuguese Brazil and reached across the Atlantic to European cities such as Pisa, Seville, Leghorn, and Amsterdam. Perhaps most critically, they controlled much of the slave trade along the African coast. This was an early capitalist global trading network.

Many of the Portuguese merchants started as slave traders. Indeed, the trade in African slaves formed the core of the nation's Atlantic business.[24] From slave trading, Portuguese merchants expanded into European textiles, the importation of Chinese silk in exchange for Mexican silver, and the highly lucrative commerce in cacao.[25] It seems that, in all of these trading arenas, they simultaneously managed both licit and illicit trading practices.[26]

When Portugal was incorporated into the Spanish empire in 1580, the Portuguese nation gained access to the rich resources and markets to be found in the Spanish colonies. For New World traders, the nation's trading networks were very profitable. For example, Simón Váez Sevilla, the paterfamilias of one of Mexico City's most prominent families and the husband of one of the persons investigated in this study, Juana Enríquez, held a fortune estimated at 200,000 pesos. According to one scholar's estimate, this is comparable to about $132 million U.S. in 2019.[27] And Váez was not unique. Váez's wealth put him on par with Manuel Bautista Pérez, the leader of the crypto-Jewish community in Lima. Given the Portuguese merchants' extensive trading experience and competitive advantage via control of the African slave trade, it is perhaps not surprising that the nation came to occupy "the keystone position in the much larger arch that connected the silver mines and plantations of the Americas to the manufacturing sectors of northern Europe."[28]

Spain attempted to harness the potential of the burgeoning Atlantic economy with methods such as the double fleet system and the sale of *asientos,* or trade monopolies. Enforcement was provided by the two key judicial institutions of the Spanish empire: the Casa de la Contratación and the Inquisition. Despite these efforts, it was clear to many that the colonies were hemorrhaging money through contraband, and many pointed to the Portuguese as the primary culprits. While this charge was not without basis, it was only when anxiety regarding the loss of tax revenue to contraband trade was wedded to Spanish society's broader antipathy toward Judaism and Jews that the situation became dire for the Portuguese community. In particular, anti-Jewish fears surrounding the Portuguese, many of whom were of *converso* descent and thus suspected of being "secret Jews," provided the Spanish Crown the opportunity to utilize a powerful institution, the Inquisition, to achieve a political and economic end: the destruction of the Portuguese merchant networks.[29] In short, while it is not surprising that resentment arose against these nouveaux riches of Portuguese descent and humble beginnings, it was their status as New Christians, of Jewish ancestry and questionable

Catholicism, that made the Mexican members of the Portuguese nation most vulnerable.

The Portuguese nation functioned through ties of kinship, culture, and association as much as through shared economic interest. Jonathan Israel describes the community in this way:

> Clearly it was in part a highly effective commercial network; partly, it was also a closely-knit patchwork of family relations, a socially cohesive if geographically scattered group which tended to marry and reproduce mainly from within their own ranks. But above all it was a network based on a common background, experience, and emotion, a part of a vast trans-Atlantic clandestine diaspora based on a shared experience of concealment, subterfuge and persecution which remained a living force for some eighty years down to, and indeed even after, the Auto General de la Fé, in Mexico City, in 1649.[30]

It was the construction and maintenance of this "common background, experience, and emotion" that made this wildly successful commercial enterprise work, and that is where the women in these communities performed critically important functions. In this community, the practice of crypto-Judaism provided much of the social and psychological "glue" that held its widely disparate parts together. By necessity, these rituals took place within the privacy of the home. As synagogues had been closed and declared illegal with the expulsion of Jews from Spain in 1492 and the forced conversion of Jews in Portugal in 1497, whatever Jewish practice remained in Iberia or its colonies was relegated to the home environment. Traditionally, most female ritual practice in normative Judaism takes place within the home, so women experienced far less disruption in their religious lives than did men, whose synagogue-based social and institutional practice of Judaism disappeared practically overnight.[31] As Alberro notes, this led to a distinct shift in gendered relationships with religiosity: women tended to be the practitioners of crypto-Judaism, while men tended toward assimilation by becoming either less observant or indifferent to religion altogether.[32] This is not to say, however, that no *converso* men were deeply invested in crypto-Jewish religious practice; many were. As men typically lived "out in the world" more than women, however, it meant that greater efforts at dissimulation were required in order to avoid detection.

Nonetheless, it was largely the sense of a shared religious identity, along with its clandestine ritual practice, that held the commercial networks of the Portuguese nation together. What emerges from the documentary record is that crypto-Judaism often worked as something of a calling card.[33] For example, if you were a young, crypto-Jewish man on the make who decided to leave Seville to pursue opportunities in New Spain, you were instructed to go to the home of one of the crypto-Jewish merchant community leaders in New Spain, such as Simón Váez

Sevilla. Váez, or a man in a similar position, would then set you up in some form of trade or at least provide you with the support and contacts you needed to get settled. One contemporary observer, Matías de Bocanegra, described how crypto-Jewish newcomers to Mexico were aided in settling their new land by the merchant leaders: "[Simón Váez Sevilla] dealt with the other judaizers [sic] who arrived and came to his house with recommendations from Leghorn, Pisa, Spain and other parts where the great majority of them lived. He was like a leader of them all and he accommodated them and spread them around the country in business as traders."[34]

A critical aspect of these business relationships was the establishment of trust, and in the Inquisition documents it appears that one of the most important ways in which trust was established was through participation in crypto-Jewish rituals performed within the privacy of the home. By participating in these clandestine rituals, crypto-Jews shared the risk. On one hand, a participant could denounce to the Inquisition anyone he had witnessed practicing secret Jewish rituals. On the other hand, such a denunciation would also implicate the informer. Perhaps most important, every participant became forever vulnerable to future denunciations by every other participant. Through the group practice of a heterodox, illegal, and secret religion, a communal web of shared vulnerability was created. Additionally, this shared vulnerability may have contributed to greater trustworthiness in mercantile fiduciaries, or factors. If one was potentially vulnerable to a charge of heresy, one might be less likely to betray the merchant one was representing.

In any case, it is clear that these rituals were generally led by women. Crypto-Jewish merchant leaders at times held an enormous amount of influence within their communities and the broader trading network, and this leadership tended to function through a gendered division of labor that held men responsible for the world of commerce and women responsible for the world of sacred ritual. I argue that both roles were indispensable to the overall functioning of the community.

The Bocanegra Report: Three Generations of Váez-Enríquez Women

For historians interested in the experiences of women in colonial Mexico, the Portuguese crypto-Jewish community is very intriguing, for it seems that women exercised an unusual degree of agency within a complex social and economic milieu.[35] Surprisingly, this may have not been all that unusual in Mexico City at this time. Amos Megged argues that, beginning around the middle of the seventeenth century, the counter-Reformation Church and Inquisition in Mexico became preoccupied with the threat of a "growing penumbra of alternative ritual frameworks."[36] These alternative frameworks were frequently led by women of the lower castes and represented a challenge to the Church's monopoly on formal liturgy, rites, and principles.[37] They also challenged the supremacy of the priest as an intermediary between the human and the divine, as others assumed these abilities outside the realm of the Church. That these ritual leaders were typically female, while the priests were exclusively male, points to the significance of gender in this phenomenon. Thus, it seems that in New Spain at this time there existed a plethora of female-led alternative ritual havens that, even when ostensibly "Catholic," operated beyond the pale of accepted Church practice. Therefore, the phenomenon of female leadership among the crypto-Jewish community of New Spain is consistent with similar trends toward alternative religiosity more generally.

Of the three factions within the Portuguese community of Mexico City, the largest by far was that of the Váez-Enríquezes.[38] While some observers saw Simón Váez Sevilla as the leader of the faction, others, such as Gregorio de Guijo, in his diary of important events that took place in New Spain during the 1640s, instead described Váez's *wife,* Juana Enríquez, as the leader.[39] Most likely, both were considered leaders within their community, and each shouldered responsibilities within a gendered division of labor that placed Simón in charge of things directly related to commerce and Juana in charge of things related to religious observance. Thus, this was perhaps more a marriage of equals than we might normally assume for this time and place.

As noted earlier, one of the more useful documents for investigation of the role of women in the Portuguese community of seventeenth-century Mexico City is the recounting of the 1649 auto-de-fé by Matías de Bocanegra. As a Jesuit, Bocanegra was probably not officially part of the Inquisition.[40] His document was basically a report to the Crown as to what had transpired in the auto, but it also provides insight into how the persecuted persons were commonly perceived and of what they had been found guilty. It is a bit unclear how Bocanegra obtained the information upon which the report is based. While he surely consulted the *procesos,* or trial records, it is unlikely that he read through the thousands of folios produced in the interrogations of the 1649 penitents. He also included information that was unlikely to have been gleaned from the *procesos,* such as common perceptions of the accused. These popular perceptions more likely represented what he himself had heard and thought about the matter.

An especially fascinating aspect of Bocanegra's report is the description of three women representing three generations of the Váez-Enríquez family: Blanca Enríquez, Juana Enríquez, and Leonor Váez Sevilla. Blanca Enríquez was the mother of Juana Enríquez. Juana Enríquez was the wife of Simón Váez Sevilla and the mother of Leonor Váez, who died of illness at the age of twelve, well before the 1649 auto. One of the longest *procesos* in the Mexican Inquisition files of the 1640s is that of Juana Enríquez. The Inquisitors' preoccupation with Juana suggests her significance to the crypto-Jewish community as a ritual and social leader—prominence of which the Inquisitors were apparently well aware. Had the Inquisitors somehow been unaware of her elevated status within the community, they would have quickly learned of it, as many of Juana's friends and family were coerced into denouncing her.

Also highly esteemed was Juana's mother, Blanca, who had died before the persecutions of the 1640s and was burned in effigy in the auto of 1649. Like Juana, Blanca was seen as a ritual and social leader, who had special status as a survivor of torture by the Inquisition in Portugal. Her arms bore scars from the ropes of the rack, and some women in the community held her up as a role model for not breaking under torture as they sat in the Inquisition's secret prisons facing the grim prospect themselves.[41] We even get some information about Blanca's mother, Juana Rodriguez. Bocanegra's account provides insight into how these women were perceived as especially threatening to the colonial order.

Blanca Enríquez was described by the Inquisitors as a *rabina,* or female rabbi, a woman who had turned her home into a "synagogue" and who repeatedly led ritual services such as prayers, fasts, funeral observances, and Jewish holiday celebrations.[42] The vitriol she elicited among some members of the Old Christian community of New Spain is suggested by Bocanegra's description of her:

> Doña Blanca Enriquez says she was born in Seville . . . but doubtless she was born in Marialbar, Portugal. . . . She was the root and trunk of such great numbers of Jews. . . . Her wicked mother, Juana Rodriguez, took advantage of her and . . . applied herself in teaching her so that she made her daughter into one of the greatest and most diabolical Jewesses . . . that ever lived. She [Blanca] . . . attained such eminence that no one in the Jewish quarters of Italy or Amsterdam could have had better teachings than those from her mother. . . . [She was] equal to anyone who was able to pursue learning in public synagogues. . . . Blanca corrupted her husband . . . and some of her daughters while in Spain. . . . If she knew that some book was prohibited by the Inquisition, for that very reason she sought it out and read it. This would fill her with more vigor and deadly venom against the Catholic religion.[43]

This woman was filled with "vigor and deadly venom," had personally created "great numbers of Jews," and threatened the Catholic Church by reading banned books. This passage demonstrates that the Inquisition and Bocanegra highlighted Blanca's literacy, her zeal for reading banned books, and her questioning mind in their portrayal of her as a wicked woman. Furthermore, she was seen as "equal to anyone," that is, men, who had been trained in places where Judaism was permitted. One of the more intriguing aspects of Bocanegra's account is the claim that Blanca was highly educated by her mother. Historians have begun to dismantle the conventional wisdom that elite early modern Spanish women were overwhelmingly illiterate, as scholars continue to find compelling evidence for literacy derived from a system of home-based schooling.[44] What is suggested in this passage is the informal but perhaps sophisticated education of a girl by her mother. In any case, it is clear from the Inquisition documents that Blanca was indeed literate, as were at least two of her daughters, and that their literacy was seen as a threat by the Inquisition. Juana Enríquez appears to have deliberately hidden her literacy until near the end of her trial and imprisonment. She finally signed her name before she was released in 1649.[45]

The passage also reveals the common trope of a "wicked mother" who "took advantage" of her innocent daughter and turned her toward the "evil" of Judaism. This story of powerful and persuasive mothers or grandmothers corrupting their descendants appears regularly in the Inquisition files. For example, in the *proceso* of Gaspar Váez Sevilla, son of Juana Enríquez and grandson of Blanca Enríquez, he pleads his case by claiming the understandable gullibility of youth, asserting that he was a victim of his grandmother's indoctrination into Judaism when he was a boy.[46] We also see in Bocanegra's account a preoccupation with women's abilities to create life. Blanca was the "root and trunk of great numbers of Jews." This indicates that her power to create heterodox life through childbirth, as well as by persuasion and conversion, was a source of concern for the Inquisitors. Thus, Bocanegra suggests a Church-based moral anxiety about maternity in general.

Yet another common trope revealed by the passage is an echo of Eden: the idea that wives could sway their husbands away from God and toward evil. For example, Bocanegra declares that Blanca "corrupted" her husband to Judaism. Similarly, in the *proceso* of the swashbuckling merchant Thomas Nuñez de Peralta, son-in-law of Blanca, he claimed he did not know that his wife, Beatriz Enríquez, was Jewish until *after* he had married her. Thus, he depicted himself as the victim of marriage under false pretenses and explained his turn to Judaism as simply a way to preserve domestic harmony.[47] Thus, we see that even the family members of the accused at times portrayed the women in their lives as powerful, persuasive, and heterodox.

As mentioned earlier, the Mexican Inquisition in the 1640s was especially interested in Juana Enríquez. The Inquisitors described her as an especially "zealous and fervent Jewess."[48] Bocanegra's account of Juana at least partially explains the Inquisition's intent focus upon her: it appears that she had captured the public's imagination as both a community leader and a woman of style, grace, and status. Furthermore, it seems that her imprisonment and sentencing as a Judaizer shocked and surprised Mexico City's locals:

> Doña Juana Enriquez was born in Seville about 1602. She is the daughter of the famous dogmatizing rabbis, Antonio Rodriguez Arias and Doña Blanca Enriquez. . . . She had a grand manner when she fasted. She observed Saturdays with baths and other rites and Jewish ceremonies. . . . [A]mong the Judaizers of this kingdom, she came to be acclaimed as the perfect and saintly Jewess because they saw her as a great faster and reciter of prayers. She was so ceremonious and punctiliously bathed herself and cleaned so much before celebrating the Jewish holidays. [She was also venerated] because of the many charities she dispensed to those who observed her lapsed law. . . . [And] she attended all of the funerals and interments of those of her nation. Maybe, because of her false zeal, many died as Jews. She made them give heed to the Law of Moses with their last breaths, telling them that it was necessary for their salvation. A woman could not be more daring! . . . Her evil deeds and transgressions caused a great deal of wonder in the whole city where she had been seen and applauded for the splendor of her dress, the ostentation of her coaches, the maids she kept, and the great vanity of her personage as though she were a great lady and a noble matron.[49]

Here, Bocanegra describes Juana as a "grand" and highly devout woman whose conspicuous consumption of luxury items made her the object of local envy. Thus, her Jewishness is conflated with material prosperity, which in turn suggests high status. Bocanegra does his best to undermine this status by denigrating her "vanity of personage *as though* she were a great lady and noble matron" (emphasis added). In other words, Juana was not a great lady or a noble matron; rather, she had deceived the community into thinking she was. In doing so, she had subverted the "natural" order of things. As the *limpieza de sangre* (blood purity) statutes limited the display of the trappings of wealth to hereditary nobles, for Juana to both display wealth *and* be Jewish, or of "impure" blood, represented a real challenge to legal proscriptions designed to maintain colonial social hierarchy.[50] Thus, Bocanegra iterated through his description of Juana the dangerous potential of material wealth—and stylish women—to confuse the natural order of things.[51] This preoccupation with the potential for misreading social hierarchy via the accumulation and/or display of wealth as characteristic of Jewish people is, of course, nothing new in the annals of European history, but its connection here to female power and fashion in Mexico City is perhaps a less-known tale.

Yet we might also ask this: if, as is suggested by the documents, it was a poorly kept secret that Juana was a *conversa,* if not covertly Jewish, then why the "great deal of wonder" at her denunciation and imprisonment? Likely, it was a reflection more of the sense of violation of the norms associated with her elite status than of genuine surprise at her purported Jewishness. As mentioned earlier, status in early colonial Mexico was signaled primarily by wealth and place of birth, and there was less emphasis on religious orthodoxy per se. In other words, the "wonder" was sparked by the fact that Juana had so effectively played the part of wealthy nobility, with her pretty dresses and fancy carriages, despite the fact that she was of a lower caste. The relative indifference toward heterodoxy is supported by those scholars who have seen in the New World a modus vivendi that held that one need only be publicly Catholic—what happened in private mattered far less.[52] This allowed Indians, for example, to maintain some pre-Columbian traditions within the safety of their homes while being perceived as committed Catholics outside the home. It appears that this arrangement worked for crypto-Jews as well—at least for a while. Of course, one key difference is that crypto-Jews were subjected to the Inquisition, whereas Indians were not. But perhaps a more important difference was the material prosperity that a few crypto-Jews began to enjoy and display in the mid-seventeenth century.

So perhaps the "wonder" was also sparked because this persecution represented a real change in the status quo and was a signal that religious orthodoxy was going to become far more critical to the maintenance of status in New Spain than it had previously been. Indeed, some scholars have argued that it was precisely in the 1640s that attitudes regarding elite identity shifted toward a preoccupation with religious orthodoxy and away from simply being wealthy and Iberian. This would prove especially true for the creoles. Scholars such as Richard Greenleaf and Solange Alberro have noted the ways in which creole identity in Mexico, the basis upon which national identity was constructed at the time of independence, centered upon issues of religious orthodoxy.[53] While these issues are beyond the scope of this essay, Bocanegra's brief description of Juana epitomizes one of countless moments in which the populace in seventeenth- and eighteenth-century New Spain was instructed by local officials that *limpieza de sangre* and religious orthodoxy trumped place of birth, race, or wealth in defining who belonged to the dominant group. Alberro and Greenleaf note that this emphasis on religious orthodoxy particularly benefited creoles, who could not change their place of birth but who could fashion a sense of religious superiority as a way to strengthen their position against competing peninsulars. This shift in religious sensibility and creole identity would come to be manifested in the cult of the Virgin of Guadalupe, which emerged so concomitantly with these persecutions that it is likely that the two phenomena are linked.

The Inquisition documents reveal much about women's roles within the Portuguese community. In particular, the records suggest a high level of female participation in recognizably Jewish practice. For example, it appears that Juana and other women led prayer services for men and women, performed funerary rituals, observed the Sabbath and annual holidays such as Purim and Yom Kippur, and initiated newcomers and children into Judaism.[54] As mentioned, this substantive knowledge of Jewish practice in part stemmed from the fact that Mexico City's Portuguese population had connections with Jewish communities throughout Europe, especially with those of Italy and southern France. And it was not only the transatlantic connections with these communities that facilitated the transmission of information regarding Jewish practice, as some members of Mexico City's Portuguese community had previously resided in openly Jewish communities in European cities such as Leghorn, Pisa, Bayonne, and Bordeaux.[55] This meant that the community comprised, in part, individuals who likely had extensive Jewish knowledge.

One intriguing aspect of this phenomenon is that most of these individuals who had extensive Jewish knowledge were male, yet it appears that women led most of the ritual services in New Spain. Why were men within this community so willing to allow women to occupy positions of ritual leadership? Part of the answer lies in the fact that men within elite crypto-Jewish homes tended to be away from home for extended periods of time as part of their commercial activities, leaving women in charge of running the household for months or even years at a time. While men were away, elite women not only saw to their domestic duties but were also charged with helping to maintain the religious and social ties that bound the nation together. Thus, it may, somewhat ironically, have been the patriarchal exigencies of colonial crypto-Jewish merchant life that kept elite women within the home and men outside it, allowing some women to become community leaders.

From Bocanegra's account, we learn of the youngest of the Váez-Enríquez women, Leonor:

> Leonor Vaez Sevilla was a maiden born in Mexico City where she died at the age of twelve. . . . Beginning a year and a half prior to her decease, she followed the practices of the law of Moses. She had been taught by that nefarious, perfidious Jewess, her grandmother, Doña Blanca Enriquez. Although she was at such a tender age, she became so consumed in this [Judaism] that her grandmother held her up as an example to the other members of the family. She became the most punctilious in the observance of their fasts and ceremonies. Since she was the daughter of such parents, one could not expect more than this of the viper of hell.[56]

This description of Leonor illuminates how initiation into Judaism tended to follow matriarchal lines. Mothers and grandmothers were typically the ones to initiate their descendants into the clandestine religion.[57] This initiation made everyone concerned more vulnerable to the hostile world around them. It also forged a bond of shared risk that could intensify, for better or for worse, the relationship between parent and child. Typically, children were told around adolescence that the "Law of Moses" was the true law. Presumably, initiating younger children would have been too risky. In the case of Leonor, we see an enthusiastic embrace of the religion, with additional training and schooling provided by her grandmother. For Leonor, it seems that the conversion to Judaism led to a heightened intimacy between the generations, as mother and grandmother brought a child into a secret and educated her in Jewish lifeways. And finally, we once again see in this passage an iteration of a broader Inquisitorial anxiety toward women as mothers, as they were depicted as able to create "vipers of hell" by both nature and nurture.

Conclusion: *Las Rabinas*

Consideration of these descriptions of women from three generations of *conversas* points to some tentative conclusions. The first is that the women of this community, a sizable minority of whom not only could read and write but were even well read, performed a range of social and religious functions. They acted as ritual guides and experts, headed charitable organizations, and helped arrange marriages. They were seen as initiators and educators regarding crypto-Jewish practice. Moreover, they led the observances of Shabbat, fast days, and funerals.

Second, it is likely that women played an important role within the Portuguese nation. The Portuguese nation was built out of interactions among the men and women of Jewish and crypto-Jewish communities, and these interactions took place largely within the privacy of the home. The documentary record of Inquisition trials attests to the ways in which newcomers to these communities participated in crypto-Jewish ritual. The underlying purpose of participation in such rituals was clear: to establish trust and a shared vulnerability through a clandestine, highly risky ritual observance. This observance—at least in New Spain—was typically led by women. In other words, it was in part through these social and ritual functions that women helped to forge that "common background, experience, and emotion" that Jonathan Israel speaks of, which bound together the Portuguese nation as "a closely-knit network that was simultaneously religious, social, and commercial."[58]

The third broad point that emerges from this material is that there seems to have been a commonly held perception among at least elites in New Spain that these were powerful—and dangerous—women. Guijo identified Juana Enríquez as the "leader" of the Váez Sevilla faction. Bocanegra described Blanca Enríquez as the "root and trunk of such great numbers of Jews," a woman who, through her mother's education, had become a "venomous" threat to Catholicism. Her daughter, Juana, was "seen and applauded . . . for the great vanity of her personage" and was also perceived as a woman who "could not be more daring" as she instructed others in Judaism and performed sacred rites. Leonor Váez Sevilla was the offspring of that "viper from hell," Juana, and was therefore almost biologically determined to be heterodox. And the Inquisition documents themselves, with their intense focus on the activities of women and the use of the term "rabinas"—female rabbis—to describe some of these female leaders, suggest an elite, male, Old Christian preoccupation with the threat of heterodox, *female* power that remains an understudied aspect of the history of colonial Mexico.

The experiences of these three generations of *conversas* add to our understanding of what some feminist scholars have referred to as a "patchwork of patriarchies," the idea that not all patriarchies are created equal.[59] Even more than this, the experiences of elite crypto-Jewish women in seventeenth-century New Spain bolster Kimberly Gauderman's bold and controversial thesis that the Habsburg era in Spain and the colonies was not truly patriarchal. She argues that the Habsburg-era Spanish home and society were not truly patriarchal because power was structured more as a web of connected and counterbalanced threads than as a horizontal body that centered authority at the head.[60] In particular, wives countered their husbands' power through a range of legal rights, especially those related to the protection of their dowries and the ability to determine who would inherit their property.

While in general I maintain that Spanish America was indeed patriarchal, in that men qua men generally held positions of dominance over women in nearly all aspects of life, it seems that these *conversas* exercised considerable power and authority within their homes and community. Thus, their experiences seem to echo Gauderman's findings that elite colonial women in Spanish America tended to live in homes that were not fully or essentially patriarchal. Unlike the women Gauderman describes, however, these *conversas* did not rely primarily upon Spanish legal protections for their power. Rather, they fashioned a space that straddled two worlds, the legal and the extralegal, and it was in this alternative realm that they found greater autonomy and freedom from patriarchal constraints.

Therefore, it appears that the crypto-Jewish home could function as a site of resistance to dominant religious and cultural mores, as well as a place for establishing and maintaining business and communal connections. Crypto-Jewish women at times assumed religious and social roles that gave them a strong position within their households, within their communities, and within the dynamic and global commercial network known as the Portuguese nation. In doing so, they engaged in a creative act that restructured and redefined various aspects of the world they had been born into, including but not limited to conceptions of God, the nature of religious authority, the caste and gender ordering of society, and the particulars of individuals' social and moral obligations to themselves, their families, and their communities.

Erika Gasser

"The Refuse of the whole Creation"

Manhood, Misogyny, and Race in an Anglo-Caribbean Travel Narrative

The Condition of an Author, is much like that of a Strumpet, both exposing our Reputations to support our Necessities, till at last we contract such an ill habit, thro' our Practices, that we are equally troubl'd with an Itch to be always Doing; and if the Reason be requir'd, Why we betake our selves to so Scandalous a Profession as Whoring or Pamphleteering, the same excusive Answer will serve us both, viz. That the unhappy circumstances of a Narrow Fortune, hath forc'd us to do that for our Subsistance, which we are much asham'd of.

Edward Ward, preface to *A Trip to Jamaica* (1698)

As historians pay increased attention to the ways that Native and African women figured materially and discursively in the European colonization of the Caribbean, these women appear, paradoxically, as both marginal and central to that project.[1] This contradiction emerged in published narratives about Jamaica when, for example, English men invoked gender both to support and to disparage the colonial project. This essay examines how gender and race factored in English travel writing about Jamaica at the turn of the eighteenth century, taking as a case study the Grub Street scribbler Edward "Ned" Ward, whose venomous *A Trip to Jamaica* (1698) launched his career. In many ways, *A Trip to Jamaica* is an unlikely place to look for reliable historical information about late seventeenth-century voyages by sea, those who took them, or even their destinations. Indeed, it is hard to be sure that Ward even made the journey at all.[2] Few literary scholars have found much in Ward's writing to recommend it, either. While both historians and literary scholars refer to Ward's vibrant descriptions of social life in London and his status as one of several emerging Grub Street scribblers, he largely remains a supporting rather than a central figure.[3] But, as a case study, Ward and his first successful text suggest a great deal about how gender and race factored in English travel writing at the turn of the eighteenth century, and his bilious prose nonetheless illuminates the power and flexibility of formulaic literary misogyny. Though a hack, Ward provides an angle from which to analyze how a fraught manhood rested discursively upon disgust for women—whether English, Native, African, real or imagined. In addition to having launched Ward's career, *A Trip to Jamaica* raises profitable methodological questions about the historical value of popular satirical pamphlets in shaping and reflecting English views of colonial subjects. Ultimately, Ward's published battles with other writers reveal his own simultaneous struggle to produce a profitable body of work and to embody a profitable manhood.

Misogyny and Satire at the Turn of the Eighteenth Century

When treating the subject of eighteenth-century satire, historians and literary scholars have emphasized a somewhat later period than the moment under investigation here; this is understandable given the incredible productivity of Grub Street writers in the 1720s and 1730s, the rise of the Scriblerus Club, and Alexander Pope's *Dunciad,* which took authors like Ward to task.[4] Even an introduction to the full subject would be impractical in this format, so this essay focuses on some of the historical texts that provided a direct foundation for Ned Ward's *A Trip to Jamaica.* In many ways, Ward's work was not new. In his misogyny and satire we can see echoes of the classical works of Juvenal and of contemporary works by John Dryden, John Oldham, Thomas Brown, and the knot of pamphlets published in the 1680s and 1690s that traded on "satyr" against women.[5] Furthermore, Ward's critical scrutiny of the English en route to New World colonies in *A Trip to Jamaica* reflected earlier works like Edmund Hickeringill's *Jamaica Viewed* (1661) and contemporary works such as Aphra Behn's *Oroonoko,* published as a novel in 1688 and performed as a play in 1696, and Mary Pix's comedy *The Innocent Mistress* (1697).[6] The success of *A Trip to Jamaica* eventually enabled Ward to transition from scurrilous pamphlets and travel narratives into proto-journalism. His well-known periodical, *The London Spy,* also attracted more attention from scholars. But his early poetry and prose managed to shock rather than to surprise.

Any reader of Ward's writing will find him more comprehensible in relation to the authors whose styles he emulated. The ancient satires by Juvenal (c. 55–127 C.E.), which were populated by myriad degraded women, surely figured among Ward's models. In just a few pages of Juvenal's sixth *Satire* one encounters prostitutes,

Portrait of Edward "Ned" Ward (1710). National Portrait Gallery, London.

whores, Amazons, wives, poisoners, dames, harlots, and strumpets without any sense that the author has wearied of the repetition. Dryden's publication of a translation of Juvenal's satire in 1693 surely helped fuel contemporary imitators.[7] In an overview of Juvenal's female archetypes, Dryden wrote that "Those who pass for chast[e] amongst them, are not really so; but only for their vast Dowries, are rather suffer'd, than lov'd by their own Husbands. That they are Imperious, Domineering, Scolding Wives. . . . That they deal with Jews, Diviners, and Fortune-tellers: Learn the Arts of Miscarrying, and Barrenness. Buy Children, and produce them for their own. Murther their Husbands sons, if they stand in their way to his Estate: and make their Adulterers his Heirs."[8]

Dryden expressed disapproval of Juvenal's malice toward womankind but concluded, first, that Roman women must have embodied the vices of that notoriously infamous age, and, second, that "the Species of those Women is extinguish'd; or at least, that they were never here propagated." While Dryden assured his audience that whatever "Roman Ladies were, the English are free from all his Imputations," the exuberance of the original left a more lasting impression.[9] That exuberance of unleashed misogyny gives Ward's writing its uneasy momentum and places him alongside the range of writers who used the problem of sex as a fruitful subject for invective.[10]

However Dryden advocated the superiority of early modern English women over their Roman precursors, at the turn of the eighteenth century satirists continued to propagate many of the same charges. After 1695, when Parliament opted not to renew the Licensing of the Press Act, a market for all sorts of printed material flourished in London, and Ned Ward strove to make a name for himself by writing what would sell. While his drive for profits undoubtedly overtook any concern with accuracy in reporting, Ward's obsessive reliance upon gender as the primary language of meaning and power, in his writing about both himself and others, made his work revealing despite itself. As befit satire, he represented women and men in ways that obscured complexities and resorted to familiar types. In *A Trip to Jamaica,* this approach is mirrored by a similar erasure of Jamaica and race; the West Indian colonies and everything they represented were translated to English readers only as implicit suggestions that traded on inherited assumptions about whiteness, Englishness, and power. Ward's scurrilous writing therefore provides an example of how satire enabled the pursuit of multivalent arguments and objectives and provided context for emerging ideas about England's colonization of the West Indies. Even the silences and empty spaces in Ward's invoked Jamaica allow glimpses of the ways that language structured power relations among the writer and his subjects.

Manhood and Misogyny in the Writings of Edward Ward

Edward "Ned" Ward came to London around 1690 in anticipation of receiving a patrimony from his grandmother.[11] His hopes were dashed, however, when the grandmother left the estate to the daughter who lived with her; this was surely an example, from Ward's perspective, of a tragic misdirection of resources. Ward found himself with a rapidly dwindling fortune and threw his lot in with his scribbling peers, mostly men of university training (unlike himself), who wrote pamphlets and lived off the inconsistent profits from their sales. Ward's first foray into this world was a poem, *The Poet's Ramble after Riches, or a Night's Transactions upon the Road Burlesqu'd* (1691), which anticipated the work for which he would later become famous.[12] Between 1691 and 1698, Ward likely produced other works, but it is difficult to be confident of any attributions other than that for 1695's *Female Policy Detected, or the Arts of a Designing Woman Laid Open,* which had ten editions.[13] Howard Troyer, Ward's main biographer, minimized the text's significance in part because portions had been cribbed from earlier sources and also because Ward did not acknowledge it after he was in a position to do so—something he took care to do with *The Poet's Ramble after Riches.*[14] Nonetheless, the misogynistic *Female Policy Detected* provided the most direct context for *A Trip to Jamaica* (1698), and the subsequent edition of *Female Policy Detected* (1702) demonstrated that, no matter what his subject, Ward used women as the contested medium for his broader satire. Ned Ward makes an unlikely character on which to base historical inquiry, but this most unreliable of writers recaptures a kind of world and text in which gendered language allowed even lowly men to leverage power among themselves by deriding others.

Female Policy Detected outlined the sufferings of men at the hands of designing women, in chapters about their allurements, inconstancy, love, revenge, pride, and ingratitude. Purportedly to prevent young men from falling victim to the wrong sorts of women, Ward wended his way through the "Subtile Stratagems and Devices, by which they oft Trepan Unwary Youth into a State of Misery."[15] In the edition from 1702, Ward appended a more virulently misogynistic section lifted almost entirely from Joseph Swetnam's *The Arraignment of Lewd, Idle, Forward and Unconstant Women* (1615), which had set off a pamphlet war of its own, and Jacques Olivier's *A Discourse of Women* (1660).[16] While the passages were not of Ward's making, his borrowing suggests that he found in the earlier language not only fodder for profitable controversy but also much that continued to resonate. The reader hears the familiar paradox of woman's frailty and irrationality, coupled with her apparently limitless power to manipulate, dominate, and degrade men sexually and emotionally. Several passages relied heavily on metaphor, since the images and comparisons between women and animals, nature, and objects were likely to strike a chord with readers and make the work memorable and amusing. One such passage states,

> It is of a truth said, *That an old Dog, and an hungry Flea bite sore;* but in my mind a froward Woman biteth more sorer; and if thou go about to master a Woman, hoping to bring her to humility; there is no way to make her good with Stripes, except thou beat her to Death; for do thou what thou wilt, yet a froward Woman in her frantick mood will pull hale, swear, scratch, and tear, all that stands in her way.[17]

The passage transitions quickly from comparing women to parasitic insects to casually suggesting that beating a wife to death might represent her husband's only release from her clutches. While the passage originated in Swetnam's work, both the metaphors and the clash of sudden extremes permeate Ward's writing, even in the parts that aim to provide political or economic commentary.

In *Female Policy Detected,* Ward turned again to the legacy of Juvenal and the words of Swetnam to document the philosophical and scriptural premises of women's evil nature. Perhaps to spark controversy and reach for laughs, Ward replicated Swetnam's list of men's disempowering experiences for which women were to blame by inquiring,

> And what shall we term her but the Offspring of Satan, whose Head, Hands, Heart, Mind, and Soul is evil? For Women are called the Hook of all Evil, because Men are taken with them Fish: For Women have a Thousand ways to deceive thee, and all such Fools as are Suiters unto them . . . some they please with Kisses; They lay out the Folds of their Hair, to entangle Men in their Love; betwixt their Breasts is the Valley of Destruction, and in their Beds is Hell, Sorrow, and Repentance. Eagles eat not Men till they are dead, but Women devour them alive. . . . [T]hey are ungrateful, perjured, full of fraud, flouting and deceit, unconstant, waspish, toyish, light, sullen, proud, discourteous and cruel.[18]

After paraphrasing these striking accusations for several pages, Ward reproduced some of Olivier's accounts of evil, manipulative women who brought about the destruction of innocent men. Though misogynist literature does not reliably reflect the condition of actual women's lives, the authors' preoccupation with women's inherent wickedness strongly suggested that there was no significant ill that could not be laid at women's feet. Ward's use of Olivier's and Swetnam's prose shows the longevity and continuity of this brand of literary misogyny and suggests his drive to spark both controversy and the profits that accompanied it.

Following the description of historical women traitors, Ward returned to Swetnam's dire description of women's bodies to illustrate how all that dazzled the eye constituted in reality nothing more than a trap. Men who were moved by women's beauty were "Giddy-headed" and "so foolish, that they think themselves happy." In addition, he cautioned:

> Although Women are Beautiful, shewing Pity, yet their Hearts are Black, swelling with Mischief; not much unlike unto old Trees, whose outward Leaves are Fair and Green, and yet the Body rotten . . . for they will allure thee with Amorous Glances of Lust, and yet kill thee with bitter Looks of Hate; they have Dimples in their cheeks to deceive thee, and wrinkles in their Brows to betray thee: They have Eyes to intice, Smiles to flatter, Embracements to provoke, Beckens to recal, Lips to enchant, Kisses to enflame, Tears to excuse themselves.[19]

Here Ward reiterated the idea that women's most pleasing attributes were nothing but calculated wiles to prey upon men. At the conclusion of the first edition, Ward provided two poems meant to commend virtue and "dispraise" vice, but while the former allowed for the possibility of a decent wife, the latter left the reader with weighty misogynist tropes. By the time Ward made the additions to

Female Policy Detected in 1702, he had established that female corruption began in the body and radiated outward into the litany of negative characteristics provided on every page, until the sense of persecution grew to encompass and overshadow the extensive detail.

Ward's own predilection to heap insult upon insult likely helps to explain why he found Swetnam's earlier prose so fitting. Even after an exhaustive account of women's wickedness from countless historical examples, he concluded,

> Therefore, if thou study a Thousand Years, thou shalt find a Woman nothing else but a Contrary unto Man; Nay, if thou continue with her an Hundred Years, thou shalt find in her new Fancies, and contrary Sorts of Behaviour; therefore, if all the World were Paper, and all the Sea Ink, and all the Trees and Plants were Pens, and every Man in the world were a Writer, yet were they not able with all their Labour and Cunning, to set down all the crafty Deceits of Women.[20]

Ward duplicated Swetnam's drive to set these deceits to paper, in a way that evoked his elision of "whoring and pamphleteering" in the preface of *A Trip to Jamaica.* The misogynistic element of Ward's first two editions of *Female Policy Detected* pervaded his many subsequent pamphlets that outlined women's defective natures and the curse they brought into the lives of men. However derivative this formulaic misogyny was, however profit driven, and however common throughout the culture, Ward's extensive reliance upon it made it resemble a compulsion that, like the lusts of the women he described, could not be sated even by the repetition of the desired act—in his case, to convey man's anxiety and spleen through the page.

Misogyny is a versatile device, and Ward's reliance upon it in nearly every aspect of his writing—whether to satirize the battle of the sexes or colonial efforts in the West Indies—reminds us that his society was steeped in such language and that it could serve various rhetorical purposes. While satirical, Ward's dismissal of women's humanity and individuality contributed to an ongoing cultural conversation that was conducive to violence. Even (and perhaps especially) when he rehashed previous writers' language, his claims that men were ever the victims of women's powers bolstered the idea that men had to assert the dominance that appeared too conditional on women's compliance. The tone of the early *Female Policy Detected* set the stage for *A Trip to Jamaica,* especially in the premise that independent manhood must assert total control over inferior dependents. Given the infamous measures taken to enforce racial supremacy in West Indian slavery, it is impossible that Ward did not see the overlap between racial and gendered power especially in his invocation of—even an imagined, discursive—Jamaica.[21]

Edward Ward's *A Trip to Jamaica* (1698)

Ward's *A Trip to Jamaica* married formulaic misogyny to casual racism in a way that sets this work apart from his many later publications that focused on London. Even granting that his agenda had more to do with caricaturing promotional travel literature than it did with "true" description, and even without many references to actual Africans, one hears casual racism in *A Trip to Jamaica* because Ward's disgust for and emphatic dismissal of the place rested on an accounting of the island's climate, heterogeneity, and fluid social boundaries that evoked images of island life among the black population. Ward claimed to have traveled to Jamaica in 1688 in order to escape his creditors, and one can only assume that had he managed to improve his fortunes there, his view of Jamaica's more fluid social structure might have been different. Instead, Ward strove to write his way into a better social position while accepting the system that allowed his social betters to exclude him; like many of his peers, he sought not to abolish the privileges of English manhood but rather to attain more of them for himself.[22]

When he published *A Trip to Jamaica* in 1698, Ward hit upon a formula that, while not original, sold beyond expectations. The short pamphlet went through seven editions before 1700, and Ward made sure to sign subsequent publications with the tagline, "By the Author of the Trip to Jamaica."[23] The pamphlet purported to provide an indifferent account of the journey to the West Indies and the island of Jamaica itself, but Ward's preoccupation with misogyny and manhood overwhelmed the purported subjects. In his preface, he explained that his purpose in writing was not to inform but rather to "*Entertain you with what I intend for your* Diversion, *not* Instruction; *Digested into such a Stile as might move your* Laughter, *not Merit your* Esteem."[24] By proclaiming his motives as satirical yet humble, he relieved himself of the responsibility to be substantive and provided a rationale for his reliance upon devices that he hoped would render him witty in his readers' eyes. This tentative balance between embracing everything low and straining to impress permeates *A Trip to Jamaica,* along with much of Ward's later work.

Sensationalism and exaggeration helped to sell papers, of course, and Ward replicated the conventions of the preexisting genre of misogynist pamphlets, but it would be a mistake to dismiss his works as nothing more than pastiche and plagiarism. Right from the start of *A Trip to Jamaica,* his careful selection and cooptation of others' work rendered the text more strategic than it purported to be, especially in the way that Ward mediated nearly every point through a gendered lens. For example, to emphasize his troubles with debt, he wrote that "like a Thief in a Goal, or a Whore in a Flux, I Resolv'd for the future to Reform my Life," though he acknowledged that he had "no more hopes of mending my Condition, by pursuing my intended measures, than a Good Husband has of mending a Bad Wife by winking at her Vices." A man he observed had "as peevish a Countenance, as if he had unluckily stumbled upon his Wifes Failings, and unhappily become a Witness to his own Cuckoldome," and the Thames became the "Lady Thames . . . put into a Passion, by the rude Kisses of an Easterly Wind, [who] drew her Smooth Face into so many Wrinkles."[25] Ward attempted to copy Juvenal, Swetnam, and other misogynist authors, but he took to the subject so forcefully that he eked out a kind of individual voice while doing so. *A Trip to Jamaica,* unsurprisingly, had more to say about what he already believed than about the place itself. Even assuming that Ward did make the trip, "Jamaica" was reduced to a series of conceits around which familiar English characters could be placed.

To grasp the extent of his commitment to this approach, one can review *A Trip to Jamaica* for Ward's obsessive references to women in the course of writing about things that were not women. The ocean "is of such Profundity, that, like a Misers Conscience, or a Womans Concupiscence 'tis never to be Fathom'd." He took pride in his winnings at backgammon "like the Whore who boasted of her Industry." A storm appeared "in as little time as a Girl might lose her Maidenhead."[26] Later, when describing the flora and fauna of the island, Ward wrote that island dwellers had for food sea turtle, which was "as White as a Green-sickness Girl," fowl "as dry as the Udder of an Old Woman," and "Cussue," which, while being juicy, was so acidic that it drew his tongue to his mouth "like a Hens Fundament, and made my Palate as Rough, and Tongue as Sore, as if I had been Gargling it with Allom-Water: From whence I conjecture, they are a much fitter Fruit to recover Lost Maiden-heads, properly apply'd, than to be Eaten." Coconuts' kernels, he wrote, were "as a Filbert, but (like a Beautiful Woman well Drest, and Infectious) if you venture to Taste, is of ill consequence."[27] These quips, if puerile, were nonetheless reliable humor for the day. Ward turned his travel account into a series of vignettes that rested upon familiar misogynist tropes because even on uncertain ground—particularly if he never actually stepped upon that ground—jokes about women and sex never disappointed.

Like many writers who found fruitful subject matter in a shipload of people closely confined, Ward used the conditions of that "little world" as a way to cast aspersions on the larger one.[28] He informed the reader that they had aboard "three of the Troublesome Sex, as some call them, (tho' I never thought 'em so) whose Curteous Affabillity, and Complaisancy of Temper, admitted of no other Emulation, but to strive who (within the bounds of Modesty) should be most Obliging." In addition to hinting at the expanded possibilities of social interactions aboard ship, Ward's claim never to have considered women troublesome set him up as a reliable and impartial narrator, and, to those who already knew him, it winked. The passage goes on to explain:

> One Unfortunate Lady was in pursuit of a Stray'd Husband, who, in Jamaica, had Feloniously taken to Wife (for the sake of a Plantation) a Lacker-Fac'd Creolean, to the great dissatisfaction of his Original Spouse, who had often declar'd (thro' the sweetness of her Disposition) That if he had Marry'd another Handsomer than her self, it would never have Vex'd her; but to be Rival'd by a Gipsy, a Tawny Fac'd Moletto Strumpet, a Pumpkin colour'd Whore; no, her Honour would not suffer her to bear with Patience so coroding an Indignity. The other two were a pretty Maid, and a comely Widow; so that in these three, we had every Honourable State of the whole Sex: One in the state of Innocency, another of Fruition, the third of Deprivation; and if we'd had but one in the State of Corruption, a Man might have pleas'd himself as well in our Little World, as you Libertines do in the Great One.[29]

This section demonstrates Ward's skill at invoking sex and race to mock, while also disingenuously distancing himself from base presentiments. He satirized the married English woman because of her irrational response to her husband's choice of mistress and also by having a string of curses come from a supposedly respectable woman's mouth. The passage poked fun at conventional presumptions about the hurt feelings of one who has been wronged, substituting instead the more intimate furies of a woman scorned. Ward conveniently fitted out the ship with one of every "honorable" female archetype, women who existed to the extent that their male contemporaries made use of them. Women such as these were types, so ready-made that they were destined to people the ship of Ward's crossing whether or not he actually made the trip.

The aforementioned storm also provided the necessary setting for Ward's next encounter with the woman whose husband had married the Creole woman; Ward claims they both sought cover in the ship's gun room, and he recorded a moment of distress in which she prayed,

> And if Thou hast Decreed, that we shall Perish in this Tempest, I most humbly beseech Thee to Punish with Pox, Barrenness, and Dry-Belly-Ach, that Adultrous Strumpet, who, by Robbing me of my Husband, hath been a means of bringing me to this untimely End; may her whole Life be a continued course of Sin without a Moments Repentence, that she may Die without Forgiveness, and be Damn'd without Mercy. In which Interim a Sea wash'd over our Fore-Castle, run Aft, and came down the Whip-scuttle; she concluding we were going to the Bottom, Shreek'd out, and fell into a Fit; whilst I, thro' my Fear, together with my Modesty, scorn'd to take the Advantage of so fair an Opportunity.[30]

In addition to learning more about the scorned wife's caustic hatred of the Creole woman, Ward provided the reader with a humorous scene in which the wife was terrified, shrieked, and fell into a panic. While he claimed to pass on it, he slyly reported this scene as a fair opportunity for a seduction that, in late seventeenth-century fashion, blurred the line between it and assault.

The mention of the Creole woman constituted the only reference to a woman of color to appear in Ward's tale, and his other references to Africans in Jamaica were similarly empty. He wrote of "Negroes" who carried their owners about when the latter were ill or who had to move the colony's refuse from one place to another and of the proverbial "Ethiopian" who was unable to change his color. The absence of any reflection upon the condition of African men and women in one way mirrors his use of types to stand in for British characters. The difference lay in the fact that while sailors, such as the kidnapped Irishman meant to be sold as a servant, were also types, they did not stand in as a representation of their kind in the same way as the rhetorical "Negroes." Even though Ward mocked everything and reveled in the weaknesses and foolishness of all sorts of English men, those critiques turned on their capacity for individualism. All women were implicated in his misogynistic jokes, and all people of color, however murkily conjured, were potential degraded "slaves," despite the fact that the supposedly biracial Creole woman evidently had a plantation in her name. In fact, Ward's only explicit reference to slavery came when he described a fearful moment on board when the crew expected to skirmish with the French and faced "great Danger of being knock'd on the Head, or made Slaves."[31] Like many of his contemporaries, Ward sidestepped slavery so completely that he registered no disjuncture when invoking an Englishman's lament about his own imminent "slavery" even while surrounded by truer examples.

After jauntily describing his journey, Ward finally prepared his reader for an account, composed "without Malice or Partiality," of Jamaica itself. Jamaica was, he elaborated,

> The Dunghill of the Universe, the Refuse of the whole Creation, the Clippings of the Elements, a shapeless Pile of Rubbish confusd'ly jumbl'd into an Emblem of the Chaos, neglected by Omnipotence when he form'd the World into its admirable Order. The Nursery of Heavens Judgments, where the Malignant Seeds of all Pestilence were first gather'd and scatter'd thro' the Regions of the Earth, to Punish Mankind for their Offences. . . . The Receptacle of Vagabonds, the Sanctuary of Bankrupts, and a Close-stool for the Purges of our Prisons. As Sickly as an Hospital, as Dangerous as the Plague, as Hot as Hell, and as Wicked as the Devil.[32]

The abrupt transition after his claim to impartiality helped to make Ward's slanderous list funny, and it invited the reader to wonder at the reason for such effusive hatred. Some of Ward's terms also reflected the language he used elsewhere to describe women. His reference to the "Chaos" that existed before God formed the heavens and earth, for example, resonated with customary associations of women with chaos. Even when taking Ward's other satirical publications into account, few other subjects came as close as Jamaica did to representing and embodying women's deceits, sins, and lies. In addition to bringing Ward his first success, *A Trip to Jamaica* also showed that colonies, like women, were entities whose possession appeared to require unremitting domination by English men.

It is possible that Ward relied so heavily upon misogyny because he intended to pander to his audience, and whores were a reliable laugh. This premise supports, although it does not necessarily rely upon, the idea that Ward was simply a bad writer. Alternatively, Ward may have wielded his pen at women's expense so relentlessly that he moved beyond the standard "war of the sexes" rhetoric and revealed himself as an ambitious writer who expanded the conversation about Jamaica at home even as he used cheap tricks. Ward depicted his journey to Jamaica as a dangerous but amusing lark, and women (real and imagined, English and African) were his currency. He used them as the focal point for his disgust and diminished them through constant comparisons between his lot and theirs; Ward claimed that a writer, like a whore, was itching "to be always doing." His cheerful references to what we would see as sexual assault and his use of sex-based stereotypes that were tired even in the late seventeenth century created an affable veneer that obscured how intently he leveraged his manhood and potential access to patriarchal power. His aggressive criticism of other men and his posturing with his own critics showed that he was palpably aware of his own literary and monetary shortcomings. There was some comfort to be taken, then, in superiority to women and how easily it could be merged with superiority to slaves, however abstract they were in Ward's imagined Jamaica. It may seem trivial to consider Ward's forms of misogyny, which reflected preexisting cultural norms rather than creating new ones, and his racism, which appears casual in comparison to that of the Englishmen who wielded direct colonial power during this period. Nevertheless, Ward's work provides an opportunity to gauge how the languages of misogyny and racism worked at varying levels of discourse and demonstrates how the continued intermingling of these languages contributed to colonial attitudes in the metropole.

Manhood in, and in response to, Ward's satire

Far more explicit than the potential implications of Ward's construction of Jamaica was his struggle to achieve viability as a writer—a project that rested upon an ongoing contest over viable manhood. Ward and his scribbling companions constantly argued over authorship, wit, and credit; the authors' very survival hinged on their ability to convince their readers and peers that they were men of parts who were respected by honorable men. This often necessitated a delicate balancing act between an aggressive defense of one's self-fashioned identity and body of work on one hand and a performance of self-deprecation and respect for one's superiors on the other. In 1698 Ward found himself in a war of words with an anonymous adversary over the authorship of certain pamphlets that described travels to the Netherlands. Their largely forgotten dispute serves as a reminder that gender—specifically the way the authors laid claims to a viable, if not always "respectable," manhood—permeated the very nature of hack writing, publishing, jesting, and profiteering.

After the success of Ward's *A Trip to Jamaica,* this other author, along with his publisher, decided to recycle parts of Owen Feltham's writings about his travels in the Low Countries. Felltham's works had been published in four different formats between 1648 and 1697, and some of these had multiple editions. After Felltham died, in 1668, publishers continued to rehash his work under slightly different titles, up to and including 1699's *A Trip to Holland,* which explicitly echoed the title of Ward's recent success.[33] The preface of the 1699 edition immediately acknowledged that the timing was no accident. "Certainly," its author asked, "a Trip to Holland may be as grateful as one to Jamaica?" Having thus situated the text, he embarked upon an attack on Ward, claiming,

> And if I am not so Witty as the Plantation Author I am certain I am somewhat Wiser. He takes the liberty of abusing his own fellow Subjects, and consequently beshits his own Nest, but I fall upon a Nation which shits upon all the world beside . . . and I think nasty terms are fitly apply'd to such nasty People. I am afraid our West-India Poet is some transported Fellon, who being sent to the Plantation for a Venture, lit on a bad Master, and with a true New-Gate Courtisie to revenge his Spleen on one House, he squirts his Excrement against a whole Island. But no more of his Trip: it has Sold very well, and it's my business to sell mine if I can, and like a true Author Preface it heartily, or the Ignorant Puppy my Chap will never buy it.[34]

One of the prerogatives of scurrilous manhood was to express scorn and disgust at the bodies of others and to align one's enemies with the base habits of known inferiors. The preface's author simultaneously admitted his desire to emulate Ward or at least to benefit from his success by proxy and reveled in the dismantling of Ward's self-fashioning as a respectable man—if one in some financial straits.[35] The ensuing struggle between the men, captured in print, demonstrates how the authorial gaze so easily slipped from an exotic subject, such as the inhabitants and environment of a Caribbean island, back to the familiar battleground for manly status and viability in the market.

Ward replied to his challenger in a double-sided broadside called *A curry-comb for a cocks-comb: or, the Trip to Holland detected,* which was signed "By the Author of the Trip to Jamaica."[36] Unsurprisingly, he took issue with the published challenges to his identity and status and labored to regain the upper hand. Because

Ward intended not only to defend himself but also to destroy his opponent's claims of qualifying to pass judgment, he gestured to the customs of publishing as a way to present the preface's author as an outsider who allowed self-interest to propel him into a society whose rules he did not understand. From the start, Ward blasted his opponent with a smug self-description that restored his relationship with his critic to acceptable terms, writing,

> As a true bred Mastiff walks with Patience thro' a Country Town, each whistling Cur, in Emulation of his Greatness, runs Yelping at his heels, till at last provoked by the insolence of some forward Mungril, who being Ignorant of his Strength, and thoughtless of his Courage, attempts to bite him by the Breech, which occasions the disdainful Animal to turn back his Head and Grin; and when with Contempt he has view'd his feeble Adversary, he holds up his Leg and Scornfully Pisses upon his Trembling Assailant.[37]

In order best to squelch the accusations against him, Ward assumed the stance of the mighty English mastiff, and a "true bred" one at that. The dog's powerful size and strength allowed him to jog unperturbed through throngs of lesser beings and to drench his cowardly challengers with his scorn. For all of the momentum of this image, Ward nonetheless cast himself as a dog, and the scatological reference both made a claim to superior status and also set it safely within a realm available to an ambitious scribbler. Whether or not Ward intended it, he retaliated in a way that suited the vicissitudes of manhood; the contest among his peers was crucial, but to overestimate one's own position was the surest path to destruction.

Having found success in animal metaphors thus far, Ward continued by referring to the preface's author as "Puppy" and "Ape." These epithets helped Ward transition from hurling outright insults to casting aspersions on the author's wit and honor; he claimed to be "sorry a Man who deals in Books should discover his Wit to be so little, or his Necessity so great, as to force him" to use tactics "which every Prudent Author ought to Condemn, and every Honest Bookseller Detest." After this moralizing, Ward stated that his opponent was a "little shallow-brained Lampooneer" who was "carry'd beyond his Tallent" as he "compos'd his Dunghill of Reflections." He added, "I must confess, till now, I could not think there was such a Cocks-Comb of the Trade."[38] Each of these charges allowed Ward to suggest that the anonymous author fell short in wit (an unpardonable sin to hack writers), ethics (of questionable use in practice but of great use in accusation), and means. Worst of all, he was a "Cocks-comb," a conceited fop or fool, whose overestimation of his talents rendered him laughable and the subject of scorn by a community of witnessing peers.

The effectiveness of Ward's address lay in the combination of an ad hominem attack with the invocation of imagined others—the true men who Ward implicitly claimed were in agreement with him at the other man's expense. It was this real or imagined community that allowed Ward to give sanctimonious advice: "I would advise him for the future, to confine his Scurrilous and Obscene Dialect within its proper bounds; and never presume to attempt any thing beyond a *Bloody Murther, Bawdy Ballad,* or a *Last Dying Speech and Confesion.*" To fail to do so, Ward warned, might lead to "the disgrace of his Family, and scandal of the Purchasers, he may chance to fall into the hands of as scurvy a Poetaster as himself; and become the lamentable Subject of a doleful Ditty."[39] Here Ward returned his opponent's lack of literary skill to the forefront, establishing himself simultaneously as fit to judge and as a representative of that invisible community of readers and writers who undoubtedly shared his opinion of the preface's author as a mere poetaster.

The anonymous author lost no time in responding to Ward and published *The curry-comb turn'd to its right use; Or, the powder-monkey to a Jamaica ship, dress'd with it.* Again, in lieu of naming himself, he used the byline "By the Author of the Trip to Holland," which conveniently advertised the pamphlet at the same time it detracted from Ward's charges of plagiarism. From the beginning, the author joined Ward in the struggle by each to "unmake" the other as a man via the conventions of satire and insult. The title doubled back upon Ward's and reduced Ward to a "Powder-Monkey," which in its nautical meaning connoted a young boy tasked with menial errands on the ship. To accentuate the reversal, the author posited that

> The fiery Plantation Author perhaps may be angry, that I liken him to so little an Animal as a Monkey in the Title, when in his Tower-bill Simile he assumes to himself the mighty Image of a true bred Mastiff; tho' where his Breeding is I can't tell; for I understand at the Derby Ale-house that his Friends never bred him a Scholar, but where his want of it appears may be easily discernable, even by our Author, who has none.[40]

The author followed his reversal of animal types with a classic sneer about Ward's social status and quality. "Breeding" had the additional benefit of implying animal husbandry at the same time that it suggested that Ward lacked the kind of manly community to protect him from such charges. For this group of scribbling men, jockeying for position was a full-time occupation, and each battle was characterized by intricate advances and retreats. The author allows Ward friends, if slightly indifferent alehouse friends, who, even in their own mediocrity, recognized that Ward was nothing special. The author then brought the reversal to conclusion: Ward's lack of breeding was discernible even to those without any themselves, a group into which he strategically placed himself. For both authors, success or failure rested on an ability to invoke a community of friends, to claim wit, to boast of success, and to demonstrate a thick skin against opponents' disdain. This challenge required that scribbling men like Ward be both presumptuous about themselves and blisteringly dismissive of others, while at the same time claiming greater modesty and moderation than were displayed by the fops, fools, and knaves who populated their pages.

In his rebuttal, the anonymous author did not resist the urge to return Ward's attack. "As he has describ'd me to be a Little, Shallow-brain'd Fellow, so it will not be out of the way to give a Description of him,"[41] the author wrote, and then composed a piece that linked mockery of Ward's appearance with dullness, poverty, and foolishness. He began with Ward's face, stating,

> It is Russet-colour'd, with Pock-holes in it; and as that is somewhat broader than ordinary, so his Skull, whose Emptiness is the only Argument of a *Vacuum* in Nature, is proportionable. His body is a long Ox's Bladder, blown up with the Wind of *Derby*-Ale: His Legs too have partaken of the same *Flatus;* and he looks like a Man who Cudgels People as much as he talks of it. For his Apparel, it all came out of one Shop: No one has the Impudence to call his Wigg a Second-handed one, for it was the Cast-off of some *Valet de Chambre,* and he had it from his Master, the Broker from him, and he from the Broker. . . . His Cravat and Ruffles, for I must tell you, when he came to Bully me, he had Hand-Cuffs, look'd as if they had the Yellow-Jaundice, and yawn'd at as many Holes as his own Jamaica did when it had an Earthquake, which he calls the *Dry Belly-Ach.*[42]

There were cheap laughs in such a description, as well as scatological barbs that transformed a high-minded opponent back into a body, one with wind, pockmarks, and substandard fashions. The anonymous author here unmade Ward as a kind of honorable man, a status that both men claimed for themselves and worked strenuously to deny to others. Just as Ward's misogyny began with women's bodies and radiated outward, so too did the kind of gendered posturing Ward and his opponent used against each other. There was less cultural weight behind these threats than in Ward's misogyny, but these clashes did have consequences for the men involved. Interestingly, while the author claimed that the two men actually met and faced off, just as with Ward's entire *A Trip to Jamaica,* the narrative could have been written in precisely the same way even if no such encounter had taken place.

While we can extrapolate some of the ways that formulaic misogyny and manly posturing likely affected the spaces inhabited by English men and women, it is trickier to consider the lived reality of Africans in England the 1690s. Some had been sent to England as servants, especially but not exclusively in hubs like London and Bristol. When wealthy planters returned to England with slaves in tow, they helped reinforce the idea of Africans as possessions.[43] Still, at this point even in London many English people were more likely to have had contact with

Africans' discursive existence than their actual one. In a limited but nonetheless significant way, the struggles of English hack writers indirectly created a context for ideas about Jamaica and the colonial project there. Even in texts as disconnected from reality as *A Trip to Jamaica,* when Ward and his opponents grappled over their respective places among other struggling scribblers, they also shaped the context into which ideas about "real" Jamaicans and people of African extraction would enter.

Conclusion: *A Trip to Jamaica* without Jamaica

Edward Ward's *A Trip to Jamaica* reveals more about the ways that misogyny and contested manhood operated in the production of hack writing at the turn of the eighteenth century than about Jamaica per se. While Ward participated in an ongoing conversation about England's presence in the West Indies, his translation of Jamaica for an English audience consisted primarily of overlaying customary scripts with old jokes in the context of a trip to someplace new. The absence of slavery and actual women in Ward's narrative only underscores how removed his account was from the lived reality of the place. This sense was only compounded by the absence of anything a historian might look for in terms of context: what of the slave revolts, the maroon communities, the aftermath of the earthquake that destroyed Port Royal in 1692, piracy, the end of the Royal African Company's monopoly on the slave trade in 1698, and the considerable degree to which Africans outnumbered Europeans there by the eighteenth century?[44] If Ward did actually travel to Jamaica, it is difficult to imagine that these realities did not feature in his conversations with other English colonists. It may not be reasonable to have particular expectations about what a satirical travel narrative "should" contain, but if part of Ward's goal was to ridicule the idea of the West Indies as a land of opportunity, a few barbed comments about the impediments to that success would have been warranted. If Ward went to Jamaica and saw sugar plantations, slaves, and divisions among the white population, why omit these details so completely?

John Richardson, in his study of the role of slavery in the work of Jonathan Swift, Alexander Pope, and John Gay, argues that English writers made implicit references to slavery because they felt uneasy with the idea of slavery and its relationship to their own customary freedoms. When these three authors did make explicit references to slaves, Richardson found that "they contained their dislike, and perhaps their guilt, by using the word in a way that made slaves despicable and deserving of their situation."[45] This formulation sounds a good deal like what Ward achieved through his obsessive reliance on the language of manhood and misogyny. Whatever Ward actually thought about women, in his writings he continually reclaimed the prerogatives of manhood by repeating that women were deceitful and disgusting by nature. This does not seem far from Richardson's outline of the contemporary writers' rationale about slavery: "slaves are by nature slaves, or their actions have made them deserve to be slaves, or their enslavement has reduced them to slaves."[46] The power play was also apparent in the facile way Ward and other English men invoked their own "slavery," whether prompted by unwanted legislation, French capture, or submission to a woman's charms. Without equating English women and enslaved African men and women, it is nonetheless clear that writers like Ward used similarly slippery means to justify the marginalization of those others.

If Ward never actually made the trip to Jamaica, it might initially seem *less* likely that the reader would learn about topics such as slave revolts, sugar, or piracy. However, given the degree of borrowing and outright plagiarism in pamphlets like Ward's, anything in printed or conversational circulation was potentially available. Ward would still have been able to draw broad satirical conclusions about the role of the English in the West Indies, the strangeness of the animals and food, or the society among whites of different sorts. Ward managed to do this in his other travel narratives, even when he patently borrowed from other writers and made only halfhearted attempts to claim that a true voyage had taken place. For example, in *A Trip to New England,* published immediately on the heels of *A Trip to Jamaica* in 1699, Ward mocked Puritans, praised Indians, and described lobster, moose, and porcupine; the details are there because he lifted them from John Josselyn's accounts of his travels in 1638 and 1663.[47] Because of Josselyn's material, Ward included a section on Indian women that was entirely complimentary, followed by his own claims about degraded female colonists. Ward's embellishments of Josselyn's texts fell along predictable lines; he did not address the debate about the nature of Native women, but he did profess that in New England the English women "like Early Fruits, are soon Ripe and soon Rotten," and continued from there.[48]

Regardless of whether or not Ward stepped onto Jamaican soil, his narrative transformed his fortune, spawned countless imitators, and put him in a position from which he was able to find his greatest success with his quasi-journalistic *The London Spy,* the first installment of which was published in November 1698, followed by a second just a month later.[49] While the premise was not particularly original, with *The London Spy* Ward hit on a way to make his winning formula apply to lands that both he and his readers knew far better than the West Indies. Greater familiarity made the satire all the more recognizable, controversial, and profitable. As Troyer points out, Ward found a way, despite considerable logistical difficulties, to profit from a periodical publication ten years before *Tatler* and *Spectator.*[50] Ward was able to turn his *Trip to Jamaica* into a platform from which to launch a career, as well as countless insults, but the curious absence of Jamaica in that publication makes it a difficult source on which to rely for information about those who lived there. But even without such content, Ward used the idea of a journey to Jamaica as a device to create space for his misogynist exploration of human frailty. While actual Jamaicans seemed incidental, Ward trafficked in deep-seated, shared assumptions about race, gender, and sex as a way to fashion himself into a writer. His text contributed to a conversation in London that underscored such assumptions and allowed English men and women to laugh or rage about the story on the surface while they trafficked in the dark messages and darker absences that lay beneath.

Elizabeth Neidenbach

"Inhabitant of Saint-Domingue, today refugee in this place"

Atlantic Networks and the Contours of Migration among Free Women of Color during the Haitian Revolution

On February 27, 1811, a free woman of color named Jeanette Azulima recorded her last will and testament with a notary in New Orleans. After first resettling in Cuba, this "*ancienne habitante de Saint Domingue*" arrived in the Crescent City between 1809 and 1810, along with 9,000 other former residents of the French colony. Azulima owned land in all three locations and recorded her intent to distribute her property among various free black beneficiaries living in New Orleans, Haiti, Savannah, and France.[1] Through her choice of legacies, beneficiaries, and testamentary executor, Jeanette Azulima's will describes a set of social contacts, highlighting a network that connected refugees throughout the Atlantic world.

The upheaval caused by the Haitian Revolution forced tens of thousands of inhabitants to flee the colony and resettle on neighboring Caribbean islands, in North American port cities, and in France. Free women of color like Jeannette Azulima made up a significant proportion of the refugee population. Until quite recently, however, scholars have paid little attention to this group of Atlantic migrants.[2] This essay adds to the growing body of scholarship on Saint-Domingue's free women of color among the refugees through an analysis of notary documents recorded in Cuba, Charleston, and New Orleans. These records allow us to reconstruct the migration experience of free women of color between 1791 and 1810. Able to hold property but possessing only tenuous social power, these women used legal documents to secure and record their lives. Such documents detail individuals' movement, property, and social relationships and, in turn, reveal the effects of revolution and relocation on the lives of free black women.

"Costumes de Affranchies et de Esclaves des Colonies." I. Illustration by Nicolas Ponce in Recueil des vues des lieux principaux de la colonie Françoisede Saint-Domingue (Paris, 1791). Courtesy of the John Carter Brown Library at Brown University.

"Costumes des Affranchies et des Esclaves des Colonies." II. Illustration by Nicolas Ponce in Recueil des vues des lieux principaux de la colonie Francaise de Saint-Domingue (Paris, 1791). Courtesy of the John Carter Brown Library at Brown University.

Accounting for the ways these refugees experienced gender, race, and dislocation, this essay recovers, in the networks of women of color from Saint-Domingue, an important set of actors in an Atlantic world reshaped by revolution.

Migration Patterns

The Haitian Revolution began in 1791 as a massive slave revolt in the French Caribbean colony of Saint-Domingue and ended with the creation of the independent nation of Haiti in 1804. The violent conflict thus endured for thirteen years, involving varying alliances among the colony's three social groups—whites, slaves, and free people of color—as well as international forces.[3] Throughout this time, tens of thousands of inhabitants left the island for safer shores. Exact numbers are difficult to determine because refugees often moved around, both between points of refuge and back and forth to Saint-Domingue, before settling permanently.[4] Although the migration was concentrated in certain locales, particularly New Orleans, ports up and down the eastern seaboard, Cuba, Jamaica, and Santo Domingo (the present-day Dominican Republic), all felt the impact of the dispersal of Saint-Dominguan refugees.[5]

Identifiable waves of migration occurred at particular points during the Revolution. Following the slave uprising on the northern plain, the initial emigration took place in the first two years of the conflict and culminated in 1793 when 10,000 people fled the burning city of Cap Français in ships bound for the United States' eastern coast.[6] The next wave took place in 1798, after Toussaint Louverture defeated the British troops that had occupied parts of the south, the west, and the strategic northwestern port of Môle-Saint-Nicolas since 1793. About 2,000 residents followed the English to Jamaica at that time.[7] The final exodus of inhabitants from the island occurred in 1803, this time coinciding with the evacuation of Napoleon's expeditionary forces, which had been sent to take back command of the colony from Louverture in 1802. Following the defeat of the French by the black "indigenous army" under the command of Jean-Jacques Dessalines, thousands of people migrated to Cuba and to U.S. port cities such as Charleston and Savannah.[8]

Louisiana became the final home for a substantial number of Saint-Dominguan refugees, but for most it was a secondary destination.[9] The largest influx of refugees to New Orleans arrived from Cuba in 1809 and 1810. Following the outbreak of war between Spain and France, roughly 9,000 people sailed for New Orleans. Disembarking over a period of only a few months, they had an immediate impact on the city's demography. The surge of émigrés more than doubled the population of the city, while the number of free people of color increased from 1,566 in 1805 to 4,950 in 1810—accounting for almost 29 percent of New Orleans's total population.[10]

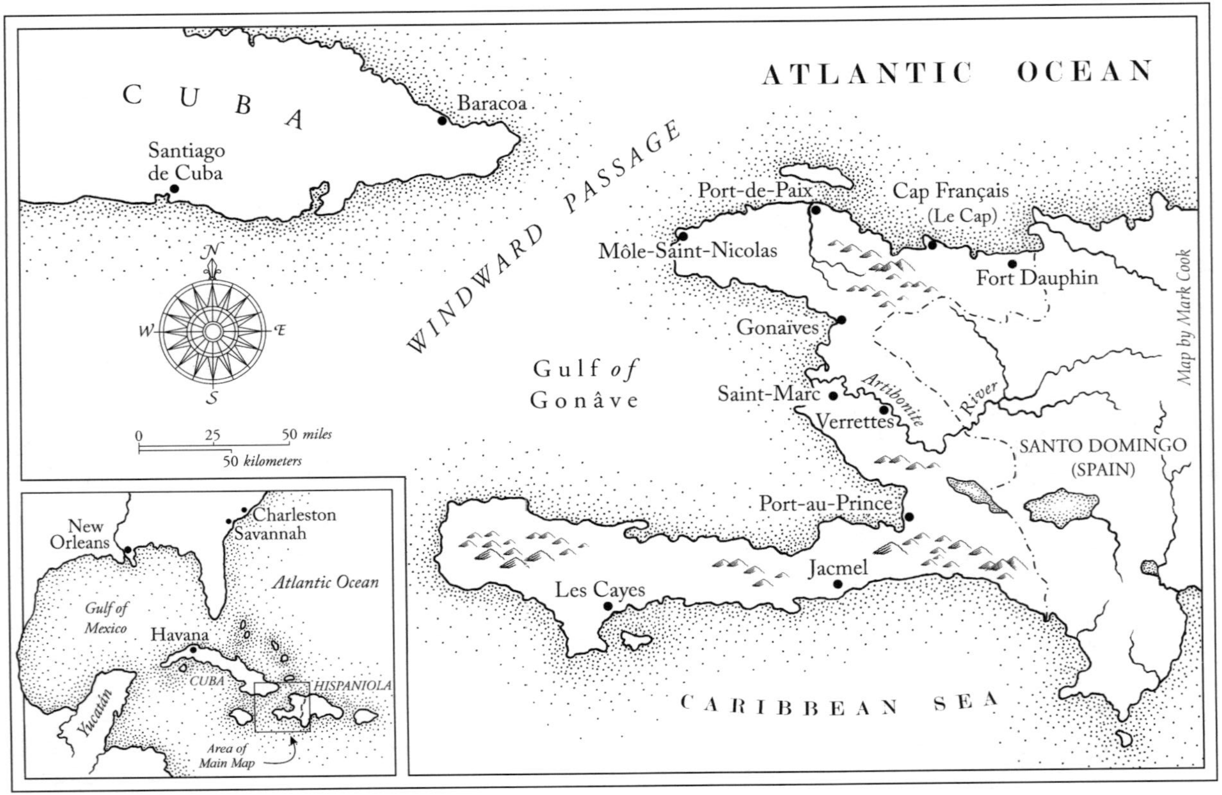

Map of Saint-Domingue by Mark Cook (2019).

Detail from "Pillage du Cap Français en 1793." Engraving proof from painting most likely by J. L. Boquet (1795). Courtesy of the John Carter Brown Library at Brown University.

The sudden growth in the city's free black population should have been greater than these figures indicate. The mayor's office provided an official count that divided the refugees from Cuba almost evenly into thirds under the labels "White People" (2,731), "free Colored and Black People" (3,102), and "Slaves" (3,226).[11] Slavery, however, had been abolished in Saint-Domingue in 1794 by the French Republican government and was prohibited by the Haitian constitution. For those individuals categorized as "slaves," then, the mayor's report enacted an unfortunate reversal of status. Regarding the 1794 emancipation decree as illegitimate, Louisiana territorial officials accepted the purported claims of ownership by some refugees over others. Once a person was labeled as a slave, it was difficult for anyone to alter the classification. A few people claimed as property successfully sued for their freedom, but many more spent the remainder of their lives enslaved in New Orleans.[12]

Whether identified as "free" or "slave," the vast majority of nonwhite refugees who arrived from Cuba were women and children. Of the adults regarded as free people of color, the 1,377 women substantially outnumbered the 428 men.[13] These numbers may well reflect the overall pattern of migration among free black

"Incendie du Cap Français: le 20, 21, 22 et 23 juin 1793 ou 2, 3, 4 et 5 messidor an I.er de la République," by Pierre-Gabriel Berthault et al. Plate 81 from Collection complète des tableaux historiques de la révolution française, vol. 2 (Paris, 1804). Anne S. K. Brown Military Collection, Brown University Library.

refugees, as more men lost their lives in the war and women and children more easily gained permission to leave the island.[14] The movements of Saint-Dominguan free men of color were further circumscribed by laws passed in Georgia, South Carolina, and Louisiana. Fearing the potential of free black men to incite rebellion, the Louisiana legislature banned their entrance into the territory in 1806.[15] The law was difficult to enforce, and free men of color did resettle in New Orleans.[16] Nevertheless, the initial numbers of Saint-Dominguans from Cuba clearly indicate that the experience of free black refugees in New Orleans was conditioned, in no small part, by gender.

Sources on Paper, Resources in People

Despite the presence of free black refugees in New Orleans and other destinations, their migration experiences remain less well documented than those of white Saint-Dominguans. Unlike many white refugees, free women of color rarely left behind letters, diaries, or eyewitness testimonies.[17] They did, however, record notary documents, including declarations, procuration acts, marriage contracts, and wills, in refugee locales.[18] Often created soon after arrival, these records suggest the types of legal actions, business arrangements, and personal information that refugees deemed crucial to chronicle in the moment of flight. They also provide details about the Revolution, pointing toward the circumstances under which women fled and the routes they may have traveled.

Specific types of documents, such as freedom declarations, highlight the risks of relocation for free black women. Work by Rebecca Scott and Jean Hébrard demonstrates the importance of written documentation for refugees whose lives were in flux. In fleeing Saint-Domingue, free women of color left a place without slaves and moved through various jurisdictions—Spanish, British, and U.S. territory— where not only did slavery still exist but slave status and African descent were explicitly linked.[19] Some women turned to notaries and other official recordkeepers to document and defend their freedom. Free women of color also used notary records to protect their status as property owners. These women actively sought to manage and retain their property, particularly their former slaves, and relied on the assistance of other refugees to do so. Thus, as socially created documents, notary records reveal the human networks that free women of color formed and maintained in the course of their migration.

The documents that free women of color crafted to secure their property and establish new lives reflect the circulation of people, commodities, and ideas that characterizes Atlantic world history.[20] The tumult unleashed by the Haitian Revolution reverberated throughout the Atlantic as both people and property (most of it humans claimed as "property") were dispersed from France's most lucrative colony to other parts of the Caribbean, the United States, and Europe.[21] When former inhabitants of Saint-Domingue relocated, they remained in contact with one another. The historian R. Darrell Meadows argues that kinship ties and other social relationships among white refugees from Saint-Domingue aided their migration to North American port cities during the 1790s. Such networks, many forged long before the Revolutionary period, helped refugees flee to safety and often determined where they relocated. Once they arrived, a combination of personal relationships and "weak social ties" provided exiles with necessary means of support. Meadows finds that these connections crossed geographical and social boundaries, including those of class, race, and politics.[22]

Networks similar to those established by white Saint-Dominguans existed among free black women, connecting them to family, friends, and acquaintances in various refugee destinations. Some relationships predated migration and were continued or reconstituted in the new location. Others were created among refugees after they moved. Whether recent or long-standing, these connections were often anchored by property ownership. As refugee free women of color exchanged land, attempted to reclaim lost slaves, or bequeathed armoires in their wills, their networks linked people, places, and property in a broader Atlantic world.

The free women of color who fled the island during the Revolution were a diverse group, and the relationships they established and preserved spanned class, color, and status and stretched throughout the Atlantic. Some women were formerly enslaved (*affranchis*), while others were free by birth. They were Africans and Creoles, "*négresses*" of pure African descent and "*mulâtresses*" of various degrees of racial mixture. Differences in wealth, family status, education, and age, as well as where they lived in the colony, structured their experiences. Many owned property, including land, slaves, houses, and businesses, in addition to material goods. Others spent much of their lives *as* property. Some women did both. Despite their varied backgrounds, refugee free women of color shared similar experiences of movement and dislocation that shaped their lives during the Revolution. When they came into contact with one another in Santiago de Cuba's French Quarter, on the streets of Charleston, or at the baptismal font in New Orleans's St. Louis Cathedral, they utilized their common experiences to create and maintain new bonds.

A World in Motion

Uncovering the trajectories of refugee free women of color during the Haitian Revolution is difficult, as few documents clearly outline when and where they traveled. Timelines and courses of movement for some individuals and families can be reconstructed, however, through details included in notary records.[23] This information correlates with broader refugee migration patterns and points toward specific aspects that may have conditioned the experience for free women of color. Knowing when and where these women lived out the Revolution generates a better understanding of what their daily lives were like during the war and points toward their motivations for ultimately leaving the island.

For some women, displacement from their homes began in the early years of the Revolution. Rosalie Chesneau, a free *mulâtresse,* by 1795 had left the house she owned in the small town of Jean-Rabel and her indigo plantations in Guinaudée for the relative safety of Môle-Saint-Nicolas.[24] The British had occupied the Môle since September 1793, and almost immediately inhabitants from the surrounding area flocked there seeking provisions and aid.[25] It is unclear how long Chesneau remained at Môle-Saint-Nicolas, but she eventually relocated to Baracoa, Cuba, where she stayed until 1809. By January 25, 1810, Rosalie Chesneau was in New Orleans. She lived in the Crescent City until her death in 1833.[26]

Piecing together Chesneau's movements required multiple documents, but records for other individuals provide more direct clues. A *négresse libre* named

Marguerite Guitonne Reine recorded a marriage contract with her "future spouse," a French native named Jean Baptiste Augebert Delaunay, on April 30, 1806, in Baracoa.[27] The contract described the assets each party brought to the marriage and legitimated the seven children the couple had had together over the past fourteen years. From the listed date and location of each child's birth, a detailed picture of the family's travels over the course of the Revolution emerges.

In addition to the burden of extensive movement and its attendant upheaval, Marguerite Guitonne Reine spent almost the entire Revolution pregnant. Following the birth of their first son, Jean Baptiste Dieu-Donné, in Petit St. Louis in 1792, Reine and Delaunay had a child almost every two years. The couple was still in Petit St. Louis, a parish in the northwestern district of Port-de-Paix, in 1794, when Charles Antoine Filicourt was born. By 1797, they had moved farther west to the neighboring parish of Jean-Rabel, where they had two daughters and lived until 1800 or so. At the birth of their fifth child, Elizabeth Jeanne Nirzine, in 1801, the family was in Môle-Saint-Nicolas. In the wake of the withdrawal of French troops from the island, the couple relocated to Baracoa, where they had another daughter on November 12, 1803. Three years later, after the birth of their seventh child, the peripatetic couple recorded their marriage contract before the agent of the French government in the Spanish port town.[28] The family's sojourn in Baracoa ended in 1809. Forced out of the colony, they continued on to New Orleans. Reine gave birth to another daughter shortly before their departure. The little girl was baptized in New Orleans on September 9, 1811.[29]

Reine and Delaunay's decision to travel to Baracoa was likely based on expediency in the hectic moment of flight, although they may have known fellow émigrés already living there. Cuba served as a place of refuge for Saint-Dominguans throughout the Revolutionary period. In the early years of the war, individuals moved back and forth between Cuba and their homes, using the neighboring Spanish colony as a safe place to wait out the conflict. Following Louverture's defeat of the British and their withdrawal from the island, a large number of French residents, mostly from the west, fled to Cuba in late 1798 and early 1799. Another sizable group, this time free people of color from the south, departed in 1800 after Louverture conquered André Rigaud's army. Most of these evacuees were Rigaud's soldiers, and many of them returned to Saint-Domingue with General Leclerc's arrival in 1802. The final phase began in the summer of 1803, as the defeated French troops began to leave the island. This "great exodus," particularly from the south and west, landed thousands of refugees in Santiago de Cuba, Baracoa, and Havana.[30]

Most of the free women of color who recorded documents in Baracoa and Santiago de Cuba arrived as part of this final group of émigrés. Several women explained that their arrival directly followed the departure of the French army. In a declaration recorded on October 27, 1804, in Santiago de Cuba, Marguerite

Caillou claimed "that she was in St. Marc at the time the French army arrived in Saint Domingue and she had evacuated this city with the army[;] she took refuge [in Santiago de Cuba] during the evacuation where she has constantly remained."[31] Other women referenced the "evacuation of the French" as an explanation for how they came to be in Cuba, but where they landed on the island depended on their point of departure from Saint-Domingue.[32] For the most part, individuals who left from the west and south relocated to Santiago de Cuba, whereas those from areas in the north went to Baracoa. The position of these Cuban port cities—Baracoa on the northern side and Santiago de Cuba on the southern side—align with the correlating departure points in Saint-Domingue.

Location in the colony in the final months of the Revolution, then, determined where free women of color resettled after leaving the island. This geographic factor had consequences for the ways in which refugee communities developed, particularly those in Cuba and, later, New Orleans. It increased the chances that these women would be reunited with relatives, friends, and acquaintances, easing their transition to an unfamiliar place. As free women of color adjusted to their new surroundings, reliance on such relationships was often necessary, particularly when it came to proving one's freedom or verifying one's ownership of property.

"The Effect of the Events of the War"

The bloody conflicts of the Haitian Revolution[33] and subsequent flights to foreign places were traumatic for all refugees, regardless of race.[34] In declarations and other acts recorded in Santiago de Cuba, French officials obscured that trauma behind a boilerplate explanation of the refugees' current situation as a consequence of "the effect of the events of the war."[35] Yet, despite their formal legal structure, notary records often included descriptions of wartime events. Indeed, their creation commonly reflected the specific circumstances of the Revolution, recounting experiences of dislocation, misfortune, and loss.

For the most part, the types of acts recorded by whites and free people of color functioned in the same way and shared common themes. Statements made by both groups frequently referenced the loss of personal papers such as land titles, promissory notes, and baptism records. These kinds of documents enabled Saint-Dominguan refugees to support their claims about their previous lives, such as where they were born or which plantation they owned. The loss of such documentation hindered these claims and often required testimonies from witnesses to attest to their truth.

Yet the loss of personal papers could have dire consequences for free women-of-color émigrés when they relocated to places where slavery remained intact. Without proof of their status, these women risked imprisonment and enslavement.[36] To counteract this possibility, free women of African descent made acts that declared and substantiated their freedom. Such documents highlight the ways race affected these women's experiences of dislocation, placing burdens on them that white refugees did not face. As a result, the documents provide a glimpse of the "events of the war" that forced these women to leave their homes.

In addition to enduring the Revolution either pregnant or nursing, Marguerite Guitonne Reine likely spent much of this time unsure of her status. Reine was born a slave in Fort Dauphin, but her marriage contract made in Baracoa clearly stated that she was "free in her actions, mistress of her person, and [had] all the rights accorded to the *affranchis.*" To prove this, she submitted a manumission act made by her former mistress on September 5, 1803, which had been recorded by a notary in Cap Français and "legalized" by a judge.[37] In Saint-Domingue, Reine's status as a free woman did not require a notarized manumission act; the French Republican government's general emancipation decree had ended slavery in the colony almost a decade before. Whether or not this decree would be upheld off the island, however, remained to be seen. The timing of Reine's manumission record, coming shortly before the evacuations of Le Cap and the Môle, suggests that she sought official recognition of her freedom (and consequently her children's) before the family departed to a foreign country.[38] Distrusting the vagaries of relocation, Marguerite took care to leave Saint-Domingue as a *documented* free woman.

Other free women of color who resettled in Cuba rerecorded their emancipation acts with the French government agent there. An Arada woman named Fanchette registered hers in Santiago de Cuba on September 24, 1806.[39] Fanchette had been a slave on a plantation in Petite Rivière in the Artibonite Valley. Her master, Mr. Borin, originally emancipated her in 1781 but registered her manumission again in Port-au-Prince on July 20, 1803. He explained that this was necessary because Fanchette had lost her freedom papers "in the troubles that occurred . . . when the French arrived."[40] A month later, Fanchette deposited a copy of Borin's document with a notary in Saint-Marc. She likely left for Santiago de Cuba shortly thereafter, following the evacuation of the French army in September.[41] After three years in Cuba, Fanchette once again registered her freedom papers. The Santiago de Cuba version both pointed to the loss of the original record and reiterated the paper trail that Fanchette had established with the help of her former master before leaving Saint-Domingue. Creating an additional record of her free status in her new residence likely provided Fanchette with a sense of security.

A Congolese woman named Zaire also lost her manumission record in the final years of the war. Zaire gained her freedom from a Widow Courtin in Saint-Marc in 1788. The original document, filed with the city's public records, was destroyed in 1802 when Dessalines burned Saint-Marc to keep it out of French hands.[42] Zaire traveled to Cuba with Servais, the brother of her former mistress.

To counter a challenge by another sibling for property rights over Zaire, Servais recorded her freedom in Santiago de Cuba on September 4, 1803. Three years later, Zaire came before the French government official to register the 1803 document. Like Fanchette, she registered a previously recorded document made as a substitution for her original manumission record. Perhaps by 1806 Servais no longer lived in Cuba, prompting Zaire to make a record of her status in her own name.

That Fanchette and Zaire were African-born increased their risk of re-enslavement or possible removal from Cuba. With the influx of refugees, Spanish colonial authorities fretted over "what to do with persons of color from French ports who looked to officials as though they ought to be slaves, but were behaving as if they were free." One proposed solution, although never implemented, was deportation.[43] Fanchette and Zaire responded to Spanish officials' perceived notions of who was a slave and who was free by (re)registering their manumission papers. Both women's claims to freedom were likely bolstered by the fact that they had gained their liberty long before the general emancipation of 1794 and had the support of a former master to substantiate this in the initial absence of proof.

Formerly enslaved women were not the only ones to insist on officially registering their free status. Marguerite Caillou, "*mulâtresse née libre,*" recorded a declaration of freedom in Santiago de Cuba on October 27, 1804. Caillou explained that, as the daughter of a "free black woman" and a "white planter," she was indeed free by birth.[44] Her baptism record served as the proof of her status, but she lost her copy during the war. In order to verify her claims, three male witnesses from her home district swore that they had full knowledge of Caillou's freedom, the loss of her baptism record, and her relocation to Cuba.[45] Lacking documentation, Caillou looked to her fellow refugees to confirm her status as a free woman.

The motivation behind the decision to stay in Saint-Domingue or risk the uncertainty of migration is rarely apparent in these documents. However, Marguerite Caillou's declaration hints at a harrowing experience that may have convinced her to leave. Originally from Verrettes, a small parish outside Saint-Marc in the Artibonite Valley, Caillou had relocated to the port city and was there when French troops arrived. Caillou explained that she lost her baptism record when she was forced "in the woods by the revolting blacks and mulattoes."[46] This surely refers to Dessalines's decision to burn Saint-Marc in 1802. According to the historian Laurent Dubois, when the French appeared, "they found the town smoldering and abandoned, with the dead bodies of several hundred residents, mostly whites, left to greet them."[47] Caillou's declaration confirms this when she states that the public copy of her baptism record, archived in Saint-Marc, was "prey to the flames at the time of the burning of the city, such that it is not possible to procure a new" one.[48] Dessalines and his men left Saint-Marc with numerous white prisoners but executed them as they moved away from the coast. When the

French commander following Dessalines's troops arrived in Verrettes, he found eight hundred bodies.[49] Caillou's life was spared by her escape to the woods, but the massacre may have convinced her to leave the island. Once in Cuba, she took action to secure her free status in her new home.

By recording these documents, Fanchette, Zaire, and Marguerite Caillou took precautions against the very real threat of losing their freedom. People of African descent fleeing Saint-Domingue risked seizure and enslavement by privateers, soldiers, and unscrupulous fellow refugees. Romain *dit* Louis Hervé, the nephew of Marie Françoise Lambert, who was also from Verrettes, suffered just such a fate.[50] Romain was about twelve years old when he fled to Santiago de Cuba with relatives in 1803. A man named Albert persuaded Romain to travel with him to Charleston to "procure [Romain] a trade." Instead, Albert sold Romain "as a slave" to Gilbert in New Orleans. Prix Doucet next purchased Romain but then sold him to Jean Rodriguez by 1809. Romain disclosed his free status to each "master," but to no avail.[51] Separated from his family and without written documentation, he had little recourse to challenge his enslavement. Once in New Orleans, however, Romain may have seen someone he knew from Saint-Domingue and sent word to his aunt in Cuba.

However she learned of Romain's whereabouts, Marie Françoise Lambert went to great lengths to rescue her nephew from enslavement. First, she created written proof of Romain's status. In November 1808, she secured the testimonies of four men from Verrettes to verify that Romain was "truly free from birth." She also submitted a copy of Romain's baptism record, which reiterated his freedom.[52] Next, Lambert gave power of attorney to Antoine Rocheville de Menard, a white refugee who had relocated to Louisiana by 1806, to assist her in New Orleans. Lambert instructed that Romain be returned to her in Cuba and that legal action be taken against "Mr. Doucet," if he refused to comply.[53] Utilizing the resources available to her in Cuba, Lambert activated refugee networks between Santiago and New Orleans, enlisted associates with personal knowledge of her family, and generated significant documentation to regain Romain's freedom.

It is unclear if Rocheville de Menard followed through with Lambert's requests. Despite his aunt's efforts in Cuba, Romain remained enslaved when Lambert arrived in New Orleans in 1809. She continued to fight for her nephew's release by sponsoring Romain's petition, submitted to the New Orleans City Court on October 9. Claiming that Jean Rodriguez illegally held Romain as a slave, the petition requested that his "liberty be restored" and that he receive financial compensation "for unjust detention of his person." Lambert verified the truth of Romain's statement. On October 18, Rodriguez filed a response to the petition in which he denied any wrongdoing. He requested that the suit be dismissed and that Lambert, as "the instigator of this process," be made to pay costs and damages "for depriving him of his slave." On April 10, 1810, the judge ruled in Romain's favor, ordering that he "be restored to his former freedom" and that Rodriguez be required to pay all costs.[54] Through her determined actions, Marie Françoise Lambert successfully gained Romain's release from bondage. Her efforts reveal the multiple strategies free women of color refugees employed to keep their families together and safe in the chaotic aftermath of the Revolution.

"She finds herself currently deprived"

In the context of a revolution[55] that destroyed the institution of slavery and many of the plantations on which it functioned in Saint-Domingue, the loss of property was an experience shared by many residents who fled. This is expressed in the documents, as most acts recorded by both white and free colored refugees concerned property ownership. Some refugees arrived with a few belongings, while most left behind property, including land and people they once held as slaves. Many of these property owners believed they would one day reclaim their abandoned possessions.[56] In her testament recorded in New Orleans in 1811, a free black woman named Barbe requested that two of the eight slaves she had left in Jérémie be given to her goddaughters, if the slaves could be returned to her.[57] Through property transfers, reclamations, and intended distribution in wills, free women of color connected with other Saint-Domingue refugees throughout the Atlantic. What they brought with them and what they left behind shaped the way they understood their dislocation and could have real consequences for how they survived in their new places of residence.

Whenever possible, free women of color "forced to depart" from their homes brought money, jewelry, papers, and other personal possessions with them.[58] When Henriette Dessources disembarked from the Spanish schooner that had carried her to Charleston, she left a small trunk on board, which later could not be located. Dessources made an official declaration regarding her lost property to the French Consulate. The trunk's contents included her linens, eight silver place settings, an extra fork, and one silver soup spoon. It also held her family papers, among them her parents' marriage contract, multiple baptism records, and two land titles. Items like clothing and spoons were relatively easy to carry and useful to have and, if necessary, could be sold.[59] The personal papers Dessources brought along represented her family's life in Saint-Domingue, outlining both who they were (baptism and marriage records) and what they owned (titles). Dessources sought official recognition of her property for the practical purpose of trying to reclaim the lost items. In doing so, she created a document that became both the physical proof of the existence of absent utensils, clothing, and a trunk and a substitute record for the papers attesting to her family's free status, wealth, and history.

Dessources's missing trunk indicates the types of personal belongings free women of color carried with them. Additionally, a number of free black refugees managed to travel with individuals whom they had previously held as slaves. Despite the fact that general emancipation had been achieved in 1794, some former slaveholders took advantage of relocating to places where slavery existed to claim fellow refugees as their property upon arriving.[60] Rosalie Chesneau abandoned ten former slaves when she moved to Baracoa, but she brought along five women over whom she continued to claim ownership. One woman was a laundress and another was a "cake peddler," occupations that transferred easily to urban locales where slavery persisted. While in Cuba, one of the women had a daughter, further increasing Chesneau's workforce.[61] As property, these women provided capital and labor to help Chesneau survive in her new home. As people, they offered a personal connection to what was left behind. The women remained in Chesneau's possession when she relocated again to New Orleans in 1809. Over time, each one gained her freedom, and a few were named as legatees in Chesneau's will.[62]

Outside Saint-Domingue, claims to freedom based only on the 1794 emancipation decree left the status of people of African descent open to question and easily jeopardized.[63] Women like Fanchette and Marguerite Caillou, who could gather the necessary paperwork and witnesses to prove their freedom—by birth or by manumission from a former master—could challenge attempts to label them as slaves. Likewise, documentation aided former property owners, such as Rosalie Chesneau, to claim entitlement over former bondsmen and -women. Thus, as Rebecca Scott argues, the line between slavery and freedom for refugees of color could be "paper thin."[64]

Free women of color who had joined the ranks of slaveholders prior to the Revolution were quick to marshal their resources, both paper and human, to re-secure their rights over "enslaved" individuals lost in the midst of relocation. They recorded declarations to prove their ownership of the slave in question and procuration acts to authorize a third party to retrieve their "property." By creating such acts, free women of color actively sought to protect their interests, as slaves provided labor and oft-needed income through hiring out or sale. These women also worked to maintain their positions as property owners. To achieve these ends, they often relied on refugee networks—both within and across locations.

On March 26, 1804, Marie Jeanne Thomas, a *mulâtresse libre* from Jérémie, recorded a declaration in Santiago de Cuba to "formally protest" another refugee's claims on her slaves. According to Thomas, Mr. François Duthil had said in a recent census of Saint-Dominguans in the city that he owned Marie Joseph and her two children. Thomas was "ignorant of the motive that guided" Duthil to make such a claim, since the three slaves were born on her plantation and she had therefore always owned them.[65] To prove this, Thomas presented three witnesses from her home district in Jérémie who testified to the truth of her declaration. She could then provide their recorded statements as evidence to counter Duthil's attempt to divest her of what she considered to be her property.

Unlike Marie Jeanne Thomas, who remained in proximity to the people she claimed as her slaves, other free women of color were separated from their slaves and attempted to reclaim their human property by relying on transnational refugee networks. On January 5, 1805, Cécile Charlesteguy declared her ownership rights to a thirteen-year-old named Jean Baptiste *dit* La Guerre. Jean Baptiste was the son of Charlesteguy's slave, Charlotte, which likely explains why Charlesteguy did not have any proof of her ownership and needed third-party testimonies to attest to this fact. Charlesteguy explained that because "she finds herself currently deprived" of her property, she required this document to fulfill her "intention to reclaim it."[66] The recovery was difficult since Charlesteguy was in Santiago de Cuba and Jean Baptiste was in New Orleans. In order to regain possession of Jean Baptiste, Charlesteguy authorized "Sieur Marc Lafitte, resident in New Orleans," to act in her stead, taking the legal actions necessary to return her enslaved property.[67] Charlesteguy used refugee connections when she empowered Lafitte, a white Saint-Dominguan who had resettled in New Orleans and worked as a notary, to recover Jean Baptiste for her.[68]

Marie Louise Didier *Veuve* Renaud, a *mulâtresse libre* from Saint-Marc, also lost a slave in the midst of evacuating from Saint-Domingue. On November 5, 1804, Didier recorded a document in Santiago de Cuba asserting her claim of ownership over a boy named Rossignol Bacú. According to Didier, the twelve-year-old Creole had been transported from Port-au-Prince to Môle-Saint-Nicolas a few days before the French troops evacuated, and, once there, he was placed in the care of Dame Viard. Before Viard departed for Cuba, a French military aide named Baubin seized Rossignol and took him to Havana. There, under false license, Baubin sold Rossignol to Jean Jarreau. By the time Didier had been alerted to Rossignol's fate, Jarreau had taken him to Louisiana. In the interest of reclaiming her property, Didier furnished a declaration that included statements from three "residents of St. Marc . . . and likewise refugees in this city of St. Yago" that confirmed her as "the true and only owner" of Rossignol.[69] Whether or not she successfully recovered possession of Rossignol, Didier reinforced her own free status by recording her title to rights over the boy.

Didier's saga of dispossession highlights the vulnerability of refugees of color—former slaves and former slaveholders alike. It also illustrates how opportunities for deceit were rife in the chaos of the final evacuation of Saint-Domingue. Didier claimed that Baubin sold Rossignol to Jarreau using fake documents. Jarreau, in turn, practiced his own deception in bringing Rossignol to New Orleans. On June 18, 1804, he sold the slave he had acquired in Havana to Jean Tournoir. Rather than describing Rossignol as a Creole, the sale record lists him as "brut," meaning a recent African import.[70] Jarreau likely lied to conceal Rossignol's origins in a ploy that enabled him to enter New Orleans with a Saint-Dominguan slave. The territorial governor of Louisiana, William C. C. Claiborne, explained in 1804 that "[s]laves are daily introduced from Africa, many *direct* from *this* unhappy Country and others by way of the West India Islands. All vessels with slaves on bord [*sic*] are stopped at Plaquemine [*sic*], and are not permitted to pass without my consent. This is done to prevent the bringing in of Slaves that have been concerned in the insurrections of St. Domingo [*sic*]."[71] Despite laws that forbade the importation of slaves, the illicit trade in slaves from Saint-Domingue found a market in New Orleans.[72] A white refugee from Jean-Rabel cited the high value of slaves as an advantage to living in the Crescent City: "what's left of our Negroes is worth a lot more money, and they are more easily rented" in New Orleans.[73] As Cècile Charlesteguy and Marie Louise Didier discovered, Saint-Dominguan "slaves" also *sold* well in New Orleans even if their origin had to be masked in order for them to enter the city.

Not all free women of color were separated from people they claimed as slaves through deceptive means. On April 21, 1808, Marie Genevieve Zelime Fortunat authorized Louis Gillet, another refugee in Baracoa, to recover two slaves whom she had inherited from her mother. The slaves had been in Charleston since 1804, when Fortunat's mother entrusted them to Sieur Darquier to rent out for her financial benefit. To claim her property, Fortunat needed an agent in the American city. Since Gillet was soon to depart for Charleston, Marie Genevieve gave him the legal power to procure the slaves from Darquier. If he refused to return them, Fortunat authorized Gillet to take legal action. However, she also permitted him to sell the slaves to Darquier for a price "most favorable" to her.[74] That she was willing to sell her inheritance suggests Fortunat may have struggled financially in Baracoa and needed the revenue. Fortunat's act of procuration also demonstrates her participation in local and transnational networks that connected white, free colored, and enslaved Saint-Dominguan refugees in and across relocation points. Fortunat depended on relationships and associations formed first by her mother and on the movement of refugees between locales to better survive her migration experience.

Friends and Neighbors

Refugee social networks are visible throughout the documents recorded by free women of color in Cuba, Charleston, and New Orleans. As Marie Genevieve Zelime Fortunat's procuration act illustrates, these networks were both local and transnational. Associations among refugees, based on face-to-face interactions, helped individuals find jobs, secure housing, and subsist on limited resources.[75] After arriving in New Orleans from Cuba, Barbe, for example, settled in a house with Marie Catherine Bourguignon, another free woman of color from Saint-Domingue. It is unclear if the two women knew each other before migrating, but Barbe obviously trusted her housemate to manage her affairs after her death because she named Bourguignon as her testamentary executor in her will. Barbe owned no property in New Orleans and likely struggled while there. She owed $16 to a baker named François Lavigne. Also a refugee, Lavigne lived only a block away from Barbe and Bourguignon's residence. To get by, Barbe relied on her close neighbors with ties that reached back to Saint-Domingue.[76]

Local networks also provided support in other ways. As in some of the cases discussed earlier, the loss of previous documentation required claimants to produce alternative proofs of status or property ownership. In these instances, witnesses came forth to record sworn statements that attested to the truth of the claim. When Marguerite Caillou needed evidence that she had been born free, she had three men living in Santiago de Cuba and who had known her in Saint-Marc verify her status.[77] The legal procedure of oral corroboration by associates carried over to Cuba from Saint-Domingue.[78] In New Orleans, this means of verification in the absence of written proof was made explicit in an 1807 law that required a refugee of color to "prove his or her said freedom" before city officials "by credible testimonies."[79] What may have been a precaution on the part of Caillou in Cuba would become a necessity in New Orleans. In both places, refugees' ability to access a social network served as a valuable asset.

Networks also connected refugees across national borders. Fortunat's mother sent her slaves to Charleston with Darquier, while Fortunat took advantage of Gillet's intended trip to the city to retrieve them. When Cècile Charlesteguy needed help recovering her slave in New Orleans, she called upon Marc Lafitte, a refugee who had already relocated there, to procure her property. These relationships linked refugees across long distances and paved the way for continued business connections as well as future relocations.

Assistance with relocations proved particularly important for refugees in Cuba, as so many of them continued on to New Orleans when expelled by the Spanish from the colony. A group of refugees from Verrettes provides one example. With few plantations and inhabitants, Verrettes remained a frontier area on the eve of the Revolution.[80] Because of its small size, it is likely that most people from this parish knew of each other and utilized these associations, first in Cuba and then later in New Orleans. In her attempt to rescue her nephew from enslavement in Louisiana, Marie Françoise Lambert needed proof that Romain was free. She assembled four men from her own parish of Verrettes, including a free man of color named Henry Guilhou, to testify to Romain's status.[81] Both Lambert and Guilhou relocated to New Orleans in 1809. While Lambert died soon after moving, Guilhou was listed as a tailor in the 1822 City Directory.[82] He lived with François Verdry, another free black refugee from Saint-Marc. In his will, Verdry named Guilhou executor of his estate.[83] François Verdry's connections to Verrettes extended beyond his friendship with Guilhou. In 1815, he served as godfather to the son of Pierre Herve, from Verrettes, and Marguerite Menard, a native of Saint-Marc.[84]

If former inhabitants of Verrettes maintained social connections that began in Saint-Domingue and continued in Cuba and New Orleans, other free refugees of color created new ties in their places of refuge. From different regions of Saint-Domingue, Rosalie Chesneau and Marie Genevieve Zelime Fortunat likely did not meet until they relocated to Baracoa.[85] Upon leaving Cuba, however, the relationship they created through business arrangements continued even after they went their separate ways.

While in Baracoa, Fortunat borrowed money from Chesneau. By June 1, 1808, she had yet to repay the debt but planned to leave the island. Unsure if she would survive the trip, Fortunat left three female slaves with Chesneau and granted her permission to sell them in order to satisfy the loan. If the sale of the slaves made more money than the sum Fortunat owed Chesneau, she was instructed to give the surplus funds to Fortunat's brother and sister.[86] This suggests that Fortunat's family stayed behind in Baracoa.

In May 1814, Rosalie Chesneau registered an act of procuration with a notary in New Orleans. Granting Chesneau power of attorney, the act was recorded by Marie Genevieve Fortunat on August 7, 1813, and passed in Jérémie, a town in the southern part of the now-independent Haiti.[87] On June 13, 1814, Chesneau once again returned to the notary office in New Orleans, this time with Fortunat's brother, to record a document that acknowledged his recent receipt of $848—his share of the inheritance from his mother—given to him by Chesneau.[88] How Chesneau acquired these funds remains unclear, but evidently Fortunat trusted Chesneau to manage her affairs in New Orleans. Not only did these women remain in contact after leaving Cuba for Louisiana and Haiti, respectively, they also continued to utilize the notary system to do so. Chesneau and Fortunat's relationship exemplifies the connections among people, places, and property created by the movement of free women of color refugees in the Revolutionary Atlantic world.

Conclusion

Fleeing their war-torn island, Saint-Dominguan free women of color left a variety of recorded documents in their wake. The loss of personal papers and property and, indeed, proof of their previous lives necessitated the creation of such records. Women-of-color refugees sought protection in documentation of their status as free women and, for many, as property owners. While some women utilized notary records to defend their freedom, others used them to reclaim their property rights over their former slaves. In both enterprises, the connections created and maintained by these women in the course of their movements were vital to substantiate their assertions. The documents that free women of color deposited, recorded, and crafted are tangible evidence of individual struggles for rights and property against a backdrop of revolution. However "thin," the papers reveal elaborate efforts that mobilized refugee networks across time and sea. Tracing the contours of migration for Saint-Dominguan free women of color reveals the ways these women actively created and re-created meaningful connections in the face of dislocation.

Joshua L. Bearden

Intimate Entanglement in the Early Republic

The Gendered Politics of Nation-Building in Early America

In 1740, James Logan Colbert made his way over the Appalachian Mountains toward the Chickasaw Nation in the lower Mississippi River basin. A recently arrived Scots immigrant to the Carolinas, Colbert participated in a trans-Mississippi–Carolina trade in which Anglo-American merchants exchanged British manufactured guns, copper pots, and textiles in return for Native deerskins, beaver hides, and indigenous slaves. A small, powerful tribe, the Chickasaw had been important trading partners for Spanish, French, and British merchants since the seventeenth century. Colbert's decision to relocate to the interior of the Gulf South brought him into proximity with important mercantile contacts and allowed him to establish a solid base of support from which goods could be sent from the interior back to the ports of Charleston and Savannah in British-controlled North America.[1]

At the same time that Colbert made Chickasaw alliances, the French Juzan family did the same with Choctaw Indians. The more populous Choctaw were the southern neighbors of the Chickasaws and occupied a geographic location that easily facilitated contact with Spanish, French, and British settlers as well as other Native Americans in the South. Like many of the "Five Civilized Tribes" inhabiting the Gulf South, the Choctaw had entered into an Atlantic exchange economy over the course of the eighteenth century, and they had come to rely heavily upon French merchants in the same way that the Chickasaw had come to depend upon Anglo-Scots merchants like Colbert. Pierre Juzan, a French military officer and the progenitor of the Juzan family in the Gulf South, had been killed in a battle against the Chickasaw in 1736. His grandson, also named Pierre Juzan, exploited his family's military and commercial connections to become a leading citizen of late eighteenth-century Mobile, ultimately serving as the "Commissioner for the Indians" to the Spanish governor of Louisiana in the 1780s and conducting a lucrative trade with the Choctaw Indians. During the American Revolution, Juzan led a contingent of Choctaw Indians, free blacks, and enslaved Africans in fighting a guerrilla campaign against British interests in the Gulf South. In one memorable event, Juzan unsuccessfully attempted to kidnap James Colbert, whose raids against Spanish ships on the Mississippi became more brazen as the American Revolution created turmoil in the region. In the post-Revolutionary era, Charles Juzan, the son of Pierre, successfully navigated the unsettled political landscape of the Gulf South by calling upon his family's French, Spanish, and Native American connections. At some point in the 1780s, Charles moved into Choctaw country and established a string of profitable trading posts that brought the Juzan family into the nexus of the Atlantic exchange economy.[2]

The Colbert and Juzan families accumulated an amount of wealth that would have been the envy of any Virginia tidewater or West Indian plantation owner. One Spanish official noted that James Colbert owned "a grand house" and more than 150 African slaves. Charles Juzan owned three different trading houses, located in the Choctaw towns of Coosa, Chunky Chitto, and Tuscahoma, and his family also laid claim to a profitable plantation located on the northern periphery of the city of Mobile. The Juzan and Colbert families adopted diversified economic strategies that effectively blended plantation production with the Indian trade and that created a stunning amount of wealth and power. The descendants of these men would become some of the largest and wealthiest slaveholders and most influential political leaders among early nineteenth-century Chickasaw and Choctaw Indians. The creation of this wealth and power would not have been possible without the cross-racial intimate connections both families established with Choctaw and Chickasaw women.[3]

James Colbert and Charles Juzan both had multiple Native American wives who assisted their husbands in navigating the shifting imperial politics and economic transformations of the eighteenth-century Gulf South. Colbert married three Choctaw women, while Juzan married two sisters, Peggy and Phoebe, who were themselves the mixed-race descendants of a Choctaw woman and a French man. Men like Colbert and Juzan discovered that the Chickasaw and Choctaw synthesized power, gender, and authority in ways that drastically departed from their own Euro-American heritage. Like many of their Native American counterparts, the Chickasaw and Choctaw organized their society around a kinship structure that differed markedly from Anglo-American concepts of family and gender. The basic unit of organization in Native tribes was the clan, a group of individuals who claimed descent from a common ancestor. Clans were matrilineal in nature, with membership determined by descent through the mother's line. Birth to a Native woman was a necessary prerequisite for membership in a clan and tribe, and those who lacked vital kinship connections occupied a tenuous position that jeopardized their lives and property. Intimate liaisons with Native women provided kinship connections and security as well as material comforts such as food, shelter, and even language or translation services that an itinerant merchant found invaluable.[4]

In crossing the color line and establishing intimate liaisons with Native American women, Juzan and Colbert adopted a tactic well known to Europeans who explored the Atlantic world in the early modern period. Europeans engaged in cross-racial sexual alliances with nonwhite women in locales that stretched across the Atlantic basin and beyond. In places as diverse as Senegal, on the west coast of Africa, and the West Indian sugar colonies in the Caribbean, Euro-American men found relationships with local women necessary to navigating socioeconomic circumstances in which white European superiority was anything but ensured. Cross-racial relationships throughout the Atlantic world took a variety of forms and served a multitude of purposes. In North America, white men marrying Native American women participated in "Winchester weddings" or "left-handed marriages," while on the Gold Coast in West Africa such unions between European men and African women were referred to as "country" or "cassare" marriages. Women on the Indian subcontinent who participated in intimate liaisons with Englishmen were called "bosom friends." Such relationships could be permanent or temporary, but everywhere they served the same purpose: women provided access to local kinship networks, shared knowledge of local culture and language, and supplied basic resources such as food and shelter, all of which in turn provided European men with a defined place within local social hierarchies and smoothed the way for trade and commerce. As was the case with Colbert and his Chickasaw wives, these unions also resulted in the creation of biracial children who simultaneously bolstered and challenged notions of Euro-American cultural and social superiority.[5]

While these liaisons provided crucial support to European men as they traveled, traded, and settled throughout the Atlantic world, imperial governments often wrangled with the repercussions of such intimate entanglements for the social and political hierarchies of the far-flung places they sought to rule. Once the generations of initial contact passed, European settlers attempted to exercise more power and influence over local affairs, while metropolitan governments became increasingly concerned with enforcing patriarchal notions of family and sexuality. The imposition of European gender norms was an effort to buttress European claims to power and dominance. By deciding on the legitimacy of intimate unions and the status of their offspring, imperial authorities sought to give meaning to racial difference and construct rationales for European cultural dominance.

As the American state expanded into the trans-Appalachian frontier in the years after the American Revolution, Anglo-American settlers confronted the remnants of the multicultural mixing that had defined an earlier era. Native men, Anglo-American men, and Native women reacted to this entanglement in ways meant to bolster their own claims to power and authority in a rapidly changing world. In the process, both groups rethought what had been fundamental connections among gender, status, and economic power and fashioned new identities as they attempted to escape from the entanglement of an earlier era. This essay begins with an examination of the shifting attitudes of Anglo-Americans toward Native American culture and then proceeds to a discussion of how Chickasaw and Choctaw men blended Native and Anglo-American gender norms in ways that underwrote their power and authority. To understand the Native American female perspective, the essay also examines the lives of two women who were products of the Juzan and Colbert family's intimate entanglement in the Gulf South. Delilah Wall, born in 1795, was the daughter of Charles Juzan and his Choctaw wife Peggy Trahern. Rhoda Gunn, born in 1818, was the daughter of an Anglo-American man named James Gunn and his Chickasaw wife Molly Colbert. Rhoda's connections to the Colbert family were twofold: first, her mother was the granddaughter of James Logan Colbert through his son William; second, in 1833 Rhoda married Samuel Colbert, the grandson of James Logan Colbert through his son and namesake James Colbert. The experiences of Delilah Wall and Rhoda Gunn situate the early nineteenth-century Gulf South in a wider global context and provide historians with an opportunity to make comparative connections between the early American republic and other aspiring metropolitan governments as they sought to govern more effectively the diverse peoples of their empires. The efforts to define the meanings and consequences of intimate entanglement in the Early Republic occurred in a context in which Euro-Americans across the globe attempted to assert their cultural dominance and economic power by more closely regulating cross-racial relationships. The essay concludes by making comparative connections between the Gulf South and other Atlantic regimes of the early nineteenth century.

From "Civilization" to Relocation: Anglo-American Attitudes toward Native Americans

Enlightenment thought played a dual and contradictory role in the ways that Anglo-Americans approached Native American relations after the American Revolution. Race had been a flexible and unstable category of social difference for most of the colonial era, but Euro-Americans were adopting a more rigid approach to race by the dawn of the nineteenth century. In the seventeenth century, Europeans had been inclined to believe in a single creation and that all humanity was descended from a common ancestor; in this worldview, skin color was the product of cultural and geographic factors. Yet the late seventeenth and eighteenth centuries witnessed an increasing stratification of racial thought, especially with regard to people of African descent. The creation of slave societies that centered upon plantation production in places as diverse as the West Indies, the Chesapeake, and the Carolina lowcountry resulted in the legal codification of slavery and created a permanent, degraded status for persons of African descent. In tandem with the legal codification of racial difference, the scientific rationalism of the Enlightenment encouraged philosophers and social thinkers to systemically study, explain, and classify racial difference. The writings of men like Carl Linnaeus provided Euro-Americans with a taxonomy that rationalized white superiority and political dominance while justifying the racial subordination of nonwhite people. In *Systema Naturae* (1735) Linnaeus divided humans into four broad categories, including "*Homo sapiens europaeus,*" whom he described as "smart, inventive. Covered by tight clothing, ruled by law," and "*Homo sapiens afer,*" who were "sluggish, lazy, crafty, slow, and careless. Covered by grease. Ruled by caprice."[6] In the Euro-American mind, race transformed from a flexible cultural construct to an innate biological category that could not be transformed. The ideas of men like Linnaeus ultimately culminated in the scientific racism of the nineteenth century, in which new disciplines such as phrenology sought to further rationalize Euro-American exploitation and dispossession of nonwhite people.[7]

In the post-Revolutionary era, Native Americans occupied a liminal space in America's racial hierarchy that placed them somewhere between Euro-Americans and African Americans. The Enlightenment's emphasis on environmentalism and education led some Euro-American thinkers to conclude that Native Americans could be converted into "civilized" members of society if they would only adopt Euro-centric ideas about family organization, property ownership, and religion. Enlightenment philosophical musings about the improvability of mankind combined with government policy in the federal government's "civilization program," which traced its roots to George Washington's administration. In a 1789 report on Indian affairs, Henry Knox, Washington's secretary of war, advised the president that peaceful coexistence was preferable to hostile relations with Native Americans. In outlining his plan to the president, Knox mused, "how different would be the sensations of the philosophic mind to reflect, that, instead of exterminating a part of the human race by our modes of population, we had persevered, through all difficulties, and at last had imparted our knowledge of cultivation and the arts of the aboriginals of the country, by which source of future life and happiness had been preserved and extended."[8]

The federal government sought a cultural transformation by asking that Native Americans adopt the concept of private property and overhaul their gendered division of labor. Indian men were instructed to give up hunting and to embrace farming while Indian women adopted spinning, weaving, and "the domestic arts." Patriarchal yeoman households, anchored by private ownership of land, would replace the matrilineal clans and communal property. In his second inaugural address, Thomas Jefferson summed up his administration's implementation of the civilization program when he advised his listeners that "humanity enjoins us to teach them agriculture and the domestic arts, to encourage them to that industry which alone can enable them to maintain their place in existence and to prepare them in time for that state of society which bodily comforts adds the improvements of the mind and morals." Writing to the Delaware people in 1808, Jefferson advised them that hunting deer and buffalo would not lead to safety and security upon their lands: "it is the cultivating [land] alone which can do that—the hundredth part in corn and cattle will support you better than the whole in deer and buffalo." Jefferson explained that such a shift in attitudes would lead to unity between Anglo-Americans and Native Americans, writing, "you will unite yourselves with us, join in our great Councils & form one people with us and we shall all be Americans, you will mix with us by marriage, your blood will run in our veins, & will spread with us over this great Island."[9]

Many Native American peoples selectively adopted elements of the civilization program in ways that did not require drastic cultural reorientation. Perhaps many Native listeners scoffed at hearing Anglo-American government officials and reformers preach the virtues of "agriculture." Native American women's cultivation of the "three sisters"—squash, beans, and corn—had provided important sustenance to their families and clans for centuries. Yet the overhunting of deer and the destructive influence of the Atlantic exchange economy led many Native Americans to embrace portions of the civilization program.

The Choctaw leader Franscimastabe advised his followers in 1792 that "the time of hunting and living by the Gun . . . was near its end." Native American men would have to "live by labor like White Men. . . . The whites by recourse to money always find the means to carry on trade but the poor red men have no other recourse than peltries." Similarly, the Choctaw leader Homastubbe asked the federal government in 1809 that "ploughs may be sent us, wedding hoes, grubbing hoes, axes, handsaws, iron wedges, and a man to make wheels, and a small set of blacksmith's tools for a red man."[10] While federal officials might have interpreted such requests as evidence of the success of the civilization program, evidence suggests that Indian peoples held onto their own cultural logic and their gendered division of labor. If they asked for spinning wheels, axes, or hoes, it was because they found agricultural production more efficient with these tools; if Native leaders encouraged missionaries to settle among their people, it was because they valued the schools that would teach reading and writing to their children, not the education in Christianity and the religious conversion that were the ultimate goals of the missionaries themselves. The cultural reorientation envisioned by the federal civilization program remained elusive and was contested by Native people.[11]

Anglo-American perceptions that the civilization program had failed, combined with the new scientific racism of the nineteenth century and greed for Indian land, resulted in a turning point by the time Andrew Jackson was elected president in 1828. Anglo-Americans no longer believed Indians capable of cultural transformation, and many federal officials advocated relocating Native groups west of the Mississippi River. While Jefferson and his followers had envisioned a world in which Anglo and Indian blood would intermingle and spread throughout the continent, later settlers and politicians advocated for segregation and expressed a strict abhorrence of the idea of Anglo and Indian intermixture. In a letter to Governor William Rabun of Georgia in 1817, Hugh Montgomery expressed astonishment that some white men were "lax in their Morrels [morals] & Still Less Delicate in their taste" and would "kiss a Squaw for the privallage of their Land and Range." Montgomery urged speedy intervention by Georgia's elected officials, since "a Motly Race are propigating fast verry fast on the Chatachoochee and its waters."[12] Rabun's successor in office, George Troup, also expressed disdain for Indians in Georgia, advising Secretary of War John C. Calhoun in 1824 that "the utmost of the rights and privileges which public opinion would concede to the Indians would fix them in a middle station between the negro and the white man. As long as they survived this degradation without the possibility of attaining the elevation of the latter they would gradually sink to the condition of the former."[13] Legislators and settlers in the Gulf South quickly abandoned the idea of Native incorporation. In 1828, the state of Georgia extended its jurisdiction over Cherokee lands; Alabama and Mississippi quickly followed suit, extending their jurisdictions over Choctaw and Chickasaw lands. By 1830 Congress had enacted the Indian Removal Act, which provided Andrew Jackson and his populist followers the means and justification for expelling Indian peoples from their homelands and forcing them beyond the Mississippi.

"What is an Indian Family?": Patriarchy and Native American Men

After the passage of the Indian Removal Act, in 1830, the Chickasaw and Choctaw Indians of Mississippi and Alabama negotiated separate removal treaties with the federal government. The Treaty of Dancing Rabbit Creek (1830) required the Choctaws to give up their land and seek "suitable" land west of the Mississippi River, while the Treaty of Pontotoc Creek (1830, later amended by the Treaty of Washington in 1834) placed the same requirement on the Chickasaw Indians. The

Washington treaty provided that "heads of families, being Indian, or having Indian families," would be entitled to a reservation whose size would be based on the number of persons in the family. Families that consisted of ten or more persons would receive the most land, with a bonus paid for any families that owned African American slaves. The fourteenth clause of the Treaty of Dancing Rabbit Creek stated that "each Choctaw head of a family, being desirous to remain, and become a citizen of the States, shall be permitted to do so." Each head-of-family would receive a 640-acre land grant, with extra land provided according to the number of persons living in the household. The Choctaw treaty did not provide bounties for slave ownership, though it did specify that Indian families would be given title to the land if they occupied it for a minimum of five years. In both treaties, the Choctaws and the Chickasaws were required to live under "the laws of the whites" if they decided to remain in the Southeast.[14]

In the decade that followed the signing of these removal treaties, the U.S. federal government engaged in a series of disputes with the Choctaw and Chickasaw Indians over what they had agreed to at Dancing Rabbit Creek and Pontotoc. Both treaties required removal only if "suitable" land were found in the Oklahoma territory, and each treaty provided a method for incorporating reluctant migrants into Anglo-American society should they choose to remain behind. The promise of citizenship and land ownership for Indian heads of households was meant to ensure the end of traditional tribal governments and to force those Native Americans who remained in the South to accept Anglo-American patriarchy and patterns of land ownership. However, Anglo-Americans accused Indians of obstructing the original purpose of the treaties by not ceding their lands quickly enough, while the Indians accused Anglo-Americans of attempting to cheat them of the promised land and citizenship that had been granted through the treaties.

In 1835, a group of Chickasaw leaders petitioned Andrew Jackson to clarify the purpose of granting land to Indian families. Not only did the male leaders of the Chickasaw believe that Anglo-Americans were attempting to renege on their promises of homesteads for Indians, but they also accused the federal agents of not granting enough land to those Chickasaw who claimed homesteads under the provisions of the treaty. The Chickasaw chiefs' petition to Jackson was remarkable because it captured male Chickasaws' understandings of the gendered politics within their tribe. Central to their complaints was the very definition of "family" used to determine the size of land grants provided to the heads of Indians families. The Chickasaw men advised Jackson "that the question, 'What is an Indian family?' naturally precedes the question 'Who is the head of such family.'" Furthermore, the chiefs argued that the definition of "family" and "head of family" should be determined not by American law but by "the customs and manners of life of the Chickasaw."[15]

Of particular concern for the Chickasaw Indians was the tradition of polygamy, a long-recognized custom for Southeastern Indians. A Chickasaw man who married multiple women and had children with each formed a family unit that contradicted the Anglo-American understanding of monogamous marriage and the patriarchal family. In essence, the major failure of the treaty, according to these Indian men, was that it failed to account for the fact that a Chickasaw man could be the head of multiple families. They protested that nothing in the treaties "warranted the conclusion that the several wives of an Indian and their respective children are to be considered . . . as one family."[16] The Chickasaw argued that the answer to the question "what is an Indian family?" was not to be found in the text of the treaty, and the customs and laws of the Chickasaw mandated that "the several wives of an Indian, and their respective children, do not constitute one family, in the proper sense of the word." In arguing that their definition of family organization should prevail over that of Anglo-American men, these Chickasaw men created a new synthesis of gender and power that sought to bolster their own claims to wealth and power.

The leaders also contrasted the less rigid matrimonial connections between Indian men and women with the more binding marital contracts between Anglo-Americans. "The matrimonial connection," argued the chiefs, "is slight, it is contracted without formality, and dissolved at the pleasure of either party." The chiefs explained their matrilineal traditions to the president as resulting from the "weak" bond between husband and wife and the fact that Chickasaw men practiced polygamy.

The Chickasaw chiefs argued that an Indian father was "not considered to be under any obligation to support his children, the care and nurture of them is exclusively the duty of the mother." Wives and children also did not inherit property from their husbands or fathers, and upon a man's death "his oldest collateral relations [inherit]; and it frequently happens, that by them the wife and children are stripped of all his property." However, the chiefs also explained that Chickasaw women were allowed to have separate estates from their husbands and that a woman retained "full liberty to dispose of [her property] in any manner she may please." In the case of an Indian man who had multiple wives, the custom was for each wife to maintain a separate establishment. In this arrangement of multiple families connected by a single husband, "the home of each is regarded as her own, and is generally so known and distinguished by the community."[17] For these Chickasaw men, nonbinding relationships between husbands and wives and multiple familial households connected only by the father or husband constituted a cultural norm that they asked Anglo-Americans to respect when making land grants provided by the removal treaties.

The main concern of these Chickasaw men was that the land allotments granted under the removal treaties were not enough to allow them to care for their large families. While the land granted under the treaties might have appeared generous to an Anglo-American who maintained one wife and their children, the same could not said about the large families of Chickasaw men. The chiefs argued that the largest family size mentioned in the treaty (ten) was actually not very realistic when accounting for a husband and his multiple wives. They provided a concrete example of the well-known Chickasaw "mixed blood" Levi Colbert, the son of James Logan Colbert who had become an important mediator between the Chickasaws and the federal government in the early nineteenth century. Under the treaty of 1834, Levi gained four sections of land, one of the largest allotments granted to any Chickasaw under the treaty. Yet the men who signed this petition, including Levi's brother and a son, indicated that this would not be enough land to support Levi's extensive family, since according to these men he had "upwards of twenty children, the offspring of his several wives."[18] The land provided for Colbert might have been sufficient for a family of ten, but the same land grant seemed inadequate for a family with more than twenty children.

The chiefs presented evidence meant to bolster their own power and authority within Chickasaw culture, and they clearly attempted to modify Anglo-American notions of patriarchy to suit their own ends. They declared that problems may arise "in deciding whether the reservations are to rest in the wives as heads of their respective families, or whether the husband shall take distinct reservations in right of his several wives." The men reasoned that since the treaty required that one reservation would go to a Chickasaw man in support of his family, they could "perceive no reason, why several reservations may not be vested in him with the expectation that he will dispose of them for the support of the several families." Realizing that some Anglo-American officials might object to granting so much land to Indian men, the Chickasaws attempted to head off any objections. They argued that while "it is true, such husband may dispose his connection with one of his wives, and thereby cut off her and her children from any provisions . . . it is equally true and just as likely to happen, that an Indian husband may dissolve his connection with an only wife, and the same consequence would follow." In other words, if federal officials trusted Indian men to care for one family, they should also respect Indian men's ability to provide for multiple families with their many different wives.

In case Anglo-American officials were afraid that Indian men would shirk their duties to their families, the Indians also asserted that each man did not represent his own individual interest but spoke as the representative "of the several families of which he is the head."[19] While they recognized that matrilineal customs had allowed polygamous marriages and granted wives "separate estates," the men also presented themselves as patriarchs who spoke on behalf of their multiple families. They claimed economic power and authority over their families beyond what had traditionally existed for Chickasaw husbands and fathers. The men who petitioned Andrew Jackson to acknowledge their traditional cultural practices surrounding marriage also sought to increase their own power by adapting Anglo-American notions of patriarchy to suit their own goals.

In asking that the federal government recognize their right to form polygamous unions and establish multiple households, these Chickasaw men also sought to strengthen their economic power by deploying complex domestic arrangements. For example, Levi Colbert's four wives lived in their own separate establishments and specialized in different economic activities. His first two wives (one of whom was named Seletia) occupied a residence on the Tombigbee River and assisted in the operation of a lucrative ferry there. His third wife lived on a large livestock plantation known as "French Farm." His fourth wife, Mini-Hoyo, operated a boardinghouse and lodge at Buzzard Roost Creek at the start of the Natchez Trace. These three households operated independently of one another, but Levi Colbert was the crucial link between them. His ability to create multiple permeable households allowed Levi Colbert to accumulate wealth and prestige within the Chickasaw community. His ability to deploy familial contacts that served to enrich him throughout his varied economic enterprises would have made him the envy of any Anglo-American patriarch.[20]

Yet Levi Colbert's abilities to assume the role of the patriarch were limited. According to Chickasaw tradition, the separate households and families, as well as the associated property, would have fallen under the wife's authority. Property and wealth were generally transmitted between generations through the mother's lineage, and fathers would have exercised little, if any, control over either the property or their children. The Chickasaw men who petitioned Jackson in 1835 sought to combine both matrilineal and patrilineal concepts in a way that would ultimately bring greater power and authority to Native men. They asked the federal government to recognize Chickasaw men as heads of multiple Indian families and to provide them with the resources necessary to maintain separate establishments and the resulting children. Yet these men were just one in a cacophony of voices claiming to interpret the impact that cross-racial familial arrangements had upon the gender politics of the early nineteenth-century South. Anglo-American men acted to curtail the ability of bicultural individuals to gain power or economic status from their dual backgrounds, and they also construed the legacy of intimate entanglement in ways that allowed for the dispossession and relocation of Native Americans living in the Gulf South. In contrast, Native American women offered interpretations that allowed them to maintain some economic independence from both Native and Anglo-American men while at the same time combating the increasing racialization of Native peoples in the nineteenth century.

Delilah Wall, Native Women, and the Status of *Feme Covert*

In October 1837, Delilah Wall, the wife of a man named David W. Wall, signed a contract agreeing to pay a debt of $133.75 to a white man named Williamson. Delilah was the daughter of Charles Juzan and his wife Peggy, herself the mixed-race descendant of a white man and a Choctaw woman. Delilah described her husband David as "one-fourth Indian," indicating that not only had she descended from a mixed-race family but also that she had married into one. Prior to her marriage to Wall, Delilah had been married to a "mixed race" Choctaw man named Jesse Brashears. Upon Jesse's death, in 1827, she remarried and established a new household with David Wall near the southeastern boundary of the Choctaw Nation in the area that is modern-day Sumter County, Alabama. The couple's relationship lasted from 1828 until 1840, when David fled west into Oklahoma territory to escape prosecution for murdering a man whose identity has been lost in the historical record. Delilah apparently never again laid eyes upon her husband, though she did occasionally receive letters from him threatening to return and remove their child from her custody. When she defaulted on the debt owed to Williamson, he brought a civil case against Delilah in the Sumter County circuit court in 1840. Though perhaps he did not know this when he filed his suit, Williamson's case against Delilah required members of the Sumter County community to confront the legacy of cross-racial intimate entanglement and to adjudicate on the compatibility of Native American gender norms with Anglo-American concepts of citizenship and power. Because the case against Delilah eventually reached the Alabama Supreme Court, the decisions rendered set important precedents and assisted with the effort to codify white male superiority in the antebellum era.[21]

The Alabama Supreme Court also mediated two other civil cases in the 1840s involving Delilah Wall. In addition to the Williamson suit, a white man named Williams similarly sued Delilah for failing to pay a debt. The first names of these men have not survived in the court records, and it is not possible to conclude from the available records if there was a connection. Though the contract with Williamson had been signed before David Wall's "desertion" of Delilah and the contract in the Williams case was signed after the "desertion," both men argued that Choctaw traditions and customs denied husbands power over their wives' property. Eventually, the Alabama Supreme Court agreed that this "peculiarity" meant that Choctaw women maintained the right to contract, even after marriage. A third case, involving Delilah's stepson from her previous marriage to Jesse Brashear, reached the court in 1846; one of Delilah's creditors had seized African American slaves to settle an outstanding debt. The stepson (named only "Brashear" in the case records) argued that he took possession of the slaves soon after coming of age and "continued to exercise acts of ownership" over the said slaves. Brashear also argued that Delilah's creditors offered no evidence that Choctaw widows "became entitled to a share" of a deceased husband's property.[22]

Men and women like David and Delilah Wall and their children created uncertain gendered and racial subjectivities in the new United States. As the offspring of a Native woman and a French man, Delilah occupied an ambiguous position in the antebellum South. Because she was neither white nor red, her citizenship status and legal rights were disputed by all those involved, and she presented a quandary to the Alabama jurists who heard her case. Whose social and cultural conventions would prevail in this case? Delilah could claim, by birth and by residence, to be governed by two distinct gendered traditions, one Choctaw and the other European-American. Her ability to transcend and amalgamate multiple cultures created the possibility of destabilizing the white patriarchy that underwrote Anglo-American gender norms. Perhaps more menacing to the white men who sat in judgment of her case, inherent in Delilah's ambiguous place in the South's social hierarchy was the possibility of disrupting and confounding Anglo-American racial hegemony at the very moment that white slave owners were revolutionizing the demographics of the Gulf South. A "half-blood" Indian woman who used white gender norms to subvert responsibility to her white male creditor potentially undermined the entire foundation of male patriarchal authority over all their dependents.

Delilah insisted to the white men of the jury that Williams's suit was without basis, as she was still married to David Wall and that therefore she was "entitled to all the rights, and subject to all the incapacities of a married woman." According to coverture laws that governed the actions of white women, a married woman (legally known as a *feme covert*—literally "covered woman") had no legal identity separate from that of her husband. Married women could not own separate property or make valid contracts. A single woman (*feme sole*) maintained those rights so long as she was unmarried or widowed. Delilah supported her claim to the status associated with white womanhood by arguing that both she and David were entitled to American citizenship under the fourteenth clause of the Treaty of Dancing Rabbit Creek. The fourteenth clause of the treaty granted land to "each head of a family" who wished to remain in Mississippi or Alabama. Furthermore, the treaty promised American citizenship if the "head of a family" occupied the land for at least five years. Anglo-Americans assumed this agreement would force Native families to adopt patriarchal family arrangements centered around private property and agricultural production. Delilah and David Wall numbered among a small group of Choctaws who chose to remain in their ancestral homeland while also laying claim to American citizenship under the provisions of the Treaty of Dancing Rabbit Creek. Just as Chickasaw men had sought to define "head of family" in ways that underscored their power and status, Delilah Wall also sought to provide a definition that would grant her the maximum amount of maneuverability in the Gulf South's changing social and cultural environment.

The white claimants in these cases exoticized the marriage customs of the Choctaws in response to Delilah's claim to American citizenship and the status associated with white womanhood, and their arguments before Alabama jurists created a portrait of an "uncivilized" and "savage" people. According to these men, Choctaws "had no marriage ceremony." Men and women simply "lived together" and were considered husband and wife. According to one witness, "they married and unmarried at pleasure—a man frequently having several wives."[23] David Wall was repeatedly referred to as having "deserted" his wife and thereby severed the marriage relation. In debating the legality of polygamous marriages among non-Christian peoples, Justice Goldthwaithe declared, "a parallel case, to a Turkish, or other marriage in an infidel country will probably be found among all our savage tribes."[24] Furthermore, according to Justice Collier, "marriages among the Indian tribes must be regarded as taking place in a state of nature" because of the absence of either civil or religious institutions. In reviewing the case of Brashear's claim to the African American slaves, Justice Ormond maintained that the "necessary presumption must be, that in a savage tribe, laws do not exist, regulating the descent of property." The courts also refused to recognize the dynamic nature of Gulf South Native American society. In responding to a claim that an 1832 Alabama law extended protection only to "full blood" Indians, Justice Collier concluded that "in common parlance the word Indians" included not only full-blood Indians but also persons who "have become thus mixed, yet retain their distinctive character as members of the tribe from which they trace their descent."[25] In support of this conclusion, Collier argued that "the ignorance of the half breed is in general quite equal to that of the Indian whose blood is unadulterated."

In both cases where Delilah was sued by her white creditors, the Alabama Supreme Court ruled that Delilah's marriage was governed by Choctaw, not Anglo-American, cultural norms. Since Choctaw women maintained rights to property after marriage, the court reasoned that she was not entitled the status of *feme covert.* Furthermore, Justice Collier maintained that, because an Indian husband could "abandon" his wife "at his pleasure," such abandonment must be taken as proof of a divorce and have the same effect as a "lawful decree in a civilized community dissolving marriage." Whether married to her lawful Choctaw husband or a divorcée by Choctaw customs, Delilah Wall was not, according to the court, entitled to the civil status associated with white womanhood. Both witnesses and jurists in these cases created an essentialized identity for Delilah Wall that placed her outside the bounds of Anglo-American "civilization." For these men, her racialized identity as a Choctaw overrode her claims to the "civilized" status of white womanhood. The justices refused to entertain the notion that Choctaw gender norms were dynamic and changing in response to the vast economic dislocations of the early nineteenth century. The language used in these cases fixed women like Delilah Wall in an essentialized racial identity that permanently disempowered them.

To accomplish this essentialism, Alabama jurists had to overlook evidence that Choctaws had made efforts in the 1820s to create a centralized political system and enforce a unified code of laws. In an effort to resist Anglo-American encroachment upon their homeland, a group of Choctaw leaders wrote a constitution and code of laws in 1826 that vested legislative and executive power in a group of elected leaders. The assembly and the legal code it produced were expressions of power among a new, mostly "mixed blood" cabal of Choctaw men. Delilah Wall's then husband, Jesse Brashear, and her brother-in-law, Vaughn Brashear, were both signatories to the code adopted in 1826. The laws governing marriage and family life vastly departed from previous Choctaw tradition of matrilineal kinship and clan-based inheritance. Rather than allowing goods and wealth to pass down through the wife's or mother's clan, the new laws mandated that the wife and children of a man dying without a will would "inherit all his livestock and estate." The deceased father or husband's property would be divided into thirds, allowing for his wife and children to share in the property. This arrangement closely mirrored white women's dower rights in Anglo-American culture. Furthermore, Indian men were required to make provisions for their families, as "every individual's will must provide for his wife and children." The law also provided protection for Choctaw women who married white men. The law gave these women an interest in the property of the couple, declaring that "the woman has a right to their property; they [the couple] cannot sell it frivolously if they are not in agreement." The substance of these laws could have been construed to uphold the Alabama Supreme Court's view that Indian women maintained property and the right to contract. Though the laws specifically mentioned only interracial marriages between Choctaw women and white men and failed to make provisions for endogamous marriage among the Choctaw, the laws provided evidence that Choctaw male legislators intended for some married women to retain property rights. However, the Alabama court chose an easier and perhaps more consequential path when they essentialized Choctaw women as "savage" and "uncivilized" people who lived in a "state of nature." This allowed the court to ignore the dramatic acculturation that some Choctaws had undergone in the early nineteenth century and to declare all Choctaws as living outside the law.[26]

The courts also rebutted Delilah's claim that the Treaty of Dancing Rabbit Creek had granted her citizenship. Justice Collier rhetorically asked, "Do our laws allow Indians to participate equally with us in our civil and political privileges? Do they vote at our elections, or are they represented in our legislature, or have they any concern as jurors or magistrates, in the administration of justice?

Are they subject to our laws of marriage and divorce, and would we sustain a criminal prosecution for bigamy, if they should change their wives and husbands at pleasure, and according to their customs, and contract new matrimonial alliances? I apprehend that every one of these questions must be answered in the negative."[27] Even though the treaty explicitly stated that citizenship would be granted to Choctaw "heads of families" after fulfilling a five-year residency requirement, Justice Collier mused that the federal agents really should have used the words "inhabitant" or "resident" rather than "citizen of the States." Collier based his argument upon the fact that the fourteenth clause of the treaty also mandated that Choctaws who chose to remain in Alabama "shall not lose the privileges of a Choctaw citizen." This clause of the treaty was meant to provide flexibility to those Choctaws who initially remained behind but later decided to migrate to Indian Territory with the vast majority of their tribe. Yet, for Collier and the other Anglo-American men involved in this case, the bicultural identity of women like Delilah and these women's ability to claim dual Choctaw and U.S. citizenship could not be tolerated; in other words, white patriarchal identity required a polarized racial order and could not tolerate the biculturalism that had been a central feature of life in the Gulf South since the eighteenth century.

In other financial transactions, Delilah Wall demonstrated a protean understanding of patriarchy and female submissiveness. When Delilah found herself in a Southern courtroom answering for her failure to pay a prior debt, she wisely insisted that she could not be held accountable under traditional understandings of coverture; however, when transferring property to her daughter, Delilah challenged these same gendered customs. In 1837, both David and Delilah divested themselves of property, selling several parcels of land for more than $4,000 to a white man named John Foster. The Walls probably sold their property in an effort to prepare themselves to move west, where they eventually ended up (though not as a married couple).

At the same time that she became indebted to Williamson for the debt of $133.75, Delilah also transferred a large amount of property to her daughter Sebelle. Among the items transferred to her daughter were 160 acres of land, two horses, five cows, two African American male slaves named Nichorimus and Silas, and a female slave named Joana. As a condition of the transfer, Delilah declared that the property transferred to her daughter "shall not be liable for any debt or debts contracted by any husband the said Sebelle Wall may hereafter have, nor subject to be sold by any such husband, but shall belong exclusively to the said Sebelle Wall."[28] Five years before she claimed that Williamson could not sue her because she was a *feme covert* and in the very same month that she came under debt to Williamson, Delilah insisted that her daughter's property could not be subject to the same regulations. The transfer took place in a chaotic time for the remaining Choctaws in Mississippi; those who insisted on claiming their rights under the Treaty of Dancing Rabbit Creek faced enormous pressure to sell their belongings and move west. Perhaps Delilah simply included this language to protect her daughter's property from a potentially lecherous future husband who might seek to take advantage of her daughter's wealth. Whatever her motivations, Delilah displayed a calculating understanding of Anglo-American patriarchal society. Whether she was claiming to be a submissive wife in need of protection or attempting to empower her daughter to reject that very same submission, Delilah's goal always remained the same—to protect the economic well-being of herself and her family.

Delilah was not the only one capable of a flexible interpretation of the Gulf South's intimate entanglements; the Anglo-American jurists who adjudicated these cases also adopted elastic and self-serving understandings of the meanings of intimate entanglement. In 1844, two years before Delilah's case reached the Alabama high court, the justices of the Tennessee Supreme Court found that a "mixed blood" Cherokee woman named Margaret Morgan was not entitled to file a lawsuit because she *was* governed by the law of coverture. Margaret had married Gideon Morgan (described as a white man) in 1818, and, after their marriage, she inherited a number of African slaves from her mother. When some of the slaves were seized to satisfy her husband's debts, Margaret sued, claiming that the slaves were her property and could not be detained in payment of Gideon's debts. Furthermore, Margaret argued that she and Gideon were "living apart" at the time of the trial, signifying that the couple's relationship had come to an end. The Tennessee court dismissed Margaret's suit without ruling on the property rights of Cherokee women, claiming that Margaret was a *feme covert* and declaring that "there is no reason why a marriage made and consummated in an Indian nation should be subject to a different rule of action." Unlike Delilah Wall, Margaret Morgan was placed under the law of coverture and denied the right to use legal action to protect her economic power. However, the outcome was the same in both cases; Alabama and Tennessee justices defined the law in ways meant to protect the economic power of Anglo-American men.[29]

Just three years after the Alabama Supreme Court ruled that Delilah Wall could not claim the protected status of *feme covert,* the same court ruled that a Creek woman's property was controlled by her husband precisely because she *was* governed by coverture. Mary Wells, a Creek woman with "one-fourth Indian blood," married William J. Wells, a white man, in Monroe County, Alabama, in 1821. Shortly after their marriage, the couple relocated within the boundaries of the Creek nation, probably to be closer to Mary's family. The couple and their children resided there until 1828, when the family moved to the Ten Islands on the Coosa River, located on what was then the border between Alabama and Creek territory. Shortly after the family's relocation, William committed adultery and "took up with another woman." Mary responded by taking her children and returning to her father's house, back in Creek territory. At some point, William took control of the children he had with Mary and took them to Arkansas. Before her death, in 1836, Mary received a grant of land under the provisions of the 1832 Treaty of Cusseta. This treaty, like the Treaty of Dancing Rabbit Creek, required the Creeks to surrender all their lands east of the Mississippi River, yet provided individual allotments for heads of Indian families. Mary's allotment and the question of who would control it after her death became a source of dispute between William Wells and his children.[30]

When William sold the allotted land for $1,800 and pocketed the money, his children sued, claiming that under Creek customs, their mother's land rightfully belonged to them. The Macon County circuit court examined the claims of the children and ruled in favor of their father, reinforcing William's position as a patriarch with the ability to control his family's property. The children then appealed their case to the Alabama Supreme Court, insisting that their mother was the head of their family. Mary's children claimed that the federal government had already tacitly recognized their mother's position as the head of the family, since she had received an allotment under the Treaty of Cusseta, which specified that land would be granted only to the head of each Indian family that applied for such allotments. Regardless of who was the head of the family, the children claimed that their mother used Creek customs to divorce her husband in 1828, when she left her husband and returned to her father's house due to William's adultery. William countered the arguments of his children by stating that his marriage had taken place according to the customs of white Americans, and, as such, "[he] became and continued, the head of the family." Furthermore, William's case was different, he claimed, from a case that involved two nonwhites who married under Indian customs. His status as a white man should ensure his position as head of the family and his ability to dispose of family property.

Just a few years after Delilah Wall lost her claim to the status of *feme covert,* the Alabama courts were again asked to litigate a case that resulted from cross-racial marriages challenging Anglo-American concepts of property and patriarchy. The justices of the Alabama Supreme Court sided with both the circuit court and William Wells's arguments, claiming that the Wellses' marriage had taken place according to Anglo-American customs, and therefore William had a right to control his wife's property. According to the justices of the Supreme Court, Mary's decision to leave her husband's home should be understood not as divorce but as abandonment. "Mrs. Wells . . . abandoned her husband within the jurisdictional limits of the State," reasoned the justices of the court, "and by such an abandonment unsanctioned by divorce in due form, their marriage could not be dissolved." The federal government's decision to grant land to "heads of Indian families" did not figure into the reasoning of the state supreme court, because it recognized William as the head of the Wells family. The Wells children could not expect to enjoy the property of their mother during their father's lifetime because it "vests in [the father], or his assignees, to be enjoyed until his death."[31]

At the heart of both cases was white men's ability to control property and exercise economic autonomy. In the case of Delilah Wall, it was her creditor's ability to recoup lost money, while in Mary Wells's case it was the ability of her husband to control and sell property. Both cases also revolved around an Anglo-American court's understandings of Indian marriage and divorce customs. Delilah insisted that her husband's abandonment of the family did not constitute a divorce and that her status as a married woman protected her from lawsuits from her white male creditor. In the Wall case, the courts decided that Indian customs dictated that Delilah's marriage had been dissolved by David's flight to Arkansas. Yet Mary Wells's flight from her husband did not constitute divorce because the justices considered her to be governed under American traditions, so her actions to constituted abandonment. If Delilah Wall selectively deployed her understanding of Indian and Anglo-American gender norms to her advantage, the justices of the Alabama Supreme Court did the same.

For the white men who sat in judgment of Delilah's case, her race proved a more salient identity than her gender or class status. Her Indian heritage not only excluded her from the benefits of American citizenship but also resulted in her existence outside patriarchal institutions and control. For more than three decades prior to Indian removal, federal Indian agents, missionaries, and social reformers had proclaimed that forsaking their customary understandings of gender and power was a prerequisite for Indians to gain American citizenship. By the time Delilah brought her suit in the Sumter County circuit court, public opinions had shifted to such a degree that many Anglo-Americans, particularly those who coveted Indian land in the Deep South, had come to believe that Indians were no longer capable of cultural assimilation or "civilization" and therefore must be expelled. Delilah's multiethnic background, which would have ensured her economic and social success just a few decades prior, had proven to be the source of her exclusion and expulsion.

In the person of Delilah Wall, the mixed-race descendant of Choctaws and Europeans, we see that efforts to create American hegemony rested upon a gendered discourse that defined her as "outsider" in the new nation, while also denying her any opportunity to gain economic power. Anglo-Americans had learned that regulating the descendants of eighteenth-century interracial mixing was an effective method of exercising power in the early Republic. The legal arguments deployed in cases like Delilah Wall's gave meaning to the racial difference constructed in the cultural discourse of the new science of race that emerged in the nineteenth century. In essence, Southern patriarchs created a two-tiered system of citizenship that was dependent upon the intertwined discourses of racialized and gendered difference. While the federal government had seemingly created space for Choctaw citizens by granting them property under the Treaty of Dancing Rabbit Creek, Southern courts used Native gender practices to define Natives as outside the boundaries of citizenship. White Southern patriarchs participated in the construction of a national identity that was racially and sexually encoded. Essentializing Native American women in the courtroom gave meaning and power to the new cultural discourses of scientific racism, providing important precedents for later discourses about race and gender difference that served to endorse and propagate American hegemony writ large in the coming years.

Reading the Silences: Rhoda Gunn and Covert Challenges to Patriarchy

In 1829, Rhoda Gunn married Samuel Colbert, grandson of James Logan Colbert and youngest son of Major James Colbert, thereby gaining entry into the prestigious biracial Colbert clan. While Samuel and Rhoda may have been attracted to each other because their racial status as "half breeds" provided a common racial identity, Rhoda later insisted that their marriage took place "according to the customs" of the Chickasaw nation.[32] This important phrase implied that Rhoda and Samuel understood that their marriage existed according to the traditions of matrilineal kinship and female property ownership, not those associated with Anglo-American patrilineal descent.[33] Indeed, when Rhoda married Samuel Colbert, she brought considerable property into the marriage, consisting mostly of the thirty-five African slaves she had inherited from her father. Rhoda claimed that she retained the use of the slaves even after she married, providing proof that Chickasaws incorporated new ideas about racial slavery within an old framework of gender norms.[34] Furthermore, Rhoda claimed that Chickasaw custom had no concept of coverture. After marriage, Rhoda maintained the use and ownership of her slaves, since Chickasaw wives did not automatically surrender their personal or real property to their husbands upon marriage. Whereas Delilah Wall had attempted to navigate the imposition of Anglo-American ideas about power and authority by claiming the status of *feme covert,* Rhoda denied its very existence among the Chickasaw.

The union between Rhoda and Samuel was not a harmonious one. In her divorce petition, Rhoda claimed that she cohabited with Samuel as man and wife until 1833, when Samuel deserted her and "openly lived with another woman" as his wife. The following year, in 1834, Samuel and Rhoda reconciled, and in January 1835 Rhoda gave birth to a daughter. Five months later, in the summer of 1835, her relationship with Samuel again turned sour. Samuel became violent, frequently beating Rhoda. Finally, Samuel forced Rhoda out of their home and sent her slaves with her. When Rhoda fled with her daughter and her slaves, Samuel soon tracked her down, forcibly taking control of their daughter and a number of the slaves. Claiming that "maternal feelings compelled her to return," Rhoda again attempted to cohabit with Samuel. However, Rhoda again feared for her safety and fled once more, this time seeking asylum in her mother's house.[35]

Rhoda filed for divorce from Samuel Colbert in October 1835, claiming that he kept her "in a constant state of alarm, continually threatening to remove her child from her custody." During the period of their separation, Rhoda also claimed that she maintained authority over her slaves, even though many of them continued to reside on Samuel Colbert's plantation. While the slaves lived and worked on Samuel's plantation, Rhoda "received the hire" of the slaves. What this means is not exactly clear. Perhaps Rhoda hired out the slaves and received cash payments for their work, or she may have retained the rights to the products of their labor. Again, this would have been consistent with native gender traditions that failed to recognize the existence of private property. What is clear is that the slaves continued to live and work on Samuel's plantation, but Rhoda claimed that they supported themselves and worked for her.

Not content with this arrangement, Samuel Colbert apparently schemed to confiscate the slaves of his wife, against the terms of the separation agreement they had signed. Samuel claimed that he had incurred considerable expense in clothing and feeding Rhoda's slaves who remained on his plantation, so he took ownership of three of the slaves as his personal property in order to reimburse himself for the expense. Samuel's actions imply that he continued to recognize Rhoda's rights to the other thirty-three slaves, since he claimed only a few of the slaves as reimbursement for himself. However, Rhoda claimed that "certain white men," including Beverly Mitchell, Wyatt Mitchell, and Charles F. Eastmond, conspired to deprive her of the slaves by convincing Samuel that his rights as a husband entitled him to his estranged wife's property.[36] Following the advice of his white neighbors, Samuel exercised his rights as a husband by selling the remaining slaves. Rhoda claimed that all the male parties involved, including her husband and their white neighbors, had lived within the boundaries of the Chickasaw nation and so were well aware that they made this transaction in opposition to Chickasaw customs regarding a wife's right to her personal property.

Unfortunately, the records detailing the results of Rhoda Gunn's divorce petition have failed to survive, so we have no way of knowing whether she successfully defended what she saw as her traditional rights. Eventually Samuel and Rhoda turned to a local Presbyterian missionary, Thomas C. Stuart, for assistance with their marital problems. On March 31, 1836, Samuel and Rhoda signed a separation agreement mediated by Stuart and filed in the De Soto County courthouse. Per the separation agreement, Rhoda would have custody of Susan, their daughter. The couple agreed that Samuel and Rhoda Gunn were to live "separate and apart from each other" and that Rhoda would be considered a *feme sole* from that moment forward. In this separation agreement, Rhoda agreed to let Samuel sell several of the slaves in order to raise money that would contribute to the support of their daughter.[37]

When compared to Delilah Wall's, Rhoda's actions are very revealing. Like Delilah, Rhoda Gunn used local Southern courts to protect her property. Similarly, both Delilah and Rhoda were products of the sexual entanglement that had characterized an earlier period, and their status as wives and mixed-race women became a particular problem once Southern states extended their boundaries to include the lands ceded by the Choctaw and Chickasaw natives. However, while Delilah Wall openly embraced Anglo-American notions of coverture that limited her economic freedom, Rhoda Gunn was more circumspect in her appropriation of Anglo-American gender norms.

In many ways, Rhoda Gunn asked the white men who sat in judgment of her case to rethink their traditional understandings of gender relations by suspending their Anglo-American custom of coverture. Rhoda repeatedly reminded the court that she was not asking for any radical changes in her status but that she desired what were her customary rights under Native traditions. She insisted that both Samuel and the white men who bought her slaves were well aware of the Native wife's right to control property but that they spurned this custom when they stood to benefit financially. While this request may have conformed to traditional Chickasaw concepts of marriage and property, the white men who sat in judgment of this case would have interpreted her request as an extreme shift in the balance of power between husband and wife.

Perhaps in an effort to make her bold request more palatable to her white audience, Rhoda took great care to present outward conformity to Anglo-American gender norms, with the important exceptions of private property and coverture. She highlighted her "maternal feelings" towards her daughter, and she presented a narrative of her marriage that made clear that she left her husband only once he ordered her out of his home. Even then, she returned to a difficult domestic situation in an effort to make her marriage a success, only to be forced to flee when her husband's abuse threatened her own and her child's safety. If the prospect of a wife suing a husband over property rights threatened the white men of the jury, Rhoda attempted to alleviate their anxieties by presenting a narrative that portrayed her as victimized and suffering from the abuses of an unfaithful husband. In this way, Rhoda selectively adopted the Anglo-American gender norms to which she would conform in order to maximize the amount of empathy she might generate in the white male jury.

Rhoda Gunn's selective adoption of Anglo-American customs is even more revealing when we consider what she left unsaid in her petition. When she mentioned that Samuel Colbert had "deserted" her and lived in open adultery with another woman, Rhoda was most likely exploiting the Anglo-American concept of monogamy for the benefit of her suit. Like other Native tribes in the Southeast, the Chickasaws maintained a tradition in which Native men were allowed to marry more than one spouse. Since women formed the backbone of the Chickasaw kinship structure and maintained full authority over their children and property, Chickasaw men could develop intimate relationships with a number of different wives while still maintaining the social order. As mentioned, Levi Colbert, Rhoda's kinsman, was well known for having more than one Chickasaw wife. Levi's polygamous relationships were known to more than just federal agents and government officials; members of the Colbert family's local community were also well acquainted with the complex intimate arrangements of the family. Joseph Bullen, a congregational missionary traveling to the Mississippi territory at the turn of the nineteenth century, commented upon Samuel Colbert's uncle's practice of maintaining more than one wife. Bullen approached Levi Colbert, Samuel's uncle, for assistance in getting his missionary settlement established, and, after one particular visit to Levi's home, Bullen commented that Levi, "with his two wives, appears to live comfortably: here we were politely received, well fed, and kindly treated; with him we were soon on terms of agreeable familiarity: to him the design of our mission was disclosed, with which he was evidently pleased." Similarly, Josiah Walton, a resident of Monroe County, Mississippi (home to many Colberts), recalled that "although he had a number of wives and two of them sisters, they lived as cordial and affectionately as so many sisters. They would laugh and joke [with] each other as though wives of different men, and no discord ever happened among them. Each of them had their children so trained that it seemed that all three were their mothers, and care for alike." On another occasion, Walton wrote that Levi "had a splendid dinner prepared for me and all of his family present, three grown daughters and five or six sons. The old man and his three wives were at one end of the table." Since no direct evidence exists regarding how Samuel Colbert replied to Rhoda's charges against him, it is impossible to know the full circumstances of the Colberts' intimate relationship. However, it is striking that, while she took great care to explain Native customs regarding marriage and property, Rhoda Gunn was suspiciously silent when it came the Native tradition of polygamy, accusing Samuel Colbert of "open adultery."[38]

Their actions demonstrate that Delilah and Rhoda used white cultural norms in a way that cut to the very core of Anglo-American claims to power and dominance. If the so-called gender frontier depended upon civilized whites conforming to European traditions of patriarchy and backward natives who eschewed those traditions, the life stories of Delilah Wall and Rhoda Gunn provide historians with a richer, more complex portrait of interracial mixing in the American South. In an effort to maintain their power, property, and status, some Native women were perfectly willing to embrace the basic tenets of patriarchy, even if they adapted patriarchy to suit their own ends. Their creative misunderstandings of patriarchal order allowed these women to contest the imposition of a colonial order over their families and their tribes.

At the time that the Colbert and Juzan families established a mixed-race dynasty among the Choctaw and Chickasaw, the Gulf South was a multiethnic and multinational space in which Anglo-American hegemony was anything but ensured. Spanish, French, British, and American influence could be widely felt in the area, and a variety of ethnic groups resided in the area between the Mississippi River and the Atlantic Ocean. When James Colbert made his journey into the Gulf South in the mid-eighteenth century, six out of every seven persons residing in his new home were Native American. People of European descent never composed an absolute majority of Southern residents until after Indian removal was accomplished during the administrations of Andrew Jackson and his successor, Martin Van Buren.[39] In the decade in which the Alabama Supreme Court heard the cases of Delilah Wall, the demographics of Alabama, including Sumter County, shifted decisively. Furthermore, Anglo-American attempts to spread their culture and hegemony into the American hinterlands came at a time when that very culture was under attack and advocates for reform enjoyed increasing sway. If the white men who heard the details of Delilah's and Rhoda's intimate arrangements were concerned with maintaining white patriarchal authority, they were also aware that the particular history of the colonial period and the Revolution resulted in serious challenges to the very nature of patriarchy.

The Early American Republic in a Global Context

Anglo-American men adopted a strategy of "distance and denial" that allowed them to forget the biculturalism and cross-racial intimacy that was a hallmark of an earlier era at the same time that they were forging a new polarized racial order in the Gulf South. White patriarchs in the South constituted their authority by deciding whose gendered customs would prevail in the South. Yet this story is more complicated than Anglo-American colonizers imposing a colonial order on Native American peoples. As we have seen, Native American men engaged in a process of centralizing their power and authority. In this process, they adapted gender and social roles to buttress their own claims to power and authority. In essence, both Native and Anglo-American men found power in limiting the autonomy and power of Native women.

Placing the early American republic in an Atlantic framework demonstrates that the United States had much in common with the "global gendered order" that emerged in the nineteenth century. Euro-Americans across the globe used patriarchal family norms, Westernized ideas about the gendered division of labor, and the sanctification of private property in ways that bolstered their claims to racial and political superiority in places as diverse as the West Indies, South Africa, and India. For example, the abolition of slavery in the British empire in the 1830s brought new attention to efforts to reshape the colonial social order that had dominated British slave societies for two centuries. European missionaries and social reformers attempted to restructure family life by granting African men the patriarchal privileges that had been denied to them under slavery, while "domesticating" African women by refocusing their work from field to domestic labor. Just as the U.S. federal government's "civilization program" had sought to transform Native American family life, reformers and government officials across the globe made regulation of family politics an integral part of constituting metropolitan authority. The process of instructing nonwhite people in the finer points of "civilized" family life allowed reformers and government officials to articulate a racialized national and imperial identity and also provided the framework for excluding nonwhite peoples from that identity.[40]

Mixed-race individuals, the products of an earlier era, became problematic in the disparate places that Europeans and Americans sought to rule. Persons who originated from the blended families that had made commercial ties possible in the eighteenth century blurred the lines between new polarized racial subjectivities that emerged in the nineteenth century. Women like Rachel Pringle Polgreen, a free woman of color in the Southern Caribbean who claimed Anglo and African ancestry, used blended customs to challenge the imposition of racial norms and imperial authority. Polgreen and other free women of color created novel understandings of marriage that allowed them to lay claim simultaneously to economic power and to Anglo-European notions of respectability. The "free colored moment," as Kit Candlin and Cassandra Pybus have termed the period between the 1780s and 1840s, allowed women like Polgreen to take advantage of the unsettled economic and social terrain of the era in ways that allowed them to accumulate property, wealth, and power. Likewise, the mixed-race Afro-Dutch women who participated in the slave trade on the Gold Coast embraced Christianity and European material culture partly because doing so helped distinguish them from the enslaved women they sold to Atlantic merchants. Just as Delilah Wall and Rhoda Gunn had done in the Alabama and Mississippi courts, mixed-race women throughout the Atlantic world attempted to find empowerment by calling upon their bicultural understandings of gender and power. Hybrid people practiced a flexibility of gender relations that eventually came into conflict with the rigid implantation of racial and gendered hierarchies that accompanied the settlement and growth of settler colonies, whether in the Gulf South, the West Indies, or Africa's Gold Coast.[41]

The republican state that emerged in the years after the American Revolution was embedded with ideas about egalitarianism and the great promise that "all men are created equal." The United States was in the uncomfortable position of having embraced equality for the purposes of throwing off the yoke of empire, only to later embrace methods of imperial rule in an effort to dispossess Native American peoples. The existence of the republican state was a central difference between Rhoda and Delilah's era and that of their eighteenth-century forbears. The need to define and limit citizenship in a republican state led judges and lawmakers to adopt a hierarchal and racialized vision of social order that essentialized Natives' racial differences and used their supposed racial and cultural inferiority to provide justification for political exclusion and economic dispossession. Drawing boundaries more firmly around inclusion and exclusion and formalizing legal codes gave Anglo-American men a power they had not had earlier and limited the ability of mixed-race individuals to play both sides. For Native American peoples like the Walls, the Juzans, and the Colberts, Jefferson's "empire of liberty" would put more emphasis on the "empire" while radically redefining "liberty." For nonwhite peoples, the methods and tactics of American national expansion and imperial rule were indistinguishable from those adopted by other Westernized powers across the globe in the nineteenth century.

Alicia L. Monroe

Building Black Civic Manhood

The Luiz Gama Masonic Lodge and the Beneficent Society of Men of Color in São Paulo, Brazil, 1894–1914

In 1924, José Correia Leite, coeditor of the Afro-Brazilian newspaper *The Clarion* (*O Clarim*), penned an article calling for African descendants to unite and organize a national association to improve social and economic conditions for blacks in the city of São Paulo and throughout the nation.[1] Leite argued to the newspaper readership that their common enslaved ancestors had resisted oppression and bondage and that he and his contemporaries should not "be dominated in the struggle for rights." For Leite, Afro-Brazilians across the nation would need to know and retell the history of their ancestors to demonstrate "the value of our race in the development of society" in order to more fully enact and receive recognition as citizens. He suggested to the paper's readers that such a project was inherently collective and would demand Afro-Brazilian self-advocacy. He wrote, "the good name of our people depends on our actions. . . . For this reason it is necessary [that we form] a general convocation of Negro men, and work to establish a beneficent fund, elect a directorate, send manifestos to all states of Brazil, and finally, found a society of the 'Confederation of Negro Men.'"[2]

Correia Leite's call to found a new black secular civic society was not a new proposition. An older cohort of self-identified blacks in the city of São Paulo organized at least four secular civic associations before 1915. Black-identified residents established and served as founding members in the Luiz Gama Chapter Masonic Lodge (1894), documented here for the first time; the Thirteenth of May Club of Black Men of São Paulo (1902); the Beneficent Society of Men of Color (1906); and the Federated Center of Men of Color (1914).[3]

Afro-Paulistanos created secular civic organizations in the decades after abolition to exercise the political citizenship emancipation granted them and to cultivate new spaces of mutual aid and sociability.[4] Afro-Brazilians, like other postemancipation African descendants in the Atlantic world, worked toward their social advancement by establishing civic groups designed to advance the race through mutual assistance and to combat the effects of structural inequality and discrimination prevalent as a legacy of racial chattel slavery. In this respect, the Luiz Gama Chapter Masonic Lodge and the Beneficent Society of Men of Color, the two Afro-Paulistano organizations analyzed as case studies in this essay, were quite similar to black voluntary associations in Cuba referred to as "sociedades de color" and to notable U.S. organizations such as the Black Odd Fellows and the Knights and Daughters of Pythias.[5]

In postemancipation São Paulo, black secular organizing represented a decidedly male endeavor. Organizational founders utilized voluntary associations as a means to articulate what the performance of masculinity entailed for Afro-descendant men as free people. The articulation of citizenship and civic engagement through tropes of black manhood was not unique to Brazil and, in fact, characterized postemancipation societies across the Atlantic world. As Pamela Scully and Diana Paton discuss in *Gender and Slave Emancipation in the Atlantic World,* no country in the Atlantic world extended the vote to any women when suffrage and full citizenship were extended to formerly enslaved people. Scully and Paton write, "the promise of emancipation was, to some extent, a gendered one: that is men were promised the entitlement to masculinity, of being head of household."[6] The expansion of citizenship in the Americas after waves of political abolition bound and linked masculinity and performances of patriarchy in private family settings and in public collective realms.

The masculine ideal emergent among charter members and founders in Afro-Paulistano civic groups worked to collectively reorient and recapitulate the characteristics and responsibilities that together defined manhood, particularly for middling sector and middling aspirant participants.[7] Civic groups functioned as laboratories where a segment of the Afro-Brazilian population worked out at least one conceptualization of what it meant to be an upstanding man and citizen.[8] The end of legal bondage for Africans and their descendants meant that hegemonic ideas about race, gender, and family that existed under the slave regime could be collectively and publicly recast and redefined. Founders of the Luiz Gama Masonic Lodge and the Beneficent Society of Men of Color established civic groups to lead the race by enacting a masculine ideal in which men functioned as patriarchs in households and collective associative spaces.

Slavery, Freedom, and Masculinity

Although on May 13, 1888, Brazil became the last country in the Americas to end slavery, the country's elites saw themselves in rather favorable terms vis-à-vis leaders of other former slaveholding nations in the Americas. Elite Brazilians often subscribed to the view of their country as a "mixed" society devoid of racial discrimination, however far from reality that social vision was.[9] In 1883 the abolitionist Joaquim Nabuco wrote that "slavery to our good fortune, never embittered the slave's spirit toward the master, at least collectively, nor did it create between the races that mutual hate which naturally exists between oppressors and oppressed."[10]

Despite the abolitionist's idealized assessment of race relations, racial prejudice and bias against Africans and African descendants was ubiquitous. In the late nineteenth century, Brazilians across the socioeconomic spectrum considered the African descendant population a drag on the nation's progress and modernization efforts. These attitudes were based on racist discourse and stereotypes of black savagery, laziness, vagrancy, and backwardness.[11] Few Brazilians or foreign observers saw racial mixture as a positive factor in the country's development. The Swiss scholar Louis Agassiz, who visited Brazil in 1865, wrote, "let anyone who doubts the evil of this mixture of the races, and is inclined . . . to break down all barriers between them, come to Brazil. He cannot deny the deterioration consequent upon an amalgamation of races, more wide-spread here than in any other country in the world, and which is rapidly effacing the best qualities of the white man, the Negro, and Indian, leaving behind a mongrel, nondescript type, deficient in physical and mental energy."[12] Agassiz, like a segment of the international scientific community of his day, attributed this lack of vitality to a history of racial mixture.[13]

How did Afro-Brazilian men and women define the masculine ideal in circumstances of such intense black denigration and societal racism? Did the vision of what manhood entailed for those living in bondage in the late nineteenth century in the Brazilian empire (1822–1889) inform postemancipation renderings of black masculinity? Did the visions of masculinity and manhood for associational participants differ from the visions for other sectors of the Afro-Paulistano populace?

The nexus between masculinity and slavery remains underinterrogated in Brazilian historical studies.[14] However, Sandra Lauderdale Graham, one of the few scholars to focus on concepts of gender held by nineteenth-century Afro-

Brazilians, revealed commonplace notions of manhood in a study of an ecclesiastic divorce between two African-born freed slaves, Henriqueta and Rufino, in a case from the 1850s in São Paulo. The trial chronicled a marriage broken by accusations of a husband's abuse and mutual disappointment from each spouse over their mate's inability to conform to marital expectations.[15] Case testimony strongly suggested that though women were expected to labor outside the home, the ability to secure steady work and income for household support served as a critical facet of male responsibility among free, urban Afro-Brazilians.[16]

Like the version of manliness held by Henriqueta in the 1850s, the criteria Afro-Paulistanos espoused in associational charters for men of stature focused intensely on men carrying out the role of provider for families and households. When illness, unemployment, or bereavement left families without male support, civic associations committed to helping alleviate the financial stress caused by loss of income, whether or not men had actually fulfilled such a role in the household. Founders of the Luiz Gama Chapter Masonic Lodge and the Beneficent Society of Men of Color established civic groups to lead the race by enacting a masculine ideal where men functioned as patriarchs in households and communities.

Founding Leaders and Early Members

One of the first secular associations of Afro-Brazilian men organized in São Paulo began in 1894. A small assembly met and installed a Masonic lodge in the city center, which housed eighteen active lodges at the time they met.[17] Three years later, the group registered the lodge with the secretary of state (Secretária do Governo) as required by Decree 173 of September 10, 1893.[18] The association, named the Luiz Gama Chapter Masonic Lodge (Maçonica Loja Capitular Luiz Gama), officially entered the public realm in 1897 and was one of two Masonic lodges approved that year.[19]

The Masons are a voluntary fraternal order, which began in Western Europe in the eighteenth century and spread across the Atlantic world, including the Americas.[20] In Brazil, the historian Celia Maria Azevedo confirms that Masons were organizing after 1820, but the association began a period of great expansion in the 1860s.[21] Indeed, a decade later, in 1870, every province had at least one lodge, and provincial capitals housed multiple groups.[22] Masonic lodge founders set up associations that fell under the administrative governance of the Grand Lodge of Brazil (Grande Oriente do Brasil), established in 1822, but research also suggests that other chapters were completely independent and autonomous.[23] The organizational charter of the Luiz Gama Lodge includes no evidence of affiliation with the Grand Lodge of Brazil.[24]

The name of the lodge served as a public homage to the famed Afro-Brazilian lawyer Luiz Gonzaga Pinto da Gama. Gama was born in 1830 to a freed African woman in Salvador, Bahia, and was illegally enslaved by his Portuguese father, only to be sold into the nation's interprovincial slave trade to the southeast region.[25] During his captivity in the city of São Paulo, Gama learned to read and write, and in 1848 he escaped from bondage by fleeing and joining the army. After securing documents to prove his free status and working for several years as a military clerk, he attended the São Paulo School of Law, located in the provincial capital, and became a practicing attorney.[26] Gama headed São Paulo's abolitionist movement and used public speeches, newspaper articles, and litigation to secure freedom for the enslaved.[27] Despite his many obligations as a lawyer and organizer, Gama was also a Mason, and he served as a founding and active member of the America Lodge (Loja Capitular América), established in 1868.[28]

The unique feature of the Gama Lodge, which met on the Rua das Flores, only blocks away from the meeting space of the Friendship Lodge (Loja Amizade), was the racial identity shared by multiple members.[29] Three of the fifteen founding members participated in the Brotherhood of Our Lady of the Rosary of Black Men of São Paulo and two others were members of the Thirteenth of May Club of Black Men of São Paulo, an emancipation commemoration society.[30] The highest-ranking officer, Theophilio Dias de Castro, the *venerável,* or Grand Master, of the Luiz Gama Masonic Chapter Lodge, also served as an executive officer of the Brotherhood of Our Lady of the Rosary of Black Men of São Paulo from 1904 through the 1930s.[31] These Gama Lodge members and leaders identified as black men.

Little conclusive evidence exists to document whether nonelite blacks could easily join or were consistently denied entry into Masonic lodges. Scholars of the Afro-Brazilian experience in São Paulo have shown that blacks established their own social and recreational clubs when discrimination thwarted their entry into white associations.[32] However, it remains unclear whether Masonic groups followed this pattern, since several Afro-Brazilians who reached elite status did find acceptance in some groups, as demonstrated by Luiz Gama in São Paulo, the journalist Francisco de Paula Brito, and the man of letters Francisco Gé Acaicaba Montezuma, Viscount of Jequitinhonha, both of Rio de Janeiro.[33] While the organizational statutes of the lodges active in São Paulo contained no rules explicitly barring blacks, the creation of a chapter where at least one third of the founding members were active in black-identified social spaces outside the association suggests that inclusion in Paulistano Masonic chapters was limited at best to the few blacks in white society's highest echelons.

The organizational ends of the Luiz Gama Masonic Lodge demonstrate that Afro-Brazilian participants did not create organizations that were copies of their white counterparts. Organizational leaders cultivated associations that served their unique needs and addressed communally shared difficulties. An intense focus on financial support of the ill, the bereaved, and the unemployed differentiated this lodge from others in the capital. While the Luiz Gama chapter shared and adhered to general Masonic values, including the principle of developing and furthering liberal Enlightenment ideas of knowledge, logic, and science, the clear organizational priority was mutual aid.

Afro-Brazilian marginalization and exclusion in multiracial or predominantly white organizations did not lead to policies of admission that allowed universal male access. The Luiz Gama Lodge had its own restrictive criteria for potential members. The basic criteria limited the membership to men who were literate nondependents. Members could be Brazilian or foreign born; they could be from any professional or social class, as long as they knew how to read and write.[34]

The Afro-Brazilian men who led the organization wanted to involve men of stature, and the criteria they established for member eligibility detailed the characteristics upstanding men were to possess. The founding organizers of the Luiz Gama Masonic Lodge expected group associates to display "*bons costumes*." The requirement signaled that only those meeting normative standards of public propriety in relation to comportment, decorum, and dress would satisfy the qualifications for membership. Leaders wanted the appearance and behavior of their members to signal respectability.

The spiritual lives of members also mattered to group leaders. The association's founding charter required potential members to profess a faith tradition, though it could be any of their choosing.[35] Hence, while liberal Enlightenment influence may have widened the spectrum of beliefs that could garner respect in the view of the group's leadership, upstanding men were still those who believed in God and followed programs of morality established by religious institutions according to lodge leaders.

The organizational charter established by Gama Lodge founders required members to enjoy the privileges of a citizen (*cidadão*) ensured by their age, gender and literacy.[36] The prerequisite that members must enjoy "the pleasure of civil rights" indicated that potential members had to be men who were at least twenty-one years of age and that indigents, the illiterate, and those with a criminal history were disqualified as potential members.[37] The requirement demanding that members be in full possession of their "civil rights" reinforced the connection between Masonry, autonomy, and exemplary citizenship. As the historian Alexandre Barata notes, "to be a Mason was synonymous with being a citizen" in the Brazilian Empire (1822–1889) and during the First Republic (1889–1930).[38]

The restrictive criteria established by founding Gama Lodge leaders presented barriers to entrance for all but privileged men. However, even privileged Afro-Paulistanos understood that the lives of their potential brethren might entail a variety of not-so-surprising incongruities and tensions. The literacy clause, for example, indicated that applicants were eligible for membership only "*once* one knew how to read and write"; this indicates that Afro-Brazilian men and potentially foreign-born immigrants could reasonably be expected to acquire literacy in Portuguese as adults, instead of during childhood.[39] Opening membership to those of any profession or social class while requiring literacy meant that those forced by societal discrimination to work in jobs unequal to their education would not find their employment situation an impediment to joining the lodge. Furthermore, though the Luiz Gama Masonic Lodge would not use national origin as a requirement for membership, the last names of the membership suggest that no first-generation Italian, Japanese, Middle Eastern, or Eastern European immigrants became members.[40]

While associational life provided new secular spaces for men, as demonstrated by the Gama Masonic Lodge, black civic associations had a less progressive record with regard to female incorporation. Discouraging female participation in secular black civic groups represented a reversal of previous organizing patterns common to Afro-Brazilian associational life, since women could and did join black lay Catholic brotherhoods.[41] However, even the limited roles and ways in which women participated in confraternities were further reduced in secular associations before 1915.

The Gama Masonic Lodge did not include any female members, nor did the group's leadership create a women's auxiliary association, which was a common way to provide female access to the Masonic tradition and community. There was a precedent for the creation of a women's auxiliary group in São Paulo. The Seventh of September Chapter of the Masons, the oldest lodge in the city, established a separate but affiliated organization for women.[42] The women's lodge, named the Seventh of September Lodge of Adoption (Loja de Adopção Sete de Setembro), had an all-female board of officers listed among the various associations or "societies" (*sociedades*) active in the provincial capital in 1873.[43]

Without a lodge of affiliation, Afro-Paulistano women had no independent access to the mutual aid benefits Masonic membership conferred. Men alone linked households to fraternal resource-sharing networks. In other groups, even when gender did not present a formal barrier to membership, founders created rules that limited women's participation. The following paragraphs examine how charter drafters of the Beneficent Society of Men of Color shaped policies designed to constrict and hamper female membership.

The Beneficent Society of Men of Color, which had its statutes approved by São Paulo's secretary of state on January 8, 1909, was one of two associations in this early wave of organizing that allowed both female and male participation.[44] The Beneficent Society admitted new members solely on the basis of nominations by existing associates. The associate proposing a new member's candidacy stood before the board of directors and declared the candidate's name, civil status, birthplace, profession, and current residence.[45] Potential members were to exhibit good morals and manners (*bons costumes*), to be in a perfect state of health, and to be between fourteen and fifty years old for male candidates.[46] There is no explanation of what exactly constituted a perfect state of health or which medical conditions or ailments would impede a male candidate's entrance into the association. Male candidates simply required the appearance of good health and reputable public self-presentation.

Female associate candidacy involved more restrictive and stringent entrance guidelines. Only wives, daughters, and sisters of male members were eligible to become associates, a factor that underscored the patriarchal character of secular black associational life.[47] Why were women unconnected to male participants not allowed? What kind of threat or problem did they represent in the eyes of Afro-Brazilian leaders? The problem presented by nonkin women can be explained only by gender bias, since male candidates did not need the sponsorship of a relative.

Membership criteria deviated from the general rules for female candidates in other ways as well. Admission ages for women differed slightly from those established for men. Women were to be more than fifteen years of age but under forty years old, while men could join the association between the ages of fourteen and fifty.[48] Additionally, female members were allowed to serve only in the category of "effective" members, which essentially barred them from serving on any administrative or decision-making boards.[49] Men did not have to provide documentation of their health status, but the unique article applying only to female applicants stated that "they [female applicants] should present a certificate of good health from a board certified doctor proving themselves to be in perfect health."[50]

The medical examination requirement suggests that Afro-Brazilian men may have absorbed social and medical discourses that problematized nonelite female bodies as highly susceptible to degeneration, contamination, and illness.[51] During slavery, work brought black women into public spaces, where they labored selling food and other wares or washed household laundry at public fountains, among other chores performed outside the household. Black women had little choice but to move in spaces socially constructed by elites as dirty, dangerous, and corrupting.[52]

As forced servitude began its decline with gradual emancipation programs beginning in the 1870s, controlling the bodies of poor and nonwhite women became a preoccupation for statesmen, policing authorities, and doctors who associated nonelite women with poverty, social vice, and contagious disease.[53] Abolition and contagion represented serious threats in the minds of elites, and controlling these "ills" was so important that local authorities were inspired to begin licensing and registering domestic servants, especially wet nurses (*amas de leite*).[54] According to those in government, women without masters needed monitoring, and municipal authorities fulfilled this role.

In 1876, in the city of São Paulo, for example, a new law required anyone seeking employment as a wet nurse to take and pass a physical examination in order to obtain a license indicating that the applicant had no "moral or medical reasons" that would inhibit her work.[55] In 1887, in the provincial capital of Salvador, Bahia, the city council approved a law requiring wet nurses to undergo medical "inspection," while any employee, free or enslaved, working in household service was required to register and receive a passbook to work in the city.[56] Nonelite working women's bodies underwent a new level of state management and surveillance as government legislation initiated slavery's decline.[57] As such, it is not surprising that, in the Beneficent Society of Men of Color, male candidates had only to have the appearance of good health, whereas women were required to provide scientific verification of wellness. The medical examination prerequisite captures Afro-Brazilian men attempting to exercise authority over female community members in new ways that paralleled official government policy. Black female bodies roused a level of scrutiny that black male bodies did not, though issues of health and wellness were never far from the minds of male Beneficent Society members.

Gender was not the only criterion used to restrict the Beneficent Society's membership. Age requirements listed in the admission guidelines indicate and underscore an organization committed to the support of those in the midst of their working lives. Women more than forty years of age and men more than fifty were ineligible for membership, since they were likely thought to require greater financial outlays associated with old age and declining health. The Beneficent Society cultivated a narrow conception of the able-bodied that effectively excluded older workers and women who were constructed as potential liabilities.

Associative spaces established by Afro-Paulistano men were designed to reinforce the notion that men of color were able and exemplary heads of households. Associations organized corporate rules that made the groups function as unemployment, disability, and/or life insurance policies that extended benefits to those who had previously made contributions as working members. Afro-Brazilians sought economic security and stability for themselves and their families, and they organized to protect the quality of life their gainful employment had provided if they found themselves forced out of the workforce for reasons beyond their control.

Afro-Brazilian civic association leaders expressed great concern about health problems and financial disruption caused by sickness. The first "end" of the Luiz Gama Masonic Lodge was to administer aid, medical help, and pharmaceuticals to associates who, due to illness (*molestia*), found themselves temporarily unable to work.[58] When illness struck, associates in the Luiz Gama Masonic Lodge planned to have access to professionally trained medical practitioners for consultation.[59] They likely developed such a policy because "medical care was difficult if not impossible . . . to obtain when illness struck" for the urban poor.[60] One factor contributing to the difficulty of receiving medical treatment was the small number of doctors available. In 1873, a total of nine doctors and surgeons resided in the city of São Paulo, while seven pharmacists dispensed medicine from different locations in the heart of the provincial capital.[61] A few years later, in 1878, the number of doctors serving the central city had expanded to nineteen practitioners.[62]

Hospitals in urban nineteenth-century Brazil largely served the poor and indigent; people of any means received medical care in their homes.[63] Either family members or servants ideally nursed the ill person at home, and doctors came when called.[64] Beginning in the 1870s, social organizations began to retain the services of doctors to serve their membership, and leaders of the Luiz Gama Masonic Lodge aimed to participate in this trend.[65] Reserving the services of a doctor for members would likely make physicians more accessible and would ultimately help members recover and return to work more quickly.

The second organizational "end" of the association aimed to provide financial aid for a Mason unable to have his illness cured or remedied. Associational leaders pledged that the lodge would provide a monthly pension to participating members if chronic illness or physical defects brought the member to a state of disability (*invalidez*).[66] The leadership of the Afro-Brazilian Masonic lodge planned for membership fees to function as a defense against hardship for those facing financial shortfalls due to sickness.

When maladies or other circumstances led to an indigent associate's death, the Masonic Lodge pledged to provide funerals. The group's statutes promised that the association would "hold a funeral for associates that died without resources for it."[67] The need for a secular group to provide funeral assistance for poor members represented a significant shift in funerary culture, because until the 1890s in São Paulo lay Catholic brotherhoods would have buried members, their spouses, and their legitimate children.[68] The Luiz Gama Masonic Lodge, like black and white brotherhoods in previous generations, covered the costs of securing a dignified funeral for members. Like brotherhoods, the Luiz Gama Masonic Lodge ensured that participants would receive formal, ritualized commemoration of life upon their death.

Members of the Beneficent Society of Men of Color shared concerns articulated by Luiz Gama Masonic Lodge members. The organizational objectives given in the Beneficent Society association statutes were nearly identical to the Gama Masonic Lodge organizational ends, though to date there is no evidence of member overlap. As with the Gama Masonic Lodge, the first organizational end of the Beneficent Society of Men of Color was to aid its associates with medical and pharmaceutical assistance in the event of illness. This was matched by a second provision providing a daily income of one *mil-réis* for sick members.[69]

Like the Gama Masonic Lodge, the Beneficent Society of Men of Color also made a commitment to cover the costs of member burial. Beneficent Society of Men of Color association members pledged to provide "120 *mil-réis* for the funeral and *suffragios*" of the deceased member.[70] The extension of mutual aid did not stop at the moment of death. The ability to ensure a decent burial for members mattered enough for members to direct funds for such an end. Status and respectability required particular kinds of performances during life and at death.

Both the Masonic Lodge and the Beneficent Society pledged to furnish monthly pensions for the widows and orphans of deceased members who found themselves in need upon bereavement.[71] Beyond the material support, these articles draw attention to the gender norms held by founding members. For these men, the nuclear family constituted the normative familial unit, which was to be protected with temporary financial support in cases of illness or bereavement.[72] Drafters of the two organizational charters placed men at the center of family life and income earning. In their view, upstanding Afro-Brazilian men provided income for their families, and, in their absence, association members pledged to alleviate the real or perceived stress of not having a male salary in the household.

The pension funds set aside for widows and orphans draw attention to another unspoken member characteristic. Though organizational rules did not require participating men to be married, founding leaders associated black male respectability with formal marriage. As the historian Peter Beattie notes, "marriage remained an important badge of status in post-independence Brazil; untitled Brazilians commonly identified themselves first as *casados* (married men) to establish their status as respectable members of a community."[73] In Brazilian culture, marriage conferred a level of respectability on men across classes, and Afro-Brazilian males adhered to this construction of "mature" manhood and masculinity in the postemancipation period.[74]

Afro-Brazilian men faced many difficulties in the era after emancipation, and leaders of black civic groups in São Paulo repeatedly articulated concerns about employment and arbitrary arrest. Brazilian society, from high political offices to lower labor positions, required patron recommendations, and members made a commitment to help their fraternal brethren access and retain workforce opportunities.[75] Afro-Brazilian men were cognizant of the discrimination they faced, and they worked to expand the pool of contacts who could recommend them and vouch for their character and qualifications. The Beneficent Society's organizational charter, like the Gama Masons', required members to use their social connections and influence to provide access to jobs for associates. All participants pledged to "seek honest work for associates in proportion to their power."[76] The organizational charters of black civic groups repeatedly documented members' anxieties related to labor retention, and group members generated intracommunity responses and strategies to alleviate employment insecurity.

Fear of unjust imprisonment also weighed heavily even on the minds of educated Afro-Brazilian men in the late nineteenth and early twentieth centuries. Organizing leaders of the Luiz Gama Lodge pledged to assist and protect members in case of unlawful or unjust imprisonment by authorities. One of the eight Gama Lodge group statutes called for "protection by regular means at their disposal of associates that find themselves imprisoned or jailed for unjust or illegal motives."[77] In this period, skyrocketing rates of arrest on charges of vagrancy made Afro-Brazilians vulnerable to unjust incarceration across the nation.[78] Collective support of those jailed without reason constituted the ideal response, since individuals attempting to intervene likely faced intimidation and possible arrest themselves, especially without the support of an elite patron. The Beneficent Society of Men of Color established a similar provision in which members pledged "to protect fellow associates when imprisoned or on trial, once it is established that the cause of these facts are not dishonest or dishonorable."[79]

Educational preparation represented the final issue of shared concern addressed in the early associational charters drafted by Afro-Paulistano men. The Gama Masonic Lodge pledged "to promote conferences and lectures about matters of scientific, philosophic, or artistic order to further the intellectual, ethical, and financial progress of associates in particular and of humanity in general."[80] The Beneficent Society of Men of Color proposed a more concrete remedy to facilitate access to education: founding members of the Beneficent Society of Men of Color pledged to found primary schools for the children of associates.[81]

The desire of the Beneficent Society of Men of Color's organizational leaders to establish primary schools documents their interest in facilitating literacy for Afro-Brazilian children. Public schools in São Paulo did not yet serve most people of color in 1906, the year the Beneficent Society of Men of Color was organized. Even in 1934, only 7 percent of nearly 85,000 public school children were black; poverty led families to push children into the workforce early, and the price of supplies and clothes for school attendance was prohibitive.[82] Interestingly, the education of girls was considered as important as the education of boys, even though the Beneficent Society discouraged female participation as organizational members. Unfortunately, exactly how leaders of the Beneficent Society intended to educate their children has to remain an open question, since to date there is no evidence that the group realized its corporate desire to establish a school.

The two fraternal organizations analyzed in this essay demonstrate that Afro-Brazilians wanted to be active participants in the civic sphere, with the same range of associational opportunities as their neighbors, even though they modified organizational ends of associative life to meet their daily realities. Dedication to fashioning protection from a harsh economic and social environment for

Afro-Brazilian men, however, did not mean rethinking all forms of inequality. In fact, the march toward social incorporation into the larger nation likely influenced men of color to embrace patterns of patriarchy in which the women in their families became subject to male authority in newly constricting ways.

Organizers of the Luiz Gama Masonic Lodge and the Beneficent Society of Men of Color desired to improve the lives of their organizational brethren and families. Mutual aid and social conformity were the tools that leaders considered their greatest assets in the struggle to foster their social advancement and to close the gap in the quality of life between them and their non-Afro-Brazilian neighbors. This early period of delineating manliness in the postemancipation context involved circumscribing female mobility at the same time that notions of black middle-sector masculinity embraced racial pride, heralded literacy, and worked to utilize the mutual aid tradition in an expansive way. Re-envisioning black manhood constituted a complicated process in the late nineteenth and early twentieth centuries, and Afro-Paulistanos worked diligently, though imperfectly, to formulate models of Afro-Brazilian masculinity and manhood that would facilitate economic stability as well as social and civic acceptance. Manhood meant providing income and education for one's family and helping fellow Afro-Paulistano brethren to better provide for their own.

Laura R. Prieto

Great Circle Sailing

Alice Bache Gould in San Juan, or, the Making of a Twentieth-Century Atlanticist

Great circles are important because they give the shortest surface distance between points. . . . Beginners are apt to think that a steady compass course must carry them straight.

Alice Bache Gould, "Texts and Notes Entitled Great Circle Sailing"

Alice Bache Gould leaned on an ebony cane during her regular walk through Seville. The Hotel Cristina, where she lived, was a creation of the Ibero-American Exposition of 1929, a world's fair that hoped to knit Spain and the Americas closer together. Her daily destination, in contrast, had stood for centuries, though it, too, connected Spain and the Americas. Spanish King Felipe II had constructed the opulent Casa Lonja in 1598 as a mercantile exchange. In the eighteenth century, it came to house Spain's records of colonization. With its marble staircases and vaulted ceilings, the Archivo de las Indias seemed every inch a memory palace. Gould sat there each day, focused on papers older than the Casa Lonja itself—ships' logs and viceroys' reports—while the afternoon sun blazed outside and swallows and house martins sang riotously in the archive's inner courtyard. She was eighty-four years old and at the height of her scholarly career.[1]

Gould's painstaking work had made her the leading authority on Columbus's crew. Her great gifts as a researcher were her meticulousness and her persistence since the 1910s. She had worked in almost seventy different repositories across Spain.[2] Gould may very well have crossed paths with her contemporary Fernand Braudel at the Archivo General de Simancas in Valladolid or at its overflow site in Seville.[3] Her archival research is reminiscent of the Annales school for its ambitious scope and, to some degree, for its object; although she became an expert on Columbus and Queen Isabella, her real focus was on the sailors who first voyaged from Europe to the Americas: their exact number, their individual names, and their backgrounds. She dispelled the myth that they were rough criminals and ne'er-do-wells. Her discoveries won her the admiration of Samuel Eliot Morison and other eminent historians and writers.[4] Although she died before completing her book on Columbus's transatlantic voyages, her articles in the *Boletin de la Real Academia de la Historia* won her international renown.

"Alice in Seville," as *Time* magazine called her, was not only an important early historiographer of the Atlantic, however. Gould's own life traced the first transatlantic voyages in reverse. Born in Cambridge, Massachusetts, she ventured to South America and the Caribbean and later went to live in Spain. This Atlantic context profoundly shaped her life—it brought her success and a sense of purpose. Like other young women of her generation, education, class, and ambition, Gould faced a chasm between what she *could* do and what was actually open to those of her sex. From an early age, she aspired to become a scholar, but her family and culture did not support such notions. Although she obtained a college degree and entered a doctoral program in mathematics, a university professorship evaded her. She suffered from ill health, probably depression, and what her contemporaries termed neurasthenia.

Gould transcended the boundaries that society placed on her by exploiting the contours of the United States' new colonial possessions. First, she sought relief from her illness by sojourning in the Caribbean. There, she engaged in a therapeutic imperialism, a sort of cultural tourism usually reserved for men. She accompanied a professional archaeologist in his quest for pre-Columbian native artifacts. She then became interested in public health and raised funds to build modern medical institutions in Puerto Rico. Above all, she took up a scholarly investigation of the European exploration of the New World, a journey of discovery that mirrored her own. Yet Gould never entirely abandoned her earlier expertise. She integrated her interests in mathematics and Columbus into her analysis of an ancient navigational technique based on geometry, Great Circle Sailing. To use the Great Circle method, a navigator finds the shortest distance from point to point along the curve of the earth, making regular recalculations and adjustments from waypoint to waypoint as the journey continues. It describes how Columbus sailed, and perhaps Gould found it an appealing metaphor for her own life.

Although Gould's story is her own, it refracts the ideas, expectations, attitudes, and possibilities that surrounded her. Atlantic history has often looked to individuals in order to illuminate the particularities and peculiarities of that world. Biographies and microhistories emphasize the human contingencies within vast migrations, displacements, and exchanges. Smaller stories seem well suited to the "rambling, non-linear" nature of Atlantic trajectories as well.[5] By placing individual women at the center of such studies, historians have begun to explore the ways that gender shaped the Atlantic world.[6] This approach is useful for twentieth-century subjects as well. Most Atlantic studies focus on the colonial era, the Age of Revolutions, and the Age of Sail. Experiences like Gould's demonstrate the continued fluidity and expanded opportunity that the Atlantic world afforded women into the Age of Steam. They also reveal the understudied role of the United States as an imperialist power in the twentieth-century Atlantic.[7]

Port of Origin

In some ways, Gould had an unusual upbringing. As a descendant of the prominent Quincy family, she had deep ancestral roots in New England. Despite this, however, she was never moored to one place. During her childhood, her father's scientific ambitions swept the entire family to Córdoba, Argentina, where he directed that country's first astronomical observatory. Benjamin Apthorp Gould embraced the technological innovation of astronomical photography. He began taking images of star clusters to calculate their positions with greater accuracy and published the results in the multivolume *Uranometria Argentina.*[8] His wife, Mary Apthorp Quincy Gould, helped gather a circle of Argentine scientists and cultural figures around their camp and home in Córdoba.[9] Meanwhile, the young Alice gained fluency in Spanish and immersed herself in her new environment, punctuated by periodic trips back to Cambridge, Massachusetts.[10]

Her mother's death, in 1883, dispatched Alice back to Cambridge.[11] There, Alice's life conformed to the more typical script for a young middle-class, nineteenth-century woman. As the eldest surviving daughter, she became the designated Angel of the House. Despite his fervent dedication to scientific knowledge and his spirit of adventure, Alice's father had entirely conventional expectations of his daughters. He opposed suffrage for women and urged Alice to adopt the same domestic role as her foremothers. When he returned alone to his work in Argentina, Benjamin Gould instructed the girl in what he thought was her duty: "household matters;—to sew neatly, to make dresses, sew on her father's or brother's or husband's buttons, cook or supervise the cooking and so on." These skills made for the most "wholesome knowledge," and "every lady should be familiar with them."[12] Perhaps Alice's father wrote so plainly because he saw her proclivity for intellectual life rather than domesticity.

Yet Alice encountered different influences and attitudes, especially at Miss Ireland's School for Girls in Boston. The charismatic Catherine Innes Ireland had herself been a student of the naturalist Louis Agassiz. Women's admission to higher education—whether one of the recently founded women's colleges or one of the few coeducational universities—was a new prospect, and Miss Ireland's did not

Alice Bache Gould, photograph by N. B. Lawson (Muskegon, Mich.) (ca. 1893–1894). Alice Bache Gould photographs 166.91, Massachusetts Historical Society.

structure itself as college preparatory until later. But the school's rigorous curriculum and inspiring teachers attracted other ambitious students who increasingly went to college.[13]

Supported by her peers and teachers, Alice defied her father's domestic directions as best she could. She sought a college education over his express objections. Alice attended Bryn Mawr, a women's college just opening near Philadelphia, comfortably far from Cambridge, where her bluestocking pursuits might be too conspicuous to her father's Harvard colleagues.[14] It was an auspicious choice for her. Not only did Bryn Mawr emphasize advanced scholarship, but its president, Martha Carey Thomas, too, had attended college against her father's wishes. Alice finished her degree with Bryn Mawr's first graduating class in 1889, marching alongside Emily Greene Balch, her friend from Miss Ireland's School.[15]

Determined to continue her education and become a mathematician, Gould became increasingly independent. She gained special student status in order to attend the Massachusetts Institute of Technology during the 1889–1890 term and again in summer 1904.[16] She then boldly decamped to England to study at Newnham College, University of Cambridge (1890–1893). Lacking her father's endorsement, she supported herself there by teaching. Gould spent the following year as a physics and mathematics instructor at Carleton College in Minnesota. She was one of the first women admitted to graduate study at the University of Chicago, where she began doctoral work in mathematics under E. H. Moore (1895–1897), with Brocardian geometry as her dissertation topic. Had she completed the degree, Gould would have become one of the first five or six women to earn a Ph.D. in mathematics from a university in the United States.[17]

But Gould could not seem to land what she really wanted, what would not only enable her to live autonomously but would also fulfill her intellectually: a faculty position at a university. Whatever her strong support for women's education, Gould felt that she would not be considered a serious mathematician if she taught at a women's college.[18] She sought a place at a coeducational research institution—a nearly impossible goal in a climate where even the presence of female *students* at universities still excited controversy.[19]

Gould's hopes continued to unravel with the death of her father, in 1896, and the loss of her University fellowship the following year. Her work on her doctoral dissertation stalled. Illness accompanied these frustrations. Like other women whose ambitions chafed against the conventions of gender, Gould struggled with poor health throughout her life. The causes of her symptoms were often vague. She suffered from problems with her eyes and feet, repeated bouts of influenza, and depression.[20] Jane Addams and Charlotte Perkins Gilman most famously overcame their neurasthenia and found gratifying work in the world, but many women remained trapped by their condition and never fulfilled their potential.[21]

Refusing to succumb to her physical ailments, Gould persisted in intense study.[22] This of course contradicted prevailing notions that intellectual activity endangered young women's reproductive development and threatened to incite nervous exhaustion. As she had done in her younger years, Alice surrounded herself with friends who thought differently. They admired public accomplishments in women.[23] Her friend Fanny assured Gould that "your duty is towards yourself and the career you have chosen."[24] Gould began to reconsider that choice of career, however.

Casting about for what to do, Alice turned to her interest in her family history and colonial New England. She began doing a different sort of research at the Boston Athenaeum. The editor Mark DeWolfe Howe, Gould's cousin by marriage, invited her to write a biography of her father's friend and colleague Louis Agassiz.[25] She joined two other women as authors of volumes in the series: Annie Fields on Nathaniel Hawthorne and Sarah Bardwell Elliott on Sam Houston. Alice's study would make Agassiz the first scientist among the list of "Beacon Biography" series subjects.

Various reasons may have attracted her to the particular subject, apart from Howe's commission. Likely thinking of her own debility, Alice expressed incredulity at Agassiz's hardiness as a student, though his health too suffered from overwork.[26] "These boys seem to have the knack of finding thirty-six hours instead of twenty-four. One wonders whether nervous prostration had then been invented," Alice commented. Second, Agassiz made room for women in science and education in ways Alice's own father had not. He had allowed women to attend his lectures at Harvard since the 1850s. Female students worked for him on exhibits and fossil collections at Harvard's Museum of Comparative Zoology.[27] He ran coeducational summer workshops with his second wife, Elizabeth Cabot Cary Agassiz. Elizabeth later helped found the women's school that became "the Harvard Annex" and, in 1893, Radcliffe College. Gould drew attention to this aspect of Agassiz's legacy, noting his establishment of the Agassiz School for Young Ladies, in 1855, in the chronology of his life and later commenting on how the enterprise relieved him of financial worry.[28] She mentioned his sisters' interest in natural history and botany and noted how his wife assisted him in his work.[29] In fact, writing the biography brought Alice into close contact with Agassiz's widow; Alice consulted Elizabeth's edited *Louis Agassiz: Life and Correspondence* extensively, and Elizabeth read the full manuscript that Alice produced in turn.[30]

In contrast to her inability to gain acceptance as a mathematician, Gould succeeded immediately as a scientific biographer. One reviewer pronounced the slim volume to be "the *bien être* of biography," praising it in pointedly feminine terms as "charming, stimulating, pleasant, and acceptable."[31] Still, the Agassiz biography turned out to be Alice's only published book.[32] The project gave her an occupation for a time, but she did not feel authorship was her vocation. Her poor health and the ambiguity of her future persisted. She tried to return to her doctoral dissertation in mathematics, only to succumb to fatigue and illness. Her diary of that time is largely a record of when she did *not* work.[33] She came to feel a need to leave the confined New England climate, not for England or Chicago but for another locale where her place was not so overdetermined, where, (despite) being an American woman, she might explore new horizons.

Atlantic Waypoints

The usual treatment for neurasthenic women was the now notorious rest cure, developed by Dr. S. Weir Mitchell. The rest cure required a (female) patient to remain in bed, as physically passive and intellectually inert as possible, while being periodically massaged and fed (or force-fed) a rich diet. It allowed no reading or writing. Alice Gould chose a dramatically different path: travel, which followed physicians' main prescription for neurasthenic *men*.[34] Her research on Louis Agassiz had revealed how transnationality had advantaged the eminent scientist. He trained in his native Switzerland but fell "in love . . . with his work in America," according to his widow.[35] Even his idea of a natural history museum originated in a transnational context. As Alice wrote, "the art of managing collections to the best advantage is as modern as the sister profession of the librarian; and it is hardly a boast to say that both have been chiefly cisatlantic."[36] Perhaps Alice imagined that, by leaving her birthplace and embracing the "cisatlantic," she, too, might find the passion and energy to undertake meaningful intellectual work.

Gould had already sojourned in Bermuda in December 1900. American tourists had begun visiting Bermuda in the early nineteenth century, and their numbers grew dramatically by the 1880s, after steamships made travel through the Gulf Stream more comfortable.[37] Gould kept a diary, recording her visits to Spanish Point, Victoria Park, Pembroke Church, and other popular sightseeing destinations. She noted the preserved guavas, the bananas and calabashes, the rubber and mahogany trees. She admired the vivid colors of the "turquoise blue, + white sand," coral, and "pretty gardens, [with] houses dazzlingly white against blue." Always haunted by her years in South America—to which she never returned—she mused that the "weather [is] like Cordoba [Argentina]. . . . Felt like childhood." She plunged into reading Sir John Henry Lefroy's *History of the Bermudaes or Summer Islands,* the most thorough narrative of Bermuda's early colonization available. Lefroy's account resonated deeply with Gould. She thought it "*very* interesting; [a] splendid piece of work."[38] Clearly Gould already felt an attraction to history, particularly to the exploration and colonization of the Atlantic world. But beyond that, the book may also have suggested an alternate intellectual path for her. Lefroy was a scientist of Gould's father's generation, a meteorologist who had been appointed governor of Bermuda in his fifties. Only then did he take up historical research, applying his scientific background to a new field.

By September 1902, Gould was preparing for a second Caribbean journey, one in which she would eventually find a new beginning.[39] She sailed to Puerto Rico in November, with all due propriety, in the company of her friend Susie Zebiah Preble. Like Alice, Susie was navigating Boston society as a woman with neither parents nor husband and without much likelihood of marriage; her mother, Susan, had died in 1875, and her father, Rear Admiral George Henry Preble, in 1885.[40] Gould knew at least one person in Puerto Rico: a cousin, Grace Giddings de Wolf Lugo-Viña, who had married a Puerto Rican physician years before. For this trip, Gould bought a camera. She may have sought to combat her malaise with creative expression. As Gilbert Ballet wrote in 1911, in his treatise *Neurasthenia,* "drawing, photography, and music divert and enliven these patients, especially when they have acquired some skill in the exercise of these accomplishments, and can derive from them a sensible satisfaction of their self-esteem." Though reading was dangerous, photography could help a neurasthenic heal the damage of intellectual overexertion.[41] Gould did not intend to escape her studies, however, for she also carried her "book work" on the trip.[42]

Puerto Rico was a fashionable destination for leisure travelers of the day, but it differed from other Caribbean tourist spots in many respects. Guidebooks

"Treeferns between Caguas and Cayey/Miss Preble & Miss Davis" (ca. 1903–1907). Alice Bache Gould Photographs 166.180, Massachusetts Historical Society.

warned that the savage "mongrel race" of native Puerto Ricans remained mired in disease, poverty, and illiteracy. Steamships might carry one there, but Gould would not find the hotels and luxurious amenities of other touristed islands like Cuba and Jamaica.[43] Writers promoted Puerto Rico for its verdant "natural beauty" instead: "the healing powers of Coamo Springs in the Central Cordillera, the rain forest and waterfalls at the foot of the lofty El Yunque, the wild begonias, orchids, and palm-lined beaches."[44] These were just the sort of features to which Gould had felt drawn in Bermuda. Such lush wildness made Puerto Rico seem, to Americans, an untamed place, a site for "masculine adventure."

This exoticized locale had become a possession of the United States in 1898, at the conclusion of the Spanish American War. The image of Puerto Rico's primitiveness was thus tempered with the sense that modernization was now under way.[45] Voyagers like Gould did not constitute the front line of Americanization but rather intersected with U.S. military, government officials, business interests, medical personnel, missionaries, and others who came bearing Civilization. A number of these were women, nurses and teachers in particular, who found professional opportunities within American imperialism.[46] Gould pointedly declared herself "an Anti-Imperialist" while in Puerto Rico, as she witnessed the application of U.S. power.[47] Yet she benefited from the possession of the island by the United States. The range of possibilities she encountered and even tested there mirrored the opportunities that colonialism afforded other American women and men of her generation.

Although she had gone to Puerto Rico to improve her health, Gould contracted dengue fever within the first few weeks of her arrival. She apparently suffered from the severe headache and eye pain that typically accompany the tropical disease. As part of the ordeal, she lost most of her hair, which later came in gray.[48] Her companion, Susie Preble, also fell ill. But Miss Preble became sicker, while Miss Gould became whole again. By the time Gould reported on her state to her family at home in mid-December, she had mostly recovered. "I am surprisingly well," she wrote, "except that my eyes hurt me still and my skin is all coming off in flakes, there is no trace of illness left. I *love* the place and the climate."[49] A week and a half later, she emphasized her robustness and again credited the climate for helping her heal, rather than for making her sick. "I never saw anybody recover perfect health and spirits with such a bound as I," Gould boasted to her aunt. "[Miss Preble] never saw me in such good health and spirits!! . . . a fortnight ago I was barely able to sit up in an armchair for an hour at a time—why I think it is funny. Certainly the tropics agree with me."[50] Her Aunt Fanny, in turn, was solicitous of Gould's health, expressing her "delight" at even a "temporary improvement" and her hopes that "it means more steady gain later. I cannot but think that it will come, and the enjoyment of life will open to you."[51] In their correspondence, both Gould and her aunt conflated physical and emotional health; the joy Gould was taking in her environs was a sign both of her body's revitalization and of her dissipating depression.

She threw herself into novel, even sensual, experiences. She tried new foods, including alligator pears, which she declared an "artistic pleasure," and freshly made brown cane sugar.[52] She socialized with new people, including naval officers, and later a professional archaeologist. Gould reported on flirtations at a carnival.[53] She observed a "tall and slender black man, naked except for a very slight white garment of the decollete variety, wading in the surf," who could almost be her double in his voluptuous enjoyment of nature.[54] The island's climate and culture, and especially the language of its people, evoked memories of a childhood before domestic expectations constrained her.[55] She reflected with disappointment that "I find I can understand Spanish fairly well to middling but cannot speak it at all." Nevertheless, she hoped to become more fluent and to immerse herself in the culture. "Isolated words keep popping out of the depths of unconscious memory and presenting themselves at need. I believe that if I take lessons I can pick it up quickly."[56]

Gould soon decided that "the chief trouble with me is lack of exercise," so she set to exploring her surroundings further and further from San Juan.[57] Leaving behind all vestiges of frailty, she embarked on a four-day driving tour through the mountains. She gloried in the dramatic scenery and set to surveying caves and sugar plantations. In February 1903, she sent Aunt Fanny a map with all her travels proudly marked "in crisscross." Among her stops was "Aguadilla, the post where some people suppose that Columbus landed." Her fascination with transatlantic history was growing. She also wrote animatedly of plans to see Mayaguez and Ponce.[58]

Prose did not suffice to capture Gould's perceptions and experiences. Some of her letters experimented with word-painting:

> And such flowering as the trees go through with here! The flamboyants that I was so afraid I should not see have just begun, and one behind Mrs Lugo Viña's house is like a tree daubed with vermilion. There are trees covered (as a cherry or an apple tree is covered) with flowers that look for all the world like morning glories, and there are others of a waxy consistency and so tremendous an orange in color that no paintbox could do them justice.[59]

Gould's prose shows how she struggled with comparisons and analogies to make the exotic comprehensible to her audience at home (and to herself). Like other travelers of her generation, she also turned to her camera to help capture what she saw. From the start, Gould expected little of the device: "This afternoon I have taken my first snapshot with a camera and a view of Arecibo Cathedral. It isn't likely to turn out good," she warned.[60] Indeed, the resulting images often disappointed her. The state of technology posed certain limitations. "Remember that those mountains are every shade of green & blue," she felt obliged to point out regarding her black-and-white photograph. Other challenges were more technical, as when she explained that a dark blob in the image was really a rose bush or that she could not render the sea in the distance on the photographic plate.[61]

Gould's photographic skill improved with time, and she eventually pronounced her Kodak "the most delightful possession I have had."[62] Her images of scenery, palm trees, horses, women filling gourds, and peasants eating lunch gave her exactly the "sensible satisfaction of self-esteem" that Gilbert Ballet recommended to counteract neurasthenia. Gould did not find her true identity as a

"Cayey to Guayama" (ca. 1903–1907). Alice Bache Gould photographs 166.179, Massachusetts Historical Society.

photographer, though, in the manner of Clover Adams or the Allen sisters. Perhaps the most important function of her photography was that it encouraged or simply justified her adventurous roving. Riding high into the mountains, Gould effused that the view "was like a living map, or like all the kingdoms of the world and the glory of them in a moment."[63]

Among Gould's "amusing expeditions," cave exploration tested her courage and physical endurance most. It also revealed a tantalizing possibility: an *academic* field of endeavor, unlike photography, that might put her intellectual skills as well as her historical interests to use. Gould made the acquaintance of Jesse Walter Fewkes of the Smithsonian and accompanied him on archaeological digs to find pre-Columbian native artifacts.[64]

This adventure brought Gould out of the realm of the tourist, yet exploited her affiliation with imperialism. The aftermath of the War of 1898 propelled many academic and government researchers from the United States to study its new possessions. Fewkes was building upon archaeological experience at native sites in the American Southwest.[65]

With Fewkes, Gould visited Utuado and other cave sites that contained many pottery fragments and animal bones. Pictographs ornamented the walls.[66] They had all been "previously entered by others," Fewkes admitted, and many of their original objects were long gone, so he focused on the cave floors as "most promising" for excavation. Gould fantasized thrillingly about the prospects of finding not only artifacts but human remains: "If this spot was a temple, the place around it ought to have pots and pans and bones and hatchets and idols and collars galore, and perhaps oh perhaps a skull or two. With which ladylike ambition to desecrate graves I can hardly wait for Thursday."[67]

Her most *un*ladylike ambition found fulfillment. Alice took on a project of mobilizing the local schoolchildren to help find artifacts. She proudly reported on how her mission "bore fruit . . . no fewer than fourteen hatchets for Dr. Fewkes."[68] Perhaps one of them was the singular "beautifully polished and grooved" example noted by Fewkes in his book.[69] The more "gruesome spoils" that Fewkes collected included "the remains of ten skeletons, and among them two perfect skulls, beautifully flattened as was usual according to the early historians. The bodies were in a sitting posture, five or six feet under, with pottery etc. beside them—one whole dish came out unbroken."[70]

Then Susie Preble, her traveling companion, "broke down again" in mid-February, calling an abrupt halt to their second driving tour.[71] Fewkes's wife too fell ill. "The mound isn't exhausted yet but Mrs Fewkes is," commented Gould wryly and rather uncharitably.[72] Perhaps Gould could not resist the joke, unaccustomed as she was to being the healthiest woman in the group. She measured her capacity against the women around her and felt strong and self-possessed.

"I have decided to stay on here after Miss Preble goes," she announced.[73] Gould remained until May 28, using the intervening weeks to continue her archaeological pursuits, among other pleasures:

> I have been in a cave for half a mile or more with torches . . . and I have lived through a false alarm of a cyclone; I have been to a dance on Trinity Sunday and danced with a poet who presented his own love poetry, and who has travelled more widely in the United States than I have; I am still aching from trail-riding on a pair of saddle baskets up paths so steep that a sidesaddle wasn't safe.[74]

She later elaborated that "the bats don't hit you in the face as Mr Dinwiddie has it, though one of them flew within arms length of me."[75] She also learned to be careful of tarantulas.

Gould's passion for archaeology, in both its intellectual challenges and its physical demands, suggests she might have found her vocation in the caves of Puerto Rico. As in mathematics, she would have been among the first American women in the profession, but not *the* first. She did not have a graduate degree in the field, but, before the 1930s, field archaeology valued participant observation at least as highly as specialized formal training.[76] Women thus made major contributions to archaeology in its formative years, including as excavators.[77] For example, there was Frances Eliza Babbitt, a teacher and collector of prehistoric artifacts who had presented and published her amateur research since the 1880s.[78] Though probably unknown to Gould, Anita Newcomb McGee was also the daughter of an astronomer; McGee sometimes worked with her ethnologist husband, and she founded the Women's Anthropological Society of America in 1885.[79] Zelia Maria Magdalena Nuttall was a successful, self-taught archaeologist of Mesoamerica; most of her contributions came from archival research, locating and giving new methodological value to the Codex Magliabecchiano and the Codex Nuttall.[80] Gould shared many attributes with these elite, native-born white women.

Fewkes had given Gould the unusual opportunity to obtain practical experience in the field. Most of his male peers considered women incapable of the rigors of fieldwork.[81] Even with training, the scholar Jonathan Reyman explained, "most women . . . were assigned to field laboratories where they cleaned, catalogued, and restored artifacts"—that is, they did work that resembled housekeeping and was "generally considered menial labor."[82] Fewkes incorporated—and, more unexpectedly, credited—Gould's notes from her visit to El Consejo into his published study *The Aborigines of Puerto Rico* (1907).[83] Gould had identified seven heads carved into the archway leading into the cave, designating "the original Indian entrance." Such attribution as Fewkes made to Gould was rare. Even women's important work tended to remain unpublished and overlooked.[84]

Whatever the prospects for women as archaeology professionalized, Gould "kindly" (in Fewkes's words) turned over her notes to him and did not attempt to publish them herself. Gould clearly relished the adventure of fieldwork and found the island's past fascinating. But encounters between native and European peoples captivated her more than precolonial societies did. She heard and repeated numerous stories about Columbus on the island.[85] She sometimes imagined distant events from his point of view.[86] Columbus loomed large in contemporary perceptions. Katharine R. Crowell, for example, opened her book about Puerto Rico with the spectacle of Columbus's voyages. Using Columbus as a reference point not only made the Caribbean island more familiar and relatable but also suggested that explorers, possessors, and namers from the United States were also heroic. "Columbus discovered *our* island," wrote Crowell.[87]

The project of her own that Gould began instead was an article on the early colonization of Barbados.[88] She also collected as many materials as possible on the history of Puerto Rico before U.S. occupation. The theme of exploration and discovery captivated her most. It was to lead her to her true life's work, but not until after she had navigated between waypoints from home to Puerto Rico and back and made further recalculations. Her time in the Caribbean had taught her to admire the straight yet indirect route, like the Boricuan horses that managed the rugged Puerto Rican terrain:

> No American horse could go up and down these hillsides—he would be rolling over and over in five minutes and frightened to death beside. But these nice surefooted little things ask of you only one thing, that you shall not interfere and get them all balled up with directions in detail—You indicate the path you want to follow, and the horse knits his brow in thought and starts up according to some scheme of his own—Mine saddled zigzag fashion, turning as if on a pivot, and showed his displeasure plainly when I interrupted his calculations by some of my own.[89]

Recalculations

In spring 1903 Gould returned to Cambridge. Whatever her initial intentions had been before she went to Puerto Rico, she did not return to her dissertation in mathematics. Her friend Elizabeth R. Cabot wondered whether Gould's physical strength or her intellectual capabilities might be the impediment, but she suspected that Gould's more fundamental commitment to her doctoral dissertation was really what had weakened. Gould had no better success than before in securing an academic post. In April 1905 Ellen Swallow Richards of MIT encouraged her to apply to be head of the Department of Mathematics at Vassar College. By the time Gould compiled her materials, Vassar was already in negotiations with a male applicant. M. Carey Thomas approached Gould to teach at her alma mater, Bryn Mawr, but Gould seems not to have pursued that possibility.[90]

Neither did Gould seriously pursue her new interests in photography and archaeology. She somehow obtained a "stone object" and sent it to J. Walter Fewkes at the Smithsonian; he identified it as an unusual type of ax and tried to interest her in Apache artifacts.[91] But she did not attempt any further excavations or discoveries of her own. Similarly, Gould collected more books and materials on the colonial Caribbean but did not press ahead with the article she had begun writing. She considered it incomplete because she could not document who the first English person was in Barbados.[92] Lacking meaningful work, Gould sank back into depression.[93]

The one passion that she pursued in these years was a philanthropic project. In this, perhaps oddly, she seemed at last to be falling in line with the life script for women of her class; women without husbands or children, in particular, busied themselves as volunteers, lending their abilities to a range of institutions. This was its own cure for the neurasthenic's anxiety and frustration. More conservative women gave their time and labor to churches or to city beautification projects; the more radical minority made a place for themselves in the settlement movement or as lobbyists for woman suffrage.[94]

Gould's philanthropy reached back directly to her experiences in Puerto Rico: she began raising money to support a new hospital for women and infants in San

Juan. In fact, one of the project's advantages was that it perpetuated and deepened her connection to the island. She had a familial connection to the endeavor in that José Lugo-Viña, the Puerto Rican husband of her cousin, was director of the new hospital. The gifts of modern medicine, hygiene, and sanitation were cornerstones of the "benevolent imperialism" that the United States professed to practice in its new territorial possessions.[95] The Catholic hospitals that predated U.S. occupation seemed inadequate to the task, and the occupation of nursing held no appeal for Puerto Rican women except among nuns who traditionally devoted themselves to caring for the sick.[96]

Having returned to the United States, Gould thus seemed to slip easily into the role of benevolent imperialist in relation to the nation's Atlantic possessions. She expressed frustration that the American women in Puerto Rico were not taking on the burdens of civic stewardship as they ought. "They need public spirited women among the Americans, who are mostly there under protest because their husbands are temporarily on duty," Gould wrote. "I don't know whether I came away more impressed by the selfishness and indifference of the ordinary American women down there or by the brave endeavors and the devotion of the half dozen who are attaching things outside the Government Department."[97] Her project brought her back to Puerto Rico repeatedly, as she had likely intended even during her first voyage.

Gould's position struck a chord within her social circle back in New England. Some blatantly avowed imperialism in a way Gould herself never did. Her "old friend" Helen Butler agreed that women as well as men ought to take an active role in assuming the white man's burden:

> I think that our "insular possessions" are the affair of every American. I am not of those who think that we are to be blamed for having them or that having them we should do right to drop them and leave them to their fate, but that having them we have great responsibilities toward them, which I fear are very badly fulfilled by the government - especially by Congress—and that this makes the responsibility of the private citizen the heavier.[98]

Augusta M. Brown added, in offering her "spinster's mite": "I know there is desperate need of Sanitary reform, and of trained nurses—and if the native women can be taught to do Hospital work, Successfully, & you think they *can*, all that is needed is money to teach them. The Insular Government *ought* certainly to take this work in charge. But I suppose it moves slow [*sic*] & meanwhile the need remains."[99]

A hospital built to serve women suited Gould's sensibilities. She keenly felt how her sex had reduced her own opportunities in life, up through her frustrations in finding a university position, and she had experienced the power of voluntary separatism—of sisterhood—at Bryn Mawr and within her circle of friends.

The chance to employ nurses and cultivate nurse training, especially, meant Gould could enable women to earn their own livelihoods, to master a field, to become professionals and do work of service to the world, just as she had long hoped to do. Nursing was a singular occupation in that, although dominated by women, it had decisively organized as a profession with rigorous standards and training, beginning in the 1890s.

The need for medical care that she had personally witnessed in Puerto Rico also had impressed Gould. She thus coupled the patronage of nurses with the desire to help spread the American model of medical care as a form of benevolent imperialism. As she wrote in a letter to the editor of the *Boston Evening Transcript,* "I don't believe there is a more worthy work in the world than this care of the suffering poor in Puerto Rico, and the opening of a new field of self-support for the young women."[100]

Gould pragmatically set herself to raising money. Grace Giddings de Wolf Lugo-Viña called Gould a "star collector" from the start of the fundraising in 1903.[101] Among her own early gifts to the hospital, Gould sent an operating table. Lugo-Viña later commented, "perhaps an operating table is an unusual present from a lady, but we only think of the great service it is to us three or four times a week."[102] Most of all, though, the Hospital de Mujeres y Niños de San Juan depended on Gould to pay the salary for an American nurse.[103] The hospital's ultimate goal was to train native-born women as nurses.[104] Fewer than half the initial group of nursing students passed Board exams, and racial inferiority received the brunt of the blame for this failure. Nurse Superintendent Louisa Lippitt rejoiced that the next class came from "better" stock: "I have insisted upon having white girls as I hoped to get a better educated, more reliable class."[105] Americans perceived Puerto Ricans as uncontrolled, irrational, and racially indiscriminate, all of which prolonged the period of tutelage they would need in order to become Americanized and civilized.[106] But even Lippitt recognized that more pragmatic problems challenged student achievement: there were no books from which to teach them, just weekly "lessons" (lectures) from surgeons; language barriers complicated communication between the English-speaking medical professionals and the Spanish-speaking nursing students; and the young women lacked places to live in San Juan while studying at the hospital.[107] Lippitt continued to encounter difficulties with her white students: some were very young and inexperienced, while the older ones were "not accustomed to work, are untidy and not willing to be taught and take too much upon themselves . . . nervous and inclined towards superstition."[108]

Gould did not concern herself very much with the questions of "respectability and intelligence," "conduct and appearance," that preoccupied those directing the hospital and training school.[109] Rather than take a moral position or advocate uplift, she focused on institutional challenges. She strategized how one might "induce" the Department of Education to provide the salary for a teaching nurse "if she once proves successful."[110] Gould worked to interest influential people in her project, from Puerto Rican professionals to Governor Beekman Winthrop and his wife, Melza Riggs Winthrop.[111] The Winthrops agreed that it would be beneficial for the Training School board to include prominent Puerto Ricans alongside Americans.[112] Melza Riggs Winthrop thought that support of various hospitals, including those run by different denominations, would further "help to unite all interests."[113] Gould took on the mission: she simultaneously approached Presbyterian Hospital in San Juan and the Episcopalian Hospital to offer salary support for trained nurses. Not content to limit her role to that of fundraiser, Gould concerned herself very much with the details of administration as well.[114]

Gould's appeals successfully organized other women to interest themselves and to donate thousands of dollars to a distant cause.[115] The hospital she nurtured closed in July 1907, but the same year the legislature passed a bill to fund a nurse training school.[116] By 1912, Lavinia Dock and Adelaide Nutting, leaders in nursing education and reform, were commending the "record of good work done" to bring professional nursing to Puerto Rico; twelve years later, the American Nurses' Association welcomed the Puerto Rico Graduate Nurses' Association into its fold.[117] Benevolent imperialism seemed to be achieving its ambitions of tutelage and assimilation, in part because of the concerted assistance of American women.

As the government took on a more direct role in nursing education, Gould's philanthropic focus shifted. The Anti-Tuberculosis League of Porto Rico had been established in 1906, with branches opening in Arecibo in February 1909 and in Ponce in March of the same year, bringing together American women, Puerto Rican women, and Puerto Rican male physicians.[118] The organization named Gould to its board of directors in 1909, the same year its work on the island began in earnest. The National Association created an exhibit to travel around the island, where there were "6,000 cases of tuberculosis among the million inhabitants," and then continue "to other Spanish-speaking parts of the West Indies and the United States."[119] By 1910, however, Gould had fixed her sights on another waypoint, nearing her destination.

Destination

All the while that Gould lavished her time and attention on modernizing nursing in Puerto Rico, she also nurtured her increasing interest in the history of Spanish colonization. She spent some seven years compiling material about Puerto Rican history and culture from the era before the United States took possession of the island. Her personal collection came to include manuscripts and other important primary documents.[120] She undertook this work in consultation with other researchers, many of them also amateur historians. In anticipation of her second trip to Puerto Rico, the U.S. military physician Bailey Ashford introduced her to prominent Puerto Rican intellectuals, "noted men" who included Cayetano Coll y Toste, Manuel Fernandez Juncos, and Federico Degetau.[121] Coll y Toste, for example, was not only a physician (sharing Gould's interest in medical care) but also a historian and secretary to the governor. He published historical documents from the sixteenth to the twentieth centuries in the *Boletín Histórico de Puerto Rico* from 1914 to 1918.[122]

At the turn of the twentieth century, the enterprise of history still maintained a precarious balance between amateurs and academics. The Hispanic Society of America, founded by the arts patron Archer Milton Huntington for a scholarly purpose, was formed in 1904 to promote and celebrate Hispanic culture. It filled a Beaux Arts building in Manhattan with Spanish and Latin American art and literature. Both its museum and its reference library—intended "to encourage and promote original and new investigation"—held immense appeal and relevance to Gould. She became a corresponding member in 1910.[123]

While turning increasingly to historical studies, Gould did not abandon her earlier areas of expertise. Her interests in mathematics and Columbus coincided in her analysis of an ancient navigational technique based on geometry, Great Circle Sailing.[124] Her brief period teaching navigation to naval officers—later, during World War I—suggests Gould had thought deeply and concretely about the technologies that made transatlantic voyages possible. She instructed her students in the use of compass and sextant, charts and logbooks, as well as the mathematical computations necessary to calculate sailings.[125] She was well equipped to imagine with precision the work of Columbus and his crew as navigators and sailors. In this way, the mathematical dimension of navigation likely enhanced her particular affinity for the history of exploration.

Eventually, and perhaps inexorably, Gould's fascination with the history of the Spanish Atlantic led her to the Archive of the Indies in Seville, where she began her most significant and enduring work. In 1911, Gould was delayed on her way to Rome—a much more typical destination for Americans touring Europe. Unable to continue on her planned route, Gould took advantage of the opportunity to seek out some historical documents. The Archive of the Indies housed the records of Spanish exploration and colonization. Gould hoped to find evidence to complete her article on Barbados. In the course of her research, she found an account book kept by Juan de Lepos, whom she recognized as a *tripulante,* a member of Columbus's crew. This drew her into what became her life's work: a painstaking individual and collective biography of the *tripulantes.*[126]

Gould noted how much uncertainty shrouded Columbus's life and voyages at the time.[127] Scholars disputed how many men had served on his crew and presumed them to be of low origins. Gould set out to investigate and resolve these debates with scientific precision. She spent the most time in Seville and Simancas but visited more than seventy other repositories throughout Spain. She followed the traces wherever they led her, whether to small town offices, churches, private collections, or even the jail in Moguer.[128] She periodically visited New England but always returned to Spain. She wrote from Valladolid to a friend about how she had no real home anymore; most of her possessions had remained in storage for many years.[129]

She eventually compiled the most complete and authoritative list available of individuals who sailed with Columbus. Gould worked with a range of sources, from pay lists and other archival documents, to the contemporary accounts of Fernández de Oviedo and Pietro Martire d'Anghiera, to later chronicles such as Bartolomeo de las Casas's *Historia general de las Indias* (1561). Three modern scholars—Fernández Duro, Nicolás Tenorio, and Henri Vignaud—had previously created such lists, each at variance with the others. Gould's painstaking research enabled her to eliminate twenty names from the earlier lists. Her work with the *Pagos* (accounting records) and various other archival records revealed eleven individuals unnoted by previous historians. For example, she found evidence that there were two men named Juan de la Cosa, both of whom served on Columbus's crew but at different times.[130] Gould carefully substantiated that 87 individuals had definitely served on Columbus's crew, with the possibility of nineteen others also, for a potential total of 106.[131]

Gould published her findings between 1920 and 1942 in a series of pieces in the *Boletín de la Real Academia de la Historia*.[132] She collected as much biographical detail as possible on each crew member. This not only led to the most accurate list of *tripulantes* but also illuminated the men's backgrounds. She organized her findings by individual name, in alphabetical order. Gould transcribed all available documentation for each entry on the list and discussed it in a section titled "Observations," where she articulated the interpretive problems involved and stated her conclusions. She often engaged in close analysis of language and corroboration of evidence. Gould successfully dispelled the popular assumption that, because royal orders offered amnesty to convicts, criminals must have made up the majority of the "sorry crew."[133]

Gould vividly illustrated her approach to research in an article about a separate endeavor: her quest to fill in the two weeks of Emperor Charles V's life for which his scrupulous biographer, Manuel Foronda, could not account. Gould's essay "The Adventure of the Missing Fortnight," written for a general audience, told the story of the quest. In contrast to her earlier Barbados research, which she had also hoped to publish in a popular periodical, Gould felt satisfied with her findings; she was able to answer her question with archival evidence.[134]

The mystery of the emperor's "missing fortnight" appealed to Gould's intellectual curiosity and her love of detail and precision, as well as her desire to challenge herself:

> When I first saw Foronda's book, I was studying the discovery of America in one of the larger Spanish archives; and I was somewhat disheartened by the lack of answer to the broader questions I was putting to the dusty bundles. Was it that no answer could be given? Or that I personally could not handle an archive? I wanted to test myself on something neatly asked. Spanish policies, streams of tendency, motives of legislators—all these are slippery matters; but "Where was the Emperor on August 1, 1538?"—this is so definite and safe and clear an inquiry. Either you know the answer or you don't.[135]

Although she was, as yet, in 1916, a fledgling historical researcher, Gould hoped that casting a "new eye" on the puzzle would yield results where others had failed.[136] Her "adventure" evoked Great Circle Sailing in that she did not follow a direct line from question to answer. Methodical, diligent searching led her from Simancas to the Aragonese archive in Barcelona, where she chased answers to other concrete questions unrelated to the whereabouts of Charles V. There, "sheer luck" "electrified" the drudgery of "languidly turning over successive documents": a "perfectly uninteresting" letter placed Charles V on Lerida on July 31. "A few days' livelier work yielded five signatures and three stopping-places, taking Charles as far as Saragossa on August 4. Here the trail was lost again," she recalled. But she pursued the matter further, to the Archivo Regional of Valencia, which yielded two more letters. She shared these findings with Foronda mere weeks before his appointment to the Academy of History. (Though effusively grateful to Gould, he could hardly believe "that ladies . . . should be moved to occupy themselves with such matters.") Gould concluded her "adventure," and her reminiscence of it, with one last flourish: "the audacious attempt to find something in the great Archives of Simancas where so many had looked before me; and on the way there, to travel for myself from village to village, over the road from Saragossa to Valladolid, and see for myself whether anything remained in church or town records." She guessed that along the route there might be records of the couriers who had delivered the letters. And she proved to be correct. "Reader, they had not gone! Perhaps because they were so totally uninteresting to anybody, there they were in duplicate, perfectly in order, absolutely easy to read."[137]

Gould described her research on Charles V as a contribution to the "humbler field of making tools for the historian's use"; yet that "humbler" role was an essential one. She thought of this work in scientific terms, analogous to the need for precise instruments; she appreciated how "facts in themselves unimportant" require "arduous laboring" but in the end lead to more exact knowledge, as when using a vernier scale.[138]

Gould did not turn to historical research because it was more open to women's intellectual contributions than mathematics or archaeology or photography. As with those other fields, the very process of professionalization called for women's exclusion. Amateur women historians who had thrived in the eighteenth century found themselves frozen out by the gender exclusivity of the seminar, the archive, and other scholarly credentials.[139] Domesticity was the reigning ideology that bookended Gould's life. As a young woman, she chafed against social conventions that she dedicate herself to family, hearth, and home. Her wealth and social privilege allowed her to gain precious independence after her father's death and to take advantage of expanding cultural expectations of women. She chose the archive as her "home," leaving her belongings in storage while she traveled from one repository to another. But, however twentieth-century women's reach exceeded their nineteenth-century grasp, Gould's presence in the archives still elicited surprise and suspicion.[140] The *Time* article about her in 1952 demonstrates the recalcitrance of gender ideals. Although Gould was "the world's leading expert on Columbus's crew," thus important enough to merit mention in a major news magazine, the article's opening words introduced her as a "Boston schoolmarm." The unnamed writer took relish in the irony that "Alice," more "tireless" as a researcher than even "Harvard's Samuel Eliot Morison," was applying the methods of a "good housekeeper . . . to tidy up a number of historical mysteries."[141]

Housekeeping metaphors aside, Gould's work defied the Cold War feminine mystique, just as in girlhood and young adulthood Gould did not fit nineteenth-century prescriptions of domesticity. She explored history with great self-confidence. Although she felt frustrated and disappointed that she never finished the book she planned on the *tripulantes,* Gould became a renowned and influential historian.[142] Her research projects corrected the work of accepted male experts.[143] Foronda publicly thanked her for her research on Charles V, lauding her to the Spanish Royal Academy of History as a model of correction whose labor, ability, and generosity merited imitation.[144] Gould herself later became a member of the Academia. She won the praise of the eminent American historian Samuel Eliot Morison; she aided him in his search for elusive archival documents, and he cited her research in his biography of Columbus.[145] Spain awarded her the Cross of Alphonso XII in 1927 and the Cross of Isabel La Católica in 1952. The Archives of Simancas commemorated her with a bronze plaque; her colleague Ursula Lamb, whom Gould "sheparded" through those archives, noted the plaque was "the only one, a distinction indeed, for an American woman scholar."[146]

In the end, Gould felt satisfied by the place she had made for herself in Atlantic history.[147] What was lost was the trace of how she got there. Her obituary in 1953 only glancingly mentioned Gould's own Atlantic voyages as "a few visits to the United States" from Spain in her last four decades.[148] Her time in Puerto Rico became her own missing fortnight. Yet it was that sojourn that enabled her to escape domesticity and neurasthenia. Gould remade herself by her physical and intellectual immersion in the Atlantic world. Tourism, photography, archaeology, philanthropy, and archival research each let her explore the way to a meaningful life. Her research on Columbus's crew manifested the sense of possibility and transformation in Atlantic crossings. The arc she traveled and chronicled, from New England to Puerto Rico to Spain, shows the persistent relevance and resonance of the Atlantic world as a crucible of new identities into the twentieth century. The fluidity of the Atlantic and the imperialist power of the United States gave Gould a means of escape from the constraints of gender that she would never have found had she remained moored at home.

Tessa Roynon

White Noise?

Desdemona and Transnational Voicings through Time

On May 15, 2011, the city of Vienna, Austria, hosted the world premiere of a performance piece called *Desdemona.* Formerly titled *The Desdemona Project, Desdemona* is a collaboration between the African American novelist Toni Morrison (who wrote the spoken text), the Malian singer-songwriter Rokia Traoré (who wrote both the words and music to nearly all of the piece's nine songs and who takes a leading role on stage), and the (white) American theater director Peter Sellars. The work is a response, a "talking back," or a counterpoint to William Shakespeare's *Othello;* in many ways it is a sequel to Sellars's controversial 2009 production of *Othello* at the Public Theater in New York City. Following its opening performances, *Desdemona* went on to tour metropolitan cities of the Northern Atlantic world. It played for scheduled runs of just a few nights each time in Brussels (May 2011); in Nanterre, on the outskirts of Paris (mid-October 2011); in the United States, in Berkeley, California (late October 2011, its sole contact with the Pacific region); then in New York City and back across the Atlantic to Berlin (both in November 2011). Its most recent performances were in London during July 2012, where, as part of the World Shakespeare Festival, it also came under the larger auspices of the cultural olympiad that ran parallel to the Olympic Games and the London 2012 Festival, and also in Amsterdam, in June 2013. That same month, Morrison's text was published as a book together with translations of the lyrics of Traoré's songs.[1] At around this time, Sellars stated that his plan to film the piece in Mali had not come to fruition because of the changing political situation there.[2]

Desdemona fulfils the criteria of no conventional genre but rather transcends many. Like most inter-generic works, it also eschews tidy labeling. Part play and part concert, it primarily constitutes a dialogue between Desdemona (played by

Elizabeth Marvel in Vienna and Brussels and by Tina Benko from the Nanterre production on) and Barbary (played always by Rokia Traoré). The piece is motivated by Act IV, scene iii, of *Othello,* the famous "Willow Song" scene, in which, while anticipating her imminent murder, Desdemona recalls to Emilia a song that her mother's maid, "called Barbary," used to sing to express her anguish at her own lost love.[3] Postulating from Shakespeare's lines that this remembered Barbary was both an African slave and Desdemona's childhood nurse, the Morrison/Sellars/Traoré collaboration stages a postdeath conversation between these two women. *Desdemona* gives voice to the nonmale and nonwhite perspectives on both the action of *Othello* and its ever-pertinent themes: racial, national, class, and gender difference; sexual desire; betrayal; physical violence; and the struggles for power that run through all of these. It is a work that at once creates and reflects transatlantic (and at times global) connectedness in its performance of the interactions between the Americas, Europe, the Middle East, and North and sub-Saharan Africa. It also draws both parallels and juxtapositions between the time in which Shakespeare set *Othello* (probably the early 1570s, when the Turkish/Venetian struggle for Cyprus was at its height); the time in which that play was written (around 1602) and performed (in 1604 at Whitehall); the modern centuries of the transatlantic slave trade and slavery in the Americas; the histories of both Morocco and Mali; and present-day politics across all these regions, including of course 9/11 and its repercussions.

Unsurprisingly, given its ambitious scope, the work is complex and unstable. At the same time, however, it often involves an overreaching or all-encompassing perspective that, paradoxically enough, becomes a regrettable limitedness or inflexibility. After the Nanterre/Paris production, the *Washington Post* somewhat skeptically described the piece as a "Russian stacking doll of disenfranchisement."[4] My own analysis concurs to some extent with this skepticism: in what follows, I argue that *Desdemona*'s attempt to be a mouthpiece for all those oppressed on grounds of race, class, gender, and religion, both within and beyond the Atlantic world, is problematic. In the innumerable conflations that it effects, I demonstrate that *Desdemona* is all too often "transnational" to a fault. The broad-brush universalism that it claims is somewhat redeemed, however, by the specific political and aesthetic complexities that the powerful compound of "Traoré-as-Barbary" constitutes.

In his study of the literatures of black internationalism, *The Practice of Diaspora* (2003), Brent Hayes Edwards illuminates key practices or concepts that formations of black diasporas—actual, representational, and academic or analytical—all involve. These include translation; *décalage,* meaning a gap, discrepancy, or time lag; and articulation, in the sense of both separation and linkage.[5] My ensuing discussion deploys Edwards's useful terms in arguing that while *Desdemona* is fraught with radical potential because it embodies and epitomizes these concepts in myriad ways, at the same time it undermines its own potential radicalism through the widespread and forceful erasures—often self-inflicted and often paratextual—that are brought to bear on its significant but insufficiently valued points of disconnection and discrepancy. The first part of my analysis describes the nature of the piece and its complexities, paradoxes, and occasional sterile contradictions. This section highlights its inherent unevenness and its constantly shifting, context-specific meanings, as well as some of the processes of evening out or smoothing over that its conception has entailed. The second part analyzes the problems and provocations that characterize the articulations of racial, ethnic, and national identities, differences, and similarities that *Desdemona* involves, with a particular emphasis on Sellars's paratextual discourse and Morrison's text. The third and final section begins by exploring the way the collaboration configures the politics of gender and the intersections of gender, racial politics, and global history. It argues that while Sellars's words on these themes are once again self-limiting, Morrison's perspective is at times restrictive but at others nuanced. Through detailed analysis of the ways that both Traoré's music and the complexities of her native Mali play out, it goes on to demonstrate that Traoré-as-Barbary contributes layers of meaning to the work that are not necessarily readily accessible but that repay the attention they demand.

An Overview of *Desdemona* and Its Contexts

Desdemona is by no means the first modern theatrical response to *Othello.* It is the latest addition to a provocative genealogy that includes *Not Now, Sweet Desdemona* by the South African playwright Murray Carlin (first performed in Kampala in 1968); *Desdemona: A Play about a Handkerchief* by the American dramatist Paula Vogel (first staged as a reading at Cornell University in 1987); the Canadian Ann-Marie MacDonald's *Goodnight Desdemona (Good Morning Juliet)* (first performed in Toronto in 1988); and a prequel to *Othello* titled *Harlem Duet* (first performed in Toronto in 1997 and written by Djanet Sears, who is of mixed Guyanese, Jamaican, British, and Canadian descent). The international affiliations of these playwrights and of their plays' premieres testify to the international appeal that *Othello* holds or to the fact that Shakespeare's exploration of the relationship between racial and gendered identities, power, and desire in his play appear to have multinational or transnational relevance.

The Morrison/Sellars/Traoré collaboration, however, takes the transnationalism of both Shakespeare and his previous adaptors to a new level. In the different identities of its creators and characters, in its synthesis of languages and musical traditions, and in the transatlantic as well as trans-U.S. nature of its performance history to date, *Desdemona* epitomizes conventional understandings of "globalized" cultural expression. Toni Morrison's fiction has never ignored the relationship between the United States and the rest of the world: as early as 1973, for example, in her second novel, *Sula,* Morrison described in detail one of its characters' recovery from shellshock incurred during World War I in France, before returning to focus on a small town in the author's native Midwest. *Tar Baby* (1983), meanwhile, links the Caribbean, the United States, and Paris, and *A Mercy* (2008) spans Angola, Portugal, London, and Barbados, in addition to the east coast of the United States. In the text of *Desdemona,* Morrison implicitly voices the themes of her novels in an international or global perspective: the significance of naming and misnaming; the female propensity for self-sabotage through excessive passion; the multifaceted oppression of women by men, from rape to silencing; the vulnerability of "orphans"; the violence of political subjugation; and the elusive nature of "safety" and of "home" are presented as universal, defining dilemmas of the human condition. Regrettably, however, in this collaboration the author too often exhibits a didacticism that is a more occasional lapse in her fiction. As the *New York Times* critic Jason Zindman observed, the text of *Desdemona* "comes off as an elegant lecture" and has "the whiff of a scholar's counterargument."[6] The eponymous heroine's lines are often sermonic: "Love is complete, whole, fearless," she tells Othello.[7] And her observation about war, that "I am sick of killing as a solution. It solves nothing. Questions nothing, produces nothing," buys into the discourse of "world peace," yet it is bland and impotent in its generalness.[8]

It is presumably no coincidence that a piece conceived by artists of international standing, including Traoré, whose work is categorized as "world music," should close its run as part of the *World* Shakespeare Festival, in the city that proudly boasts an authentic reproduction of Shakespeare's *Globe* Theatre.[9] A scholar of African literature with whom I held an early discussion about *Desdemona* observed that my account of its performance history—"Paris, New York, Berlin, London"—made the work sound like a designer label or an international brand.[10] It is ironic that *Desdemona,* awash in postcolonial preoccupations, has not been staged in any "peripheral" locations such as the Caribbean, Brazil, or any country in Africa (the thwarted aspiration to film in Mali aside) but instead has toured the established cultural capitals of the "Western" world. Arguably, both *Desdemona* and the in-vogue discourse of "global Shakespeare" to some extent deploy the words "world" and "global" too readily, using them as a shorthand substitution for any combination of just a few regions. While Bate and Thornton assert in their book *Shakespeare: Staging the World* (a scholarly companion to the 2012 British Museum exhibition of the same title) that "distant places and immediate histories, all thrown together: that was Shakespeare's theatre of the world" or that "in London in 1612, almost a world city, all the world was a stage and the stage was all the world," Morrison is similarly beguiled by this rhetoric, giving to her Othello flat-footed lines such as "turn away old world, while my love and

I create a new one."[11] Peter Sellars, meanwhile, has made much of the symbolic resonances of Shakespeare's "Globe." Academic discourse—this essay included—faces a similar temptation toward what is almost a new kind of colonial mapping, the conflating of all histories and locations within the euphoric term of the moment: "transnational." My hope is that my discussion pays due attention to the specificities—for example about the nature of Mali—that are contained within my own usage of the term.

Morrison's axiomatic text is to some extent ameliorated by the sound and spectacle of the piece in performance. The dark stage is bare except for two spotlighted female protagonists (one white, one black), wearing white, contemporary European-style dresses. They are accompanied by a chorus of two or three Malian women singers, clad in dresses that echo the protagonists', and by two male Malian instrumentalists (one on the *kora* and the other on the *n'goni*), who are the only ones wearing traditional Malian dress.[12] Traoré is a particularly captivating performer, and even the piece's most skeptical critics agree that her music is compelling. The sight and the sound of Desdemona and Barbary, center stage and in dialogue at their respective microphones, do initially combine to present as two women communicating across their different racial identities and geographical provenances, allied by their common gender and positioned to speak for a universal womanhood. Indeed, *Desdemona* is distinct from the theatrical adaptations of *Othello* that preceded it in the extent to which it attempts to give issues of both race and gender equal priority. It is now a theoretical truism to state that these constructs (together with sexuality and class) are inextricably linked. The problems, however, both aesthetic and political, into which certain aspects of *Desdemona* run might be seen to exemplify the risks that are often inherent in attempts to give these issues equal emphasis. On the other hand, the unconvincing nature of the reconciliation that Morrison stages between Barbary and Desdemona might also be read as her testimony to the irreconcilable nature of black and white feminisms.

Desdemona's greatest innovation is its imagining of Barbary. Depending on how one interprets the "maid called Barbary" in *Othello,* this move effects either the remembering of a forgotten, silenced, and absent presence in Shakespeare's play or the invention of a character who constitutes a historical but seldom acknowledged presence.[13] Whether she is retrieved from Shakespearean shadows (light and shadow are used to brilliant effect in the performance) or superimposed from history onto the playwright's plot, the existence of this Barbary successfully shifts the debate centered on race and gender away from the early modern playwright's emphasis on the eponymous "Moor of Venice" and toward the inclusion of a dark-skinned female slave. While Othello does not physically or literally appear in the Morrison/Sellars/Traoré piece, he is nonetheless a powerful presence in that he is ventriloquized by Desdemona. In the Nanterre (Paris) and London performances that I saw, Benko as Desdemona affected a deep-voiced West African accent as her character voiced Othello's words during their early courtship, in his account of military action with Iago (and concomitant acts of sexual violence), and in a postdeath conversation between the former lovers in which both try to rationalize their violent ends. Yet in this work, Othello's voice is deliberately overshadowed by the physical presence and spectacle, both the sight and the sound, of Barbary and all she represents.

The second major innovation in *Desdemona* is the voicing of Barbary's perspective predominantly through music or song rather than through spoken words. While Desdemona for the most part speaks, Barbary for the most part sings and/or plays her acoustic guitar, speaking only in the piece's penultimate scene. Of the nine songs that Barbary sings, seven are sung in a mixture of Traoré's two mother tongues: the Mandean language of Bambara and French, the language of Mali's modern colonizing power. Traoré-as-Barbary also sings two songs in English: one an exact transcription of Shakespeare's "Willow Song" and one for which Toni Morrison wrote the lyrics, "Someone Leans Near."[14] As must be obvious from this description, the creation or re-creation of Barbary in the *Desdemona* project epitomizes the concept of "translation" as Edwards describes it: translation of languages, of histories, of musical traditions. This process is exemplified in the songs "Othello" and "Desdemona," in which the Italianate names stand out in stark contrast to the Bambara language in which the rest of the pieces are sung. There are both benefits and risks in such multiple translations and connections.

One of the few fixed or stable elements in this piece is that only Traoré herself can play Barbary. It would be physically possible, of course, for someone else to perform Traoré's songs, but the creators' original conception would then be entirely lost. While the fact that the role of Desdemona can be played by any white actress implies that white upper-class femininity is a generalized concept here, the inextricability of Traoré from Barbary demands closer analysis of this compound identity. Traoré-as-Barbary speaks for or, more accurately, sings for at least three non-European female subjectivities at once. First, according to the work's defining premise, she articulates the experiences in early modern England of a sixteenth-century enslaved woman from the North African region known as "Barbary." The term refers to the territories historically peopled by the Berbers, and in Elizabethan England it referred to "most of the coastline between Tripoli and the Atlantic" (countries now known as Morocco, Algeria, Tunisia, and Libya).[15] Second, through the implicit transatlantic connection that the collaboration between Traoré and Morrison constitutes and the black internationalist perspective on slavery that the text and its paratexts articulate, she speaks for West Africans transported to the Americas and enslaved there and for their descendants. The third subjectivity that Barbary connotes is allied with that of Traoré herself. Traoré is the daughter of a diplomat and spent her childhood in several different European, Middle Eastern, and African nations. This background enables her Barbary to embody at once Malian womanhood and a globalized African identity.

With regard to the multiple identities and histories that inform Traoré-as-Barbary, Edwards's caveat about the shortcomings of a black internationalist perspective (and the serendipitous resonance in this context of his metaphor of the "global stage") is particularly pertinent. "As much as [the cultures of black internationalism] . . . allow new and unforeseen alliances and interventions on a global stage," Edwards writes, "they are also characterized by unavoidable misapprehensions and misreadings, persistent blindnesses and solipsisms, self-defeating and abortive collaborations, a failure to translate even a basic grammar of blackness."[16] *Desdemona* indubitably involves and provokes its share of misapprehensions, misreadings, and blindnesses. Nonetheless, where it allows or even encourages the persistence of *décalage*—for example, in the ways in which its meaning changes in different places and in different times—it is illuminating about the postcolonial world.

In introducing their anthology *Adaptations of Shakespeare,* Fischlin and Fortier summarize Derrida's theory of "iterability" or "recontextualization," expounded in his 1988 work *Limited Inc.* Derrida's point is that "recontextualization" is "the inevitable condition of texts in history." "Every act of writing, of meaning . . . loses its original context," Fischlin and Fortier explain, "which cannot entirely enclose it, and plays itself out in a potential infinity of new contexts, in which the significance of the writing will inevitably be different . . . from what it was."[17] While any new context inevitably changes a text or performance (including, of course, that of *Othello*), the new depths, angles, and "translations" that specific performance sites bring to *Desdemona* demand explication. The staging of the piece involves an overhead screen, onto which is projected the transcribed text by Morrison (mostly Desdemona's words, occasionally Barbary's). In the Anglophone United States and United Kingdom venues, these words remain in English, but in non-Anglophone countries, while Desdemona continues to speak her words in English, they are translated into the language(s) of the host country as they are transcribed onto the screen—into French in the Nanterre production that I saw, into both French and Flemish in Belgium, and into German in Austria and Berlin. Both the Bambara and French lyrics of Traoré's songs, meanwhile, are likewise translated into the host country's language before appearing on the screen.

There are several effects of these acts of translation. For example, the fact that Traoré's French lyrics did not need translating for the Nanterre performances drew attention to the colonial and postcolonial relationship between France and Mali in particular (including the late twentieth-century immigration of Malians to France) and between France and North and West Africa in general.[18] There was no typographical distinction made in the surtitles between any of the original translated languages; this implied a new kind of equal status among those languages. At the same time, as I myself am not fluent in French, the translation into French of Traoré's Bambara lyrics brought me little closer to understanding them. My own subject position made me perceive the words of Desdemona differently from the words of Barbary and also gave me a perspective that differed from that of my Francophone co-audience. As Edwards writes, "the level of the international is accessed unevenly by subjects with different historical relations to the nation."[19] In Brussels, the coexistence of simultaneous translations into both French and Flemish would have been rich with the resonances not only of the Belgian presence in Central Africa but also of historical territorial struggles between France and the Netherlands in what is now Belgium itself. In Berlin, the history and legacies of fascism and communism would have made their presence felt, while in New York City the audience would have been particularly attuned to the history of transatlantic slavery, as well as to the twenty-first-century phenomena of both radical Islam and Islamophobia, given the city's identity as the main target of the 9/11 attacks. *Desdemona,* therefore, impressed differently upon different people in the different cities in which it was performed.

Time as well as place or space has also defined the evolving resonances of the work. While the period of *Desdemona*'s touring performances—May 2011 to July 2012—coincided with the later months of the "Arab Spring" and its multiple reverberations, London in July 2012 was a city on the verge of an outpouring of Olympics-inspired celebration, of international goodwill, peace, and love. London was also, however, commemorating the fifth anniversary of the "7/7" bombings, which had occurred the very day after the announcement, in July 2007, that London was to host the 2012 Games. In addition, that the nature and conventional perception of Mali had changed so dramatically during the course of 2011 and 2012—from being a relatively peaceful, stable, and democratic nation renowned for its music (in spite of its severe poverty) to being the site of a jihadist uprising and French intervention—represented an unhappy, if not unexpected, transformation. This adds further resonances to the constantly shifting meanings of *Desdemona.*[20]

Although none of the work's creators could have known exactly the turn of events that Mali was to face during the months of their show's performance, Traoré's Malian identity cannot help but connote the recent political turmoil in her country of birth. This turmoil, in turn, brings a particularity to the text's implicit concern with Islamic extremism and with extreme responses to that extremism. Pascal James Imperato's 1989 account of Mali paints a picture of Islam as being a complex and ambivalent cultural force in that country even before the recent violence.[21] Introduced to the region via North African traders in the eleventh century, Islam exerted a strong pressure to convert and has eroded traditional

Malian arts and craftsmanship. And while for some men it has enabled freedom from restrictive societal structures, men have also adapted it in order to maintain women's lack of power. Also relevant to *Desdemona*'s exploration of Islamic identity is the complicated trajectory of the Tuareg ethnic group within Mali. A Berber people (one that therefore resonates in the name "Barbary"), this group historically exploited black Malians and was instrumental in the trading of slaves and gold from West to North Africa. While the Tuaregs were for some time an ostracized group within Mali, in late 2011 their rebels were the instigators of the uprising in the north of the country before Ansar Dine (the al Qaeda–linked jihadist group "Defenders of the Faith") took over and continued the war.[22] The discord in Mali since then obviously contributes a specific context to *Desdemona*'s exploration of war, especially in those performances (in New York, Berlin, London, and Amsterdam) that ran parallel to the conflict. That child soldiers are recruited by Saharan jihadists, for example, gives a particular poignancy to Othello's memory, in *Desdemona,* of being brutalized when sold into the army as a child.[23]

Racial, Ethnic and National Representations

Desdemona is undermined by one great irony. While as a project it aspires to give voice to women and while its central visual principle is two female protagonists at microphones, its white male director appears almost desperate to make his own voice heard. The product of an elite education (at the famous boarding school Phillips Academy in Andover, Massachusetts, and at Harvard University) and awarded a MacArthur Fellowship in 1983, Peter Sellars has made his mark as a theater and opera director through unconventional, often controversial productions of classic and "high cultural" works. *Desdemona* follows logically, then, not just from his 2009 *Othello* but also from earlier projects such as his film of Mozart's *Don Giovanni,* shot in Spanish Harlem and styled as a "blaxploitation" movie.

Sellars has surrounded *Desdemona* in a cacophonous paratext of his own articulations—a flood of explanations, clarifications, and justifications that arguably do more harm than good. It is true that his innumerable communiqués about the collaboration—Skype appearances, web postings, postperformance talks, and program notes (for example, those translated into French for the Nanterre production)—are, by their nature, insubstantial and transitory and perhaps therefore should not attract undue analysis. In the summer of 2012, however, the publication of a book version of the piece by the London-based publisher Oberon Books, in its "modern play" series, includes a four-and-a-half-page foreword by Sellars, dated June of that year.[24] This miniature essay (which is reproduced in the London Barbican program) gives both status and fixedness to Sellars's words. Its position as a foreword (rather than, say, as an afterword) in the book and as a

"Director's note" in the program gives it an air of authority, a sense that it is an endorsement or authentication. To compare it with the white prefatory authentications that validated the slave narratives of Frederick Douglass, Harriet Jacobs, and others would be to exaggerate, but it is certainly an essay that undermines its own radical aims. In its statements about Africa, race, and slavery, it exemplifies the kinds of "misreadings" and "solipsisms" in the assertion of a black internationalism or universalism against which Edwards warns. And these "misapprehensions" are, at times, reflected and amplified in Morrison's text in ways that run entirely counter to the nuanced and complex representations of racial, national, and transnational identities in her nonfiction and her fiction. At the heart of both Sellars's and Morrison's problematic discourse is their catch-all use of the term "African," the inadequacy of which their own project illuminates as well as any other.

"What was the reality of Africa for Shakespeare?" asks Sellars. "Did he know any Africans? . . . Clearly the man who called his theatre "The Globe" was interested in Africa."[25] Explicating the relationship between *Desdemona* and the "willow song" scene in *Othello,* the director continues:

> It is the word "Barbary" which triggers surprising associations. In seventeenth-century London, "Barbary" meant Africa. The Barbary pirates were hijacking British vessels off the coast of Africa, enslaving their white, British crews. In 1600, a delegation of ambassadors from the Barbary court, Africans of high degree . . . arrived in London to negotiate with Queen Elizabeth. That Shakespeare, writing *Othello* in 1603, uses the name "Barbary," implies that there is another African character in his play. . . . We are left to reflect that Desdemona . . . was raised by an African maid with African stories and African songs. . . . It was a black woman who taught Desdemona how to love, and now, Desdemona chooses to offer her love to a black man.[26]

The first problem here is the insistence that Shakespeare's use of the name "Barbary" must mean that Desdemona "was raised by an African maid." The second is Sellars's own simplistic and much-reiterated conflation of "Barbary" with "Africa" and with black skin.

There is no textual evidence in Shakespeare's play for the fact that Barbary was Desdemona's nurse. The four-and-a-half lines spoken about Barbary by Desdemona are all we learn of this character:

> My mother had a maid called Barbary,
> She was in love, and he she loved proved mad
> And did forsake her. She had a song of "willow"
> An old thing 'twas, but it expressed her fortune
> And she died singing it.[27]

There is also, therefore, no textual evidence that the "Barbary" Shakespeare references here is from either the North African region known as Barbary or from elsewhere on the African continent. Many scholars believe that "Barbary" here is a diminutive of the girl's name "Barbara."[28] But these scant textual details provide no evidence to the contrary, either; that is to say, we cannot deduce from them that Barbary was *not* Desdemona's maid or that she was *not* from somewhere in Africa. Given that Iago uses "Barbary" to refer to Othello's North African provenance in describing him as "a Barbary horse," Morrison's and Sellars's inference might be read as a fully justifiable counter to assumptions that Barbary was from Europe.[29] Their proposition does provocatively disrupt the reluctance to admit the possibility of her non-European identity, evidenced, for example, by the editor of the 1997 Arden edition of *Othello,* Ernst Honigmann. Honigmann writes, "did Desdemona's mother have a maid who was a Moor? Not necessarily: the name was in use in England. Shakespeare's lawyer . . . had a daughter called 'Barbery,' named in his will, 1617."[30]

There is also the important point that, while Shakespeare's Barbary is suggestive of a North African identity to some people and not to others, in historical terms there indubitably existed in early modern Europe women in service (both servants and slaves) who were of North or West African provenance.[31] Such women are barely acknowledged by dominant historical narratives, and their experiences are rarely voiced. To posit the existence of Barbary as a non-European servant or slave, to imagine the perspective of such a figure, and to give her voice, is therefore in itself an overdue recalibration of the past. It is a political statement akin to other recent cultural events such as the 2012–2013 art exhibition in Baltimore and then at Princeton, "Revealing the African Presence in Renaissance Europe," in which forgotten faces, such as that of Giulia de' Medici, granddaughter of an enslaved African woman, were presented to the public for the first time.[32]

Sellars's assertion about the identity of Barbary is therefore problematic, not so much for its restoration of the voice of a non-white-skinned, non-European maid but because of the nature of his assertiveness. By being absolute and dogmatic in his wording—"Desdemona . . . was raised by an African maid with African stories and songs"—Sellars inadvertently sows or provokes doubts by refusing to countenance any. His later shift to conditional syntax proves this point by contrast in that it makes all the difference to the persuasiveness of his entire premise about Barbary: "we can now *imagine* that Desdemona *could have* grown up hearing some of those stories" (my emphasis).[33] Both Sellars and Morrison further overassert their theses by unnecessarily forcing a connection between the identity of Desdemona's childhood caregiver and the fact that she falls in love with the non-European Othello. Sellars claims, "It was a black woman who taught Desdemona how to love and now, Desdemona chooses to offer her love to a black man."[34] Again, the director's refusal to be conditional works against him, and in this curiously simplistic psychoanalytical interpretation there is almost an implicit racism. Can Desdemona's love for a black man be explained only by her childhood experience? Morrison implies something similar when she has Desdemona assert, of her first encounter and falling in love with Othello, that "I saw a glint of brass in his eyes identical to the light in Barbary's eyes."[35] The character is at this moment "not yet recovered from Barbary's death"; it is as if these details justify an otherwise inexplicable or unjustifiable passion.[36]

Sellars's words on Shakespeare's understanding of the relationship between "Barbary" and the entire African continent (as well as the director's own understanding of this relationship) are also problematic. Between his program notes for the Nanterre production of October 2011 and his foreword to the book written in June 2012, however, he has at least introduced some relevant and complicating contextual detail. His earlier words in the Nanterre program are provocatively simplistic: "in the England of Shakespeare, 'Barbary' meant 'African.' . . . Shakespeare did not know (or know of) any African. Today, at the dawn of the twenty-first century, the African is very present in the world, and our shared universe has become smaller, with more integration, than even Shakespeare could have imagined in his 'Globe.'"[37] At least, in the rewriting that the later foreword involves, he has challenged his own earlier statement that "Shakespeare did not know (or know of) any African," now asking, "what was the reality of Africa for Shakespeare? Did he know any Africans?"[38]

We obviously cannot ascertain exactly who or exactly what Shakespeare "knew," yet, as Sellars goes some way to answering himself, the complex and varied nature of Africa and of its peoples was indisputably known in educated circles at the turn of the sixteenth century, and the presence in London of significant numbers of people from Africa at that time is a documented fact. Besides the well-charted visit of the Moroccan ambassadorial delegation to London in 1600–1601 (to which Sellars alludes), there is plenty of other evidence of London-based European-African encounters, represented in a range of cultural forms.[39] Bate and Thornton collate the presence of significant artifacts that testify to England's interactions with different regions of Africa: a clock shaped like an "Ethiop riding upon a rhinoceros" seen in Whitehall in 1599, for example, and a horn from the Calabar region of modern Nigeria that was inscribed and dated the same year. Bate and Thornton also point out that "the names of many 'blackamoors' . . . are to be found in the registers of the city's outer parishes," a fact that concurs with Virginia Mason Vaughan's statement in her contextual history of *Othello* that the number of black people in London was "sufficiently substantial by 1601 for Elizabeth to license sea captain Caspar van Senden to transport all Negroes and blackamoors out of England. The royal proclamation . . . followed up the Privy Council's attempt four years earlier to transport 'such slaves' back to Spain and Portugal."[40] The presence of African people in London, then, together with the anxiety and debates about human trafficking, immigration, and ethnic intermixing that resonate in *Othello,* were political and social realities in Shakespeare's time.

A range of written evidence demonstrates that, at the turn of the seventeenth century, there was also a clear understanding, or at least clear available information, about diversity within the African continent. For example, as early as 1588 or 1589, the dramatist George Peele produced "the very first representation of Moors on the early modern English stage," *The Battle of Alcazar.* This play distinguishes between two different African ethnicities: the "'barbarous Moor', the 'negro Muly Hamet' . . . and Abdelmelec, the 'brave Barbarian lord.'"[41] In 1599, meanwhile, the then Archbishop of Canterbury, George Abbott, noted in his wonderfully titled work *A briefe description of the whole world* that "although this country of Egypt doth stand in the self-same climate that Mauritania doth, yet the inhabitants there are not black, but rather dun, or tawny."[42] These examples complement the work most frequently cited by those investigating early modern European conceptions of Africa: the *Geographical Historie of Africa,* originally written in Arabic and Italian by the North African Arab scholar Al Hassan Ibn Mohammed Al Wezaz Al Fasi, now more commonly known as Leo Africanus.[43] John Pory's English translation of the work (completed in 1600) coincided with the Moroccan ambassadorial visit to London, and "its preface alludes to [the ambassador's] presence."[44]

It is widely acknowledged that the *Geographical Historie of Africa* influenced Shakespeare's conception of Othello and of *Othello.* Its relevance to my discussion of *Desdemona,* however, is somewhat different: it constitutes a long, detailed, and complex awareness of the diversity of African geography, history, and peoples at this time. Immediately following its title page is a map of the continent of Africa, which labels one northern region "Barbaria" but which clearly indicates numerous others: "Nubia," "Cafraria," and so on. The prefatory material by Richard Hakluyt, "a generall description of Africa," is as pertinent as the actual Pory translation in this regard. Hakluyt writes, for example, of "the varietiee of languages" and of "five principall nations."[45] He ascribes to a river called "Senaga or Canaga" "a separation betweene nations of sundrie colours," people on one side being "a dead ash-colour, leane, and of small stature" and those on the other being "exceeding blacke, of tall and manly stature."[46] In Pory's translation, Leo asserts from the outset that "Africa is divided into fower partes, that is to say, Babaria, Numiaida, Libya, and the lande of Negro" and goes on to describe subdivisions of "Barbarie," such as "the kingdome of Maroco," itself divided into "seven regions or provinces," as well as citing numerous names of "Negro" kingdoms.[47] In discussing the "people of Africa," he asserts a clear difference between the appearance of "the Negros or blacke Moores" and the "tawnie Moores."[48] While the book is often repetitive or contradictory and bears little

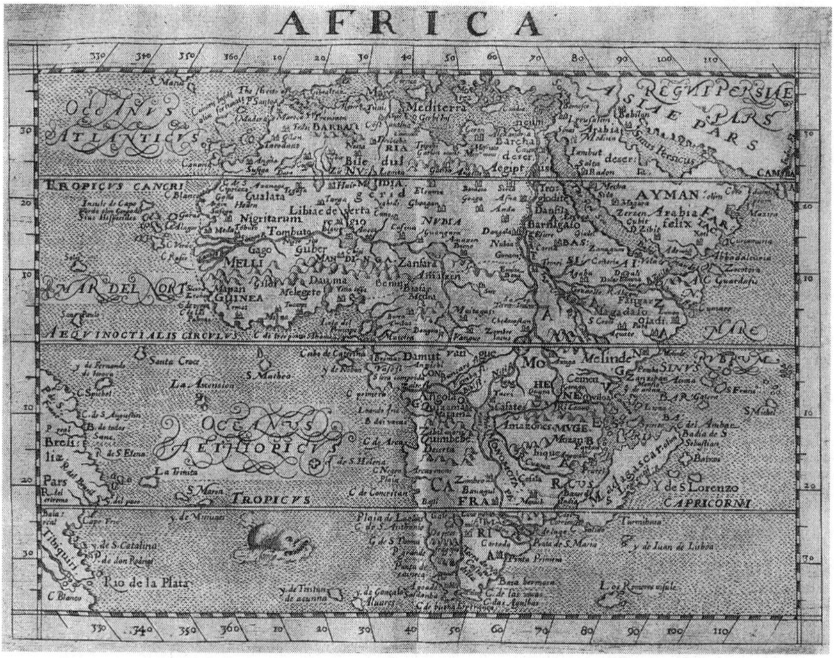

Leo Africanus, A Geographical Historie of Africa *(1601). British Library.*

resemblance to European twenty-first-century knowledge of African peoples, its existence and nature expose the oversimplification inherent in Sellars's claim that "in seventeenth-century London, 'Barbary' meant Africa."[49] As Pory's translation makes clear, in seventeenth-century London "Barbary" meant only one small area of Africa, which even within itself contained great diversity.

The irony that Sellars's use of the term "Africa" constitutes a more simplistic and broad-brush conception of the continent than that held by either Shakespeare or his contemporaries—that (in Edwards's terms) it is Sellars who attempts to smooth over or impose a prosthesis on a seventeenth-century awareness of *décalage*—raises questions as to the director's motivations. My assumption is that behind Sellars's repetitions about the "African maid with African stories and African songs" lies an anxiety about his audience acceding to the connections the project makes between African American history and culture, early modern European-North African interactions, and Mali. Sellars's detail that "Barbary pirates" were "enslaving . . . white, British crews," together with the focus on slavery in Morrison's text, suggests the collaborators' wish to address not just a black internationalist experience of slavery but also a transnational, cross-racial exploration of that institution.[50] Few would argue, I presume, with this general point that slavery is wrong; it might be more compelling, however, to tease out the specificities of slave economies in different times and places. In one sense, Mali works well as the connection between North and West Africa that Sellars intends: bordering Mauritania and Algeria to the north and Senegal, Guinea, and the Côte d'Ivoire to the south, in its position on the map it reflects exactly this transition point between North and West. Yet the director's generalities hide the fact that, from as early as the beginning of the Christian era, the territories that were to become Mali were instrumental in the trans-Saharan trade in both gold and slaves between West and North Africa.[51] In terms of the history of slavery, therefore, Mali might have as much in common with European slave traders as enablers and economic beneficiaries of slavery as it does with the African American descendants of slaves, and perhaps even more. Meanwhile, in his description of Traoré herself as "one of a new generation of African women," "musical heir to the griot traditions of the Mandean courts and the particular alchemy of Malian music that gave birth to the blues," Sellars diffuses Traoré's specific identity into a bland, generalized "Africanness" and also oversimplifies her complex relationship to Malian music.[52] His motivation, again, may be to emphasize a connection between Mali and African American history and so between Traoré and Morrison. Yet here again, he attempts to iron out discrepancies that would be more powerful left as they were.

Somewhat surprisingly, Toni Morrison's text reflects Sellars's sweeping approach to "Africa" at least as much as it complicates it. Morrison's oeuvre includes sophisticated analyses of certain aspects of West African culture, exemplified by her 2001 article on the Guinean novelist Camara Laye.[53] In her nonfiction work *Playing in the Dark,* moreover, she expounds on her groundbreaking theory of "Africanism," her term for the politically problematic Western or European tendency to use "Africanness" and "blackness" as surrogates, deployed to represent something other than themselves.[54] Yet there are some lines of the text of *Desdemona* that go so far as to exemplify the problematic features of depicting Africa or deploying "Africanness" that she has hitherto critiqued in other writers. In having Othello say to Desdemona, "I was doubted and deceived at every turn. Why? Because I am African? Because I was sold into slavery?," for example, she falls prey to the same temptation as Sellars, subsuming the specifics of Othello's experience into an implicit pan-African or African American–inflected identity.[55]

More troubling still for their recourse to the kinds of stereotype that Morrison's fiction tends to work against are Desdemona's recollections of Barbary. "Unlike the staid, unbending women of my country," she remembers, "she moved . . . [with] fluid grace," "was more alive than anyone [she] knew," and told stories about "places where . . . nature is not a crafted, pretty thing, but wild, sacred, and instructive."[56] In addition, Morrison's text repeats Shakespeare's elision of the defining experience of Barbary's life. While *Othello* reveals that Barbary "was in love, and he she loved proved mad / And did forsake her," *Desdemona* pays this detail little more attention.[57] In Morrison's text, Desdemona does relate that the forsaken maid has died of grief, but the song that Barbary sings at this moment, "M'Bifo," expresses an unhappiness that arguably articulates Desdemona's experience as much as her own: "now I know that love / can be a source of evil . . . I love you / I forgive you."[58] Even here, Barbary never gets to speak about her lover or to put her experience center stage. In some ways, therefore, both Sellars's and Morrison's conceptions of this character only reinforce her colonization, in that both, to some extent, appropriate her to explore their own interests rather than hers. Both director and author reinforce a European or white subject position, an assumption that a non-African perspective is the universal one that is exemplified by Sellars's observation, with its striking possessive pronoun that "the African is very present in our world."[59] In this they have more in common with *Othello* itself than with either Sears's *Harlem Duet,* which posits African American culture as the central and implicitly universal perspective, or Carlin's *Not Now, Sweet Desdemona,* which gives equal weight to the perspective of its white and its black protagonists.

Transnational Feminism and the Power of Traoré-as-Barbary

Not Now, Sweet Desdemona is notable for making at least a partial attempt to examine the relationship between race and gender. This same relationship plays out in the ambiguous dynamic between Barbary and Desdemona in *Desdemona* and has implications for the work's feminist agenda. As I will demonstrate, Traoré-as-Barbary succeeds in subverting, resisting, or eluding the broadbrush conceptions of both Africa and feminism to which her text writer and director at times subject her.

It is clear from Peter Sellars's foreword that, to his mind, the feminism of *Desdemona* is unambiguous and unproblematic. "In Shakespeare's late tragedies, the ideal woman . . . was mostly silent," he writes. "For Toni Morrison," he continues, "the ideal woman is not silent. Finally, she speaks. . . . Shakespeare's Desdemona is divine perfection, but Toni Morrison allows her to be human, to make mistakes, and finally, with eternity stretching before her, to learn, and then to understand."[60]

Sellars's somewhat presentist championing of Morrison's approach and apparently uncomplicated politics is echoed by most of *Desdemona*'s other promoters. In the Lincoln Center's trailer, for example, the artistic director Jane Moss describes the work as "an extraordinary piece about women. There is such performing force on the part of the women involved. There is . . . rumination on men, and violence, and Toni Morrison really evokes what this woman's life was as a Renaissance woman, which was so circumscribed that it's hard for us to imagine."[61] As with much of Sellars's prefacing, this explication adds little to a text that could hardly state more clearly the constraints on a young white woman in Venice. Yet these previews actually disguise one of the work's most interesting aspects: the persisting irresolution of Barbary and Desdemona's relationship at its end and the implications of this irresolution in terms of the potential for Barbary's empowerment.

In her opening speech, Desdemona tells us that her life was "subject to the whims of [her] elders and the control of men. . . . Men made the rules; women followed them."[62] She later states that in her childhood "constraint was the theme of behaviour" while "duty was its plot" and relates her parents' anger at her refusal of numerous suitors when she is on "the cusp of unmarriageability."[63] After describing her courtship with Othello and the "tales he told," she states that she was "captured by love and the prospect of inhabiting a broad original world where [she] could compete with the Amazons."[64] It is hard to conclude that Morrison adds significantly in any of these lines to the sense of the constraints on Desdemona that *Othello* itself presents. Shakespeare's implicit critique of Desdemona's relationship with her parents, for example, is arguably a more powerful protest.

The contemporary author again lapses into excessive explication when her Desdemona discusses Othello's loyalty to Iago: "my husband knew Iago was lying . . . so why did he act on obvious deceit?" the woman asks. "Brotherhood," she answers herself, "the quiet approval beamed from one male eye to another. Bright, tight camaraderie. . . . The wide, wild celebrity men find with each other cannot compete with the narrow comfort of a wife."[65] Morrison's interpretation of Othello's behavior here recalls her critique of the actions of the patriarchs of Ruby in her novel *Paradise* (1998) or her censure of the civil rights activist Fruit in her novel *Love* (2003) for failing to take punitive action against a co-activist rapist. But, while in those novels readers are enabled to reach this inference for themselves, in this seventh section of *Desdemona* the protagonist's words are followed by her voicing Othello's memory of his and Iago's rape of two elderly women. The combination of Desdemona's analysis of the events and a description of the events themselves is too much.

On this theme of the excesses to which male bonding can lead, there is also an interesting contrast to be drawn between Morrison's sermonizing and the approach taken by Ann-Marie MacDonald in *Goodnight Desdemona (Good Morning Juliet)*. In MacDonald's play, Tybalt and Romeo believe that the female protagonist, Constance Ledbelly, is a man. Instead of the expected fight with her/him, Romeo suggests, "now t'the baths, new friendship to baptize!"[66] Constance declines, but her comically unhappy musings on the importance of the "locker room" and of theater directors' predilection for staging all-male Shakespearean scenes in "a Roman bath" make a more powerful feminist statement about male camaraderie than does Desdemona's mournful lament in *Desdemona*.[67] Indeed, while humor is an adaptive strategy that Carlin, MacDonald, and Vogel all separately use to great effect, it is conspicuously absent from the Morrison/Sellars/Traoré collaboration as a whole.

Even Djanet Sears, whose *Harlem Duet* is the least irreverent and the most overtly painful of the adaptations I have read, employs angry humor when she negotiates the complexities of the intersections of racial and gendered oppression. In that play, Othello attempts to explain to his black wife, Billie, why he is leaving her for his white girlfriend, Mona. "The Black feminist position," he explains, "leaves me feeling unrecognized as a man."[68] When he suggests that black women used to be happy staying at home, Billie protests, "most Black women have been working like mules since we arrived on this continent. When White women were burning their bras, we were hired to hold their tits up."[69] In this graphic image, Sears pinpoints the disconnect that has long troubled Morrison and that she first articulated in a 1971 *New York Times Magazine* article. To her direct question in that essay, "What do black women think about Women's Lib?," Morrison gives her own straight-talking answer: "Distrust. It is white, therefore suspect."[70] *Desdemona* dramatizes exactly this conflict, first through the meeting of the mothers of Othello and Desdemona and then in the latter's direct conversation with Barbary.

In Morrison's text, the Venetian Madam Brabantio (Desdemona's mother) tells Soun (Othello's mother) that the pair are "enemies" because their "vengeance is more molten than [their] sorrow." In turn, Soun asserts that, despite their different religions (she prayed to her "gods" while Madam Brabantio turned to "Mother Mary"), the pair "have much to share."[71] This scene ends unresolved, however, with no guarantee that the women will find solace from their common bereavement or that they will find any mutual comfort in each other's spiritual practice. In its maintaining of an unevenness or an uncomfortable irresolution, it anticipates the piece's penultimate scene, in which Desdemona attempts complete solidarity with Barbary. Just as in the preceding scene Emilia invokes class difference to point out that her friendship with Desdemona was not straightforward, here Barbary (speaking for the first time in the piece) resists Desdemona's attempts at joyful reunion by pointing out that "you don't even know my name."[72] Morrison thereby illuminates the nonanalogous positions of the North African enslaved woman—whose real name turns out to be "Sa'ran"—and the Venetian gentlewoman. Desdemona's first speech opens with the lines "my name is Desdemona. The word, Desdemona, means misery. It means ill fated. It means doomed," and closes with the self-determining insistence "I am not the meaning of a name I did not choose."[73] By contrast, Barbary/Sa'ran unsettles Desdemona and audience members alike by pointing out (in a detail that immediately brings to mind the renaming of enslaved West Africans by transatlantic slave traders and purchasers) that her real name has been kept secret for all these years from the Europeans among whom she has had to live.

The nonwhite woman responds to Desdemona's assertion "Sa'ran, . . . you were my best friend" with the terse rebuttal "I was your slave." She insists on the permanence of irreconcilable difference: "I am black-skinned. You are white-skinned."[74] Desdemona argues that their shared gender gives them a point of communication and sympathy: "we are women. . . . My prison was unlike yours but it was prison still."[75] Yet the sense of imminent powerful female alliance is then eclipsed by the next and final dialogue, which reverts to Desdemona conversing with her ventriloquized Othello. The romantic man/woman relationship is thus privileged over the woman/woman relationship, and although the spectacle of the closing song ("Kélé Mande," or "War Is Not Good") involves only women, its words appear to apply more to Othello and Desdemona than to Barbary/Sa'ran and Desdemona. While the music at the performance's end is profoundly peaceful, a provocative irresolution persists in that complete understanding and acceptance have never been voiced or enacted between Barbary and Desdemona. The visual contrast with the piece's opening scene is suggestive: while *Desdemona* begins with Desdemona speaking and holding center stage, it ends with her lying on the floor, while the closing articulations, in musical form, belong to the still-standing Barbary.

It would be unfortunate if my own critique of *Desdemona* were (however inadvertently) to reinstate or reinforce the erasure or silencing of a hitherto marginalized woman of color.[76] Mindful of the imperative to analyze the nature of the Barbary that exists independent of Sellars's rhetoric, my thesis is that Traoré-as-Barbary is, in fact, the most successful, or the least compromised, element of this whole collaborative piece. Her success, both aesthetic and political, rests in no small part on the complexity of the racial, national, geographical, and historical identities that she encompasses. She resists oversimplification or insists on a meaningful *décalage.* Second, she embodies specific subversions and interventions through the fact that her combined voicings in Bambara, in French, and in music maintain a certain untranslatability to a European and Euro-American audience. Sellars wholeheartedly endorses Morrison's rejection of silence, and Morrison has Desdemona celebrate the fact that (in a rewriting of the *Beloved*'s "unspeakable thoughts, unspoken") "the unspeakable is no longer."[77] Traoré-as-Barbary, on the other hand, remains to some extent inaccessible, to some extent masked and in some ways silent or inaudible, unknown, unknowable, and thus "un-ownable." The multifaceted suggestiveness of this character, or of this compound of creator/character/performer, leads me to wonder whether the piece might have been better entitled *Barbary,* or even *Sa'ran.* On the other hand, it may be that Barbary has greatest effect, or the greatest power to "articulate"—in Edwards's sense of the dual process of "linkage" and "separation" that is required for "movement" or change—in the apparent shadow of the eponymous Desdemona.[78]

Specific details about Mali, about women in Mali, about Malian music, and about Rokia Traoré's position in relation to all of these details illuminate the efficacious multiplicities of the Traoré-as-Barbary figure. The traditional music for which Mali is famous is that made by the music-making group or caste known as the *jelis;* it is "essentially Africa's classical music."[79] As Lucy Durán explains, "the *jelis* are hereditary musicians, praise singers and historians, who for centuries have dominated professional music in the region and have their own repertoire and musical instruments."[80] But, as Traoré states on her website, she is "not a Malian traditional singer." She is not a *jeli* but is from the noble or "freeborn" caste or stratum of society.[81] "The Traorés were nobles, noble warriors who represented the agricultural people," she told an interviewer, Robert Ambrose, in 2001, and she was therefore somewhat transgressive in her choice of career. In her music, she says, she aims to create "something contemporary with traditional instruments."[82] In *Desdemona* and elsewhere, she combines electric guitar and other modern or originally Western sounds with traditional instruments such as the *n'goni.* Her ambivalent relationship with traditional Malian music, in that she is both shaped by it and revises or changes it, epitomizes a kind of double consciousness (or even multiple consciousness) that usefully informs the role of Barbary. In her first collaboration with Peter Sellars, which was a piece called *Wati,* staged at Vienna's New Crowned Hope Festival in December 2006, she rewrote Western tradition by reconfiguring Mozart as a *griot,* or West African storytelling musician.[83] Not dissimilarly, in her role as Barbary she revises our perceptions of both Shakespeare and the early modern world through her audacious eclecticism. This is best exemplified by a survey of the nine songs she brings together in the piece: two ("M'Bifo" and "Kélé Mandi") are her own songs from a previous album, *Bowmboi* (2003); one, "Dianfa," is from her more recent album *Tchamantché* (2009). One, "Keme Bouramah," is her version of a traditional warrior song of the Great Epic Mandingo. For "Someone Leans Near," she wrote only the accompaniment to the lyrics by Morrison; she did the same for Shakespeare's "willow song." Finally, there are three songs, all sung in Bambara, that she composed especially for the production: "Desdemona," "Othello," and "Dongori."

Traoré's Malian identity also brings to Barbary and to *Desdemona* a complex position in relation to feminism. As Imperato describes it, traditional Malian society is patriarchal and polygamous, consisting of patrilineal, patrilocal, and gerontocratic structures.[84] Yet, as Durán observes, "in Mande culture men usually play the instruments while women are the singers," and as a result "many of their songs have concerned issues that affect women adversely, such as polygamy and arranged marriages."[85] In her position at the microphone in *Desdemona,* therefore, and in singing with male instrumentalists, Traoré is in line with Malian tradition, but in accompanying herself on the guitar she breaks with it and suggests a self-sufficiency, the absence of a dependence on men. In the lyrics of her song "Dongori" (meaning "thorn"), she rewrites a traditional proverb about a woman's bridal veil being her funeral shroud, claiming instead to exemplify "self-respect" and "self-esteem" in marriage.[86] In the piece, this song appears after the conversation between the protagonists' mothers, Soun and Madam Brabantio; it speaks of Barbary's own unfulfilled aspirations for her own relationship as much as it is an implicit critique of Desdemona's submissiveness and self-denial. Barbary appears to voice the championing of women's rights that is a consistent theme of both the song lyrics and the perspective (expressed in interviews) of Traoré herself.[87]

In addition, the historical relationship between Malian and African American musical traditions, and Traoré's inevitably complicated relationship to this connection, is a powerful subtext to the transatlantic connections upon which *Desdemona* insists. "Today," writes Nigel Williamson, "it is widely accepted that the origins of the music developed by black sharecroppers in the Mississippi Delta in the early decades of the twentieth century can be traced back to Africa via the slave ships."[88] The connection between the blues and West African music is performed in famous collaborations such as that of the American Ry Cooder and the Malian Ali Farka Touré (himself a one-time mentor of Rokia Traoré), and "in recent decades the cross-pollination has grown more complicated as the music has travelled back and forth across the Atlantic."[89] In a nuance that Sellars elides in his foreword, Traoré's music (both derived and different from traditional Malian music linked to the blues) is both part and not part of this connection. More interesting still is the fact that she has forged independent links with the African American musical tradition. Growing up, she says, she tried to imitate the voices of Ella Fitzgerald and Louis Armstrong as well as those of Malian singers, and in recent years she has produced her own version of songs popularized by Billie Holliday, such as "The Man I Love" and "Gloomy Sunday."[90] Traoré's palimpsestic musical history and pedigree contribute shades and textures to the role of Barbary, enabling that character both to resist and to affirm the connections to transatlantic slavery and African American culture that are high on Sellars's and Morrison's agendas.

The musical interactions between Africa and African America find an echo of sorts in one brilliant aspect of *Desdemona*'s staging. In all performances, the floor of the otherwise bare stage is replete with candles, glass jam jars, and light bulbs, an invocation of both traditional African American and some traditional African burial practices. As Vlach has argued, "the cemetery" in "rural Afro-America" is where we find "the strongest material demonstration of African-inspired memories." Vlach links the "pressed-glass containers," "light bulbs," and "flashlights" found on some black American graves to accounts of objects found on the graves of chiefs in Kongo.[91] In both places there is a preference for objects that are

Rokia Traoré as Barbary in the Barbican production of Desdemona *(2012). Photograph by Mark Allan, markallanphotography.co.uk.*

reflective, representing "the watery transition between life and death."[92] What particularly appeals about both this aspect of *Desdemona*'s set and the complex textures of the music of Traoré-as-Barbary is that they (like African American spirituals) are a coded communication that excludes the dominant culture or that eludes those who are ignorant of what they are ignorant of. There is similar subversive potential in the fact that only those with preexisting knowledge of Malian culture can appreciate the empowering connotations of Traoré's use of the Bambara language and Morrison's choice of the name "Sa'ran." While in the context of *Othello* and of early modern Europe Barbary is at the bottom of society's hierarchy, in Mali Bambara is the dominant language (besides French) and the one that "tends to be spoken in most administrative centres because a high proportion of administrators are Bambara."[93] The name "Sa'ran," meanwhile, is traditionally one of the Keita family, one of the imperial or ruling clans.[94] Such details imply that in her homeland Barbary would be a person of high status, just as Shakespeare's Othello asserts he "takes [his] life and being / From men of royal siege."[95]

Joshua Hammer's analysis of the violence in Mali in 2012 in the *New York Review of Books,* meanwhile, testifies to recent transatlantic connections among Mali, Europe, and the Americas that are, regrettably, far less uplifting than shared musical traditions and productions. The role of France in suppressing the jihadists in Mali in 2012 and the ensuing retaliatory seizure of Western workers at the Amenas gasworks in the Algerian Sahara sheds interesting retrospective light on the Nanterre performances of *Desdemona* in October 2011.[96] Less well known, however, is that "the U.S. trained and provided supplies to Malian troops between 2005 and 2011," although this did not prove effective in safeguarding the country from the rebels.[97] And in an uncanny echo of the transcultural links forged by those who profited from the transatlantic slave trade, in the first decade of the twenty-first century "high ranking Malian officials and Muslim militants worked together in the drug trade—turning part of the Sahara desert into a transit point for cocaine between South America and Europe."[98] These new aspects of Atlantic world exchange contribute their own ironic dimensions to the figure of Traoré-as-Barbary.

The voicings that constitute *Desdemona* are sometimes radical in their power, at others frustrating in their impotence. *Desdemona*'s most self-defeating articulations are often in its all-encompassing paratexts: Sellars's assertion that "Africa was as imaginary for Shakespeare as it is for the World Bank," for example, or the baffling choice of an image of Aung San Suu Kyi for the front of the Nanterre production's program.[99] The book of the text, published in July 2012, with its crudely presented and unidentified translations of Traoré's lyrics, does violence rather than justice to the nuances, the *décalage,* of the piece in performance. These nuances in performance, as I have shown, are largely expressed by Traoré-as-Barbary, that complex compound who uses her music at once to translate difference and to insist on a potent untranslatability. In this she recalls *Beloved,* that haunting configuration of a subtler and more elusive Morrisonian prose, whose footsteps echo long after the novel's epilogue declares she is forgotten: "her footprints come and go, come and go."[100]

Notes

Introduction

1. Martin W. Lewis, "Dividing the Ocean Sea," *Geographical Review* 89, no. 2 (1999): 188–214. Alison Games, "Atlantic History: Definitions, Challenges, and Opportunities," *American Historical Review* 111, no. 3 (June 2006): 742–43; Joyce E. Chaplin, "The Atlantic Ocean and Its Contemporary Meanings, 1492–1808," in *Atlantic History: A Critical Appraisal,* ed. Jack P. Greene and Philip D. Morgan (New York: Oxford University Press, 2009), 36–38.

2. Alfred Crosby, *The Columbian Exchange: Biological and Cultural Consequences of 1492* (Westport, Conn.: Greenwood, 1972); William Cronon, *Changes in the Land: Indians, Colonists, and the Ecology of New England* (New York: Hill and Wang, 1983).

3. James Hart Merrell, *The Indians' New World: Catawbas and Their Neighbors from European Contact Through the Era of Removal* (Chapel Hill: Published for the Institute of Early American History and Culture, Williamsburg, Va., by the University of North Carolina Press, c1989); Richard White, *The Middle Ground: Indians, Empires, and Republics in the Great Lakes Region, 1650–1815* (New York: Cambridge University Press, 1991); Colin G. Calloway, *New Worlds for All: Indians, Europeans, and the Remaking of Early America* (Baltimore: Johns Hopkins University Press, 1997).

4. Marcus Rediker, *The Slave Ship: A Human History* (New York: Viking, 2007), 9–10; James Sidbury and Jorge Cañizares-Esguerra, "Mapping Ethnogenesis in the Early Modern Atlantic," *William and Mary Quarterly* 68, no. 2 (April 2011), 181–208; Karen B. Graubart, "Ethnicity," in *The Princeton Companion to Atlantic History,* ed. Joseph C. Miller, (Princeton, N.J.: Princeton University Press, 2015), 192.

5. Joyce E. Chaplin, "Race," in *The British Atlantic World, 1500–1800,* ed. David Armitage and Michael J. Braddick (New York: Palgrave Macmillan, 2002), 173.

6. *Revenge* (Sloop) Papers 1741–1801, Massachusetts Historical Society; Jane Landers, "The Atlantic Transformations of Francisco Menéndez," in *Biography and the Black Atlantic,* ed. Lisa A. Lindsay and John Wood Sweet (Philadelphia: University of Pennsylvania Press, 2013), 209–23; Jane Landers, *Black Society in Spanish Florida* (Urbana: University of Illinois Press, 1999).

7. Winthrop D. Jordan, *White over Black: American Attitudes toward the Negro, 1550–1812* (Chapel Hill, N.C.: Published for the Institute of Early American History and Culture at Williamsburg, Va., by The University of North Carolina Press, 1968), vii–xiv; Chaplin, "Race," 173–74; Joyce E. Chaplin, *Subject Matter: Technology, the Body, and Science on the Anglo-American Frontier, 1500–1676* (Cambridge, Mass.: Harvard University

Press, 2003); Martha Hodes, "The Mercurial Nature and Abiding Power of Race: A Transnational Family Story," *American Historical Review* 108, no. 1 (February 2003), 84–85; James Sidbury, "Race," in *The Princeton Companion to Atlantic History,* ed. Joseph C. Miller (Princeton, N.J.: Princeton University Press, 2015), 387–89.

8. Louis Montrose, "The Work of Gender in the Discourse of Discovery," *Representations,* no. 33, "Special Issue: The New World" (Winter 1991), 1–41; Sarah M. S. Pearsall, "Gender," in *The British Atlantic World, 1500–1800,* ed. David Armitage and Michael J. Braddick (New York: Palgrave Macmillan, 2002), 133–36; Nora E. Jaffary, ed., *Gender, Race, and Religion in the Colonization of the Americas* (Burlington, Vt.: Ashgate, 2007).

9. Pearsall, "Gender," 134.

10. Kathleen M. Brown, *Good Wives, Nasty Wenches, and Anxious Patriarchs: Gender, Race, and Power in Colonial Virginia* (Chapel Hill, N.C.: Published for the Institute of Early American History and Culture at Williamsburg, Va., by The University of North Carolina Press, 1996), 42–74.

11. Francisco Javier Cevallos-Candau, ed., *Coded Encounters: Writing, Gender, and Ethnicity in Colonial Latin America* (Amherst: University of Massachusetts Press, 1995); Karen Powers, *Women in the Crucible of Conquest: The Gendered Genesis of Spanish American Society, 1500–1600* (Albuquerque: University of New Mexico Press, 2005); Ann Twinam, *Public Lives, Private Secrets: Gender, Honor, Sexuality, and Illegitimacy in Colonial Spanish America* (Stanford, Calif.: Stanford University Press, 1999); Catalina de Erauso, *Lieutenant Nun: Memoirs of a Basque Transvestite in the New World,* trans. Michele Stepto and Gabri Stepto (Boston: Beacon Press, 1997).

12. Eliga H. Gould, "Entangled Atlantic Histories: A Response from the Anglo-American Periphery," *American Historical Review* 112, no. 5 (December 2007): 1418.

13. Gould, "Entangled Atlantic Histories."

14. David Armitage, "Three Concepts of Atlantic History," *The British Atlantic World, 1500–1800,* ed. David Armitage and Michael J. Braddick (New York: Palgrave Macmillan, 2002), 13; Isaac Land, "Tidal Waves: The New Coastal History," *Journal of Social History* 40, no. 3 (Spring 2007): 731; Peter A. Coclanis, "Drang Nach Osten: Bernard Bailyn, the World-Island, and the Idea of Atlantic History," *Journal of World History* 13, no. 1 (2002): 171; Peter A. Coclanis, "Atlantic World or Atlantic/World?," *William and Mary Quarterly* 63, no. 4 (October 2006): 741; Peter A. Coclanis, "Beyond Atlantic History," in *Atlantic History: A Critical Approach,* ed. Jack P. Greene and Philip D. Morgan (New York: Oxford University Press, 2009), 337–51.

15. Paul Gilroy, *The Black Atlantic: Modernity and Double Consciousness* (Cambridge, Mass.: Harvard University Press, 1993), 15.

16. Armitage, "Three Concepts of Atlantic History"; Patrick Griffin, "A Plea for a New Atlantic History," *William and Mary Quarterly* 68, no. 2 (April 2011): 236.

17. Jorge Cañizares-Esguerra and Benjamin Breen, "Hybrid Atlantics: Future Directions for the History of the Atlantic World," *History Compass* 11, no. 8 (2013): 597–609.

18. Luis Martin, *Daughters of the Conquistadores: Women of the Viceroyalty of Peru* (Dallas: Southern Methodist University Press, 1989); Susan Socolow, *The Women of Colonial Latin America* (New York: Cambridge University Press, 2000), 90–111; James H.

Sweet, *Recreating Africa: Culture, Kinship, and Religion in the African-Portuguese World, 1441–1770* (Chapel Hill: University of North Carolina Press, 2004); Herman Bennett, *Africans in Colonial Mexico: Absolutism, Christianity, and Afro-Creole Consciousness, 1570–1640* (Bloomington: Indiana University Press, 2005).

19. Patricia Seed, *Ceremonies of Possession in Europe's Conquest of the New World, 1492–1640* (New York: Cambridge University Press, 1995); Jill Lepore, *The Name of War: King Philip's War and the Origins of American Identity* (New York: Vintage Books, 1998); Anthony F. C. Wallace, *Jefferson and the Indians: The Tragic Fate of the First Americans* (Cambridge, Mass.: Harvard University Press, 1999).

20. Coclanis, "Atlantic World or Atlantic/World?" 741–42; Coclanis, "Beyond Atlantic History."

21. Wim Klooster, "The Rise and Transformation of the Atlantic World," in *The Atlantic World: Essays on Slavery, Migration, and Imagination,* ed. Wim Klooster and Alfred Padula (Upper Saddle River, N.J.: Prentice Hall, 2005), 1–42; Douglas R. Egerton, Alison Games, Jane G. Landers, Kris Lane, and Donald R. Wright, *The Atlantic World: A History, 1400–1888 (*Wheeling, Ill.: Harlan Davidson, 2007).

"Our Dutchmen run after them very much"

1. Allen Trelease, *Indian Affairs in Colonial New York: The Seventeenth Century*. Ithaca: Cornell University Press, 1960), 172.

2. Tom Arne Midtrød, "The Flemish Bastard and the Former Indians: Métis and Identity in Seventeenth Century New York," American Indian Quarterly 34 (Winter 2010): 83–108. Nan A. Rothschild, Colonial Encounters in a Native American Landscape: The Spanish and Dutch in North America (Washington, D.C.: Smithsonian Books, 2003).

3. Jaap Jacobs, *The Colony of New Netherland: A Dutch Settlement in Seventeenth Century America* (Ithaca: Cornell University Press, 2009), 209–211. Paul Otto, *The Dutch Munsee Encounter in America: The Struggle for Sovereignty in the Hudson Valley* (New York: Berghahn Books, 2006), 139.

The exception here is Susanah Shaw Romney, who creatively reads the absence of evidence for cross-cultural sex as an explanation for the frequent violence that characterized Dutch relations with Algonquians on New Netherland's coast and the often tense interactions between the Dutch and the Iroquois in the upper Hudson Valley. Because the Dutch did not form extensive kinship relations with either group, misunderstandings and affronts tended to snowball rather than be resolved. Cross-cultural sex emerges as central in her analysis much more for its absence than for its presence. Susanah Shaw Romney, *New Netherland Connections: Intimate Networks and Atlantic Ties in Seventeenth-Century America* (Chapel Hill: University of North Carolina Press for the Omohundro Institute of Early American History and Culture, 2014), chapter 3.

4. Rothschild briefly notes that it is strange that the Dutch men should be so averse to sex with Mohawk women when it seemed as if the same men favored concubinage with local women in Batavia, but she could offer no explanation for this divergence. Rothschild, *Colonial Encounters in a Native American Landscape,* x.

5. Wim Klooster, *The Dutch Moment: War, Trade, and Settlement in the Seventeenth Century Atlantic World* (Ithaca, N.Y.: Cornell University Press, 2016), 2.

6. Femme Gaastra, *The Dutch East India Company: Expansion and Decline* (Zutphen: Walburg Pers, 2003), 81. Klooster, *The Dutch Moment*, 121–22.

7. Daniel Livesay, "Emerging from the Shadows: New Developments in the History of Interracial Sex and Intermarriage in Colonial North America and the Caribbean," *History Compass* 13, no. 3 (2015): 122.

8. Ann Stoler has made just such a plea for comparisons between North America and the rest of the world in order to understand what might be unique about North America. Ann Laura Stoler, "Tense and Tender Ties: The Politics of Comparison in North American History and (Post) Colonial Studies," *The Journal of American History* 88, no. 3 (2001): 831.

9. This critique has been offered most vociferously by Peter Coclanis, "Atlantic World or Atlantic/World?" *William and Mary Quarterly* 63, no. 4 (2006): 725–742. Also see Alison Games, "Beyond the Atlantic: English Globetrotters and Transoceanic Connections," *William and Mary Quarterly* 63, no. 4 (2006): 675–692.

10. Natalie Zemon Davis, "Decentering History: Local Stories and Cultural Crossings in a Global World," *History and Theory* 50, no. 2 (2011): 202.

11. Charles Gehring, "New Netherland: The Formative Years, 1609–1632" in *Four Centuries of Dutch-American Relations, 1609-2009*, eds. Hans Krabbendam, Cornelis A. van Minnen, and Giles Scott-Smith (Albany: State University of New York Press, 2009) 75–79. Debates within the directorship of the WIC over whether colonization was, in fact, the best policy persisted until 1638, with one faction calling for an agricultural colony and another faction arguing that colonization would imperil the fur trade by alienating Indigenous people. By 1638, the colonization faction had clearly gained ascendancy. These debates are discussed in Van Cleaf Bachman, *Peltries or Plantations: The Economic Policies of the Dutch West India Company in New Netherlands, 1623–1639* (Baltimore: Johns Hopkins University Press, 1969).

12. Jaap Jacobs "Migration, Population, and Government in New Netherland" in *Four Centuries of Dutch-American Relations, 1609–2009*, ed. Hans Krabbendam, Cornelis A. van Minnen, and Giles Scott-Smith (Albany: State University of New York Press, 2009), 86.

13. A. J. F. van Laer, *Council Minutes, 1638–1649* (Baltimore: Genealogical Pub. Co., 1974), 4. On Kieft as a reformer, see Willem Frijhoff, *Fulfilling God's Mission: The Two Worlds of Dominie Everardus Bogardus, 1607–1647* (Boston: Brill, 2007), 346.

14. For accounts of the Munsee, see Robert S. Grumet, *First Manhattans: A Brief History of the Munsee Indians* (Norman: University of Oklahoma Press, 2011) and Otto, *The Dutch Munsee Encounter in America*. One prosecution came in 1638 against Nicolaes Coorn, a Company sergeant, for a variety of offenses that included theft, illegal private trading, and dereliction of duty, as well as adultery with "Indian women and negresses." Van Laer, *Council Minutes, 1638–1649*, 33–34. The second was in 1639 against Hans Steen. Van Laer, *Council Minutes, 1638–1649*, 43–45.

15. Van Laer, *Council Minutes, 1638–1649*, 122. It is worth nothing that the word

"adultery" (*overspel*) in early modern Dutch could encompass both the modern meaning of adultery as well as what early modern people often called fornication, that is, sex before marriage.

16. On the departure of the Munsee after 1656, see Otto, *The Dutch Munsee Encounter*, 148.

17. A. J. F. van Laer, *Van Rensselaer Bowier Manuscripts, Being the Letters of Kiliaen van Rensselaer, 1630–1643* (Albany: University of the State of New York, 1908), 442.

18. Van Laer, *Van Rensselaer Bowier Manuscripts,* 694–95.

19. Dean R. Snow, Charles T. Gehring, and William A. Starna, eds. *In Mohawk Country: Early Narratives about a Native People* (Syracuse: Syracuse University Press, 1996), 42–43.

20. E. T. Corwin, *Ecclesiastical Records of the State of New York* (Albany: J.B. Lyon, 1901–1916), vol. 1, 310.

21. Charles Gehring, ed. *Fort Orange Court Minutes, 1652–1660* (Syracuse: Syracuse University Press, 1990), 454.

22. Snow, Gehring, and Starna, *In Mohawk Country,* 91.

23. Van Laer, *Minutes of the Courts of Albany,* 86.

24. Thomas E. Burke, Jr., *Mohawk Frontier: The Dutch Community of Schenectady, New York, 1661–1710* (Ithaca: Cornell University Press, 1991), 147.

25. New York State Archives A1810, vol. 13, 116. The case of Jacob *mijn vrient* is extremely interesting. According to Stuyvesant's letter, he had stolen goods he had been given by others to trade with the Susquehannock, so he could not return to New Netherland. Instead, he seems to have taken up residence in Delaware, but in the late 1670s he settled in Maryland, where, in 1682, he was accused of plotting with the Susquehannock against the English. Part of the accusation presented against him was that he had a wife and children from that nation and so was better disposed toward them than the English. Jacob vehemently denied that he had a Susquehannock wife or children. William H. Browne, ed., *Archives of Maryland. Vol. 7. Proceedings and Acts of the General Assembly of Maryland, October 1678–November 1683* (Baltimore: Maryland Historical Society, 1889), 386–87.

26. Adriaen van der Donck, *A Description of New Netherland,* ed. Charles Gehring and William Starna and trans. Diederik Willem Goedhuys (Lincoln: University of Nebraska Press, 2008), 75.

27. David Pietersz de Vries, "Third Voyage" in *Narratives of New Netherland, 1609–1664*, ed. Franklin Jameson (New York: Charles Scribner, 1909), 231.

28. On critically reading English descriptions of Indigenous people in North America and the European agendas that these descriptions obliquely express, see Karen O. Kupperman, "Presentment of Civility: English Reading of American Self-Presentation in the Early Years of Colonization," *The William and Mary Quarterly*, 54 no. 1 (Jan. 1997): 193–228.

29. This possibility is discussed more fully in Deborah Hamer, "Creating an Orderly Society: The Regulation of Marriage and Sex in the Dutch Atlantic World, 1621–1674" (Ph.D. diss. Columbia University, 2014), 123–24, 191–92.

30. Johannes Reitsma and S. D. van Veen, eds., *Acta der provinciale en particuliere synoden, gehouden in de Noordelijke Nederlanden gedurende de jaren 1572–1620* (Groningen: J. B. Wolters, 1892-1899), vol. 2, 4.

31. For lobbying in North Holland in 1596, see Reitsma and van Veen, *Acta der provinciale en particuliere synoden,* vol. 1, 223. For activity in 1622 in South Holland, see W. P. C. Knuttel, *Acta de particuliere synoden van Zuid-Holland, 1621–1700,* ('s-Gravenhage: Martinus Nijhoff, 1908-1916), vol. 1, 40–41.

32. Herman Roodenburg, *Onder censuur: de kerkelijke tucht in de gereformeerde gemeente van Amsterdam, 1578-1700* (Hilversum: Verloren, 1990), 91–92.

33. For example, in November 1616, Amsterdam forbade Jews and Christians from having sex with one another, explicitly including sex with Christian prostitutes. Hermanus Noordkerk, *Handvesten; ofte privilegien ende octroyen mitsgaders willekeuren, costuimen, ordonnantien en handelingen der stad amstelredam* (Te Amstelredam: Hendrik van Waesberge en Salomon en Petrus Schouten, 1747-1755), vol. 2, 472.

34. E. M. Koen, "The Earliest Sources Relating to the Portuguese Jews in the Municipal Archives of Amsterdam up to 1620" *Studia Rosenthaliana* 4, no. 1 (January 1970): 33–34.

35. Roodenburg, *Onder censuur,* 183. Daniel Swetschinski, *Reluctant Cosmopolitans: The Portuguese Jews of Seventeenth Century Amsterdam* (London: The Littman Library of Jewish Civilization, 2000), 13–15, 217–18.

36. Gaastra, *The Dutch East India Company,* 85.

37. Gaastra, *The Dutch East India Company,* 86.

38. W. Ph. Coolhaas, *Generale Missiven van Gouverneurs-Generaal en Raden aan Heren XVII der Verenigde Oostindische Compagnie* ('s-Gravenhage: Martinus Nijhoff, 1960), vol. 1, 7.

39. Coolhaas, *Generale Missiven,* vol. 1, 10.

40. My thanks to Guillaume Aubert for pointing out the brutality inherent in Both's analogy to the acts of Romulus.

41. J. A. Van der Chijs, *Nederlandsch-Indisch Plakaatboek, 1602–1811* (Batavia: Landsdrukkerij, 1885–1900), vol. 1, 46–47.

42. Jakob Mooij, *Bouwstoffen voor de geschiedenis der Protestantsche kerk in Nederlandsch-Indië* (Weltevreden: Landsdrukkerij, 1927–1931), vol. 1, 102–3. The language of the consistory's decision suggests that it applied equally to both baptized men and women who sought marriages to unbaptized partners of the opposite sex. Because of the demographic situation in Batavia, in which female migration from the Dutch Republic was suppressed, when Dutch people who sought to make use of this provision almost certainly would have been Dutch men seeking to marry non-European, non-Christian women.

43. Mooij, *Bouwstoffen,* vol. 1, 221.

44. Mooij, *Bouwstoffen,* vol. 1, 215. The consistory also planned to set aside time from 8 A.M. to 9 A.M. specifically to catechize these women. Mooij, *Bouwstoffen,* vol. 1, 227.

45. Van der Chijs, *Nederlandsch-Indisch Plakaatboek,* vol. 1, 459–60.

46. Leonard Blussé, "The Eclipse of the Inibs: The Dutch Protestant Mission in 17th Century Taiwan and its Persecution of Native Priestesses," in *History, Culture and Ethnicity:*

Selected Papers from the International Conference on the Formosan Indigenous Peoples, ed. Chuen-rong Yeh (Taipei: Shung Ye Museum of Formosan Aborigines, 2006), 74.

47. Van der Chijs, *Nederlandsch-Indisch Plakaatboek,* vol. 2, 90.

48. Ulbe Bosma and Remco Raben, *Being "Dutch" in the Indies: A History of Creolisation and Empire, 1500-1920* (Athens: Ohio University Press, 2008), 35.

49. Jean Gelman Taylor, *The Social World of Batavia: Europeans and Eurasians in Colonial Indonesia* (Madison, Wis: University of Wisconsin Press, 2009), 34.

50. On Cornelia's marriage to Pieter Cnoll, see Leonard Blussé, *Bitter Bonds: A Colonial Divorce Drama of the Seventeenth Century* (Princeton, NJ: M. Wiener Publishers, 2002), 41–54. On the ongoing conflict in her marriage with Johan Bitter, see Blussé, Bitter Bonds, chapters 5–9.

51. Van der Chijs, *Nederlandsch-Indisch Plakaatboek,* vol. 1, 82.

52. The first renovation occurred in 1622. Van der Chijs, *Nederlandsch-Indisch Plakaatboek,* vol. 1, 99–102. Another renovation occurred the following year. Van der Chijs, *Nederlandsch-Indisch Plakaatboek,* vol. 1, 111. The rules against concubinage were also included in the first general legal code for Batavia which appeared in 1642. Van der Chijs, *Nederlandsch-Indisch Plakaatboek,* vol. 1, 586.

53. Bosma and Raben, *Being "Dutch,"* 13.

54. B. Watson Andaya, "From Temporary Wife to Prostitute: Sexuality and Economic Change in Early Modem Southeast Asia," *Journal of Women's History* 9, no. 4 (1998): 16. In the course of the eighteenth century, this type of temporary wife arrangement would come to be understood as dishonorable because of European influences.

55. Dhiravat na Pombejra, "VOC Employees and their Relationships with Mon and Siamese Women: A Case Study of Osoet Pegua" in *Other Pasts: Women, Gender and History in Early Modern Southeast Asia,* ed. Barbara Watson Andaya (Honolulu: Center for Southeast Asian Studies, 2000), 200–205.

56. Pombejra, "VOC Employees," 208–9.

57. Wim Klooster and Gert Oostindie, *Realm between Empires: The Second Dutch Atlantic, 1680–1815* (Ithaca: Cornell University Press, 2019), 99. The Dutch began to trade for enslaved people at Elmina in 1650, but during the seventeenth century, gold and ivory remained far more significant. In the eighteenth century, the slave trade at Elmina would become more significant to the Dutch, though much of the trade was still carried out by coasting ships on the Gold Coast rather than directly through the personnel at the fort. Klooster and Oostindie, *Realm between Empires,* 82–85.

58. Natalie Everts, "A Motley Company: Differing Identities among Euro-Africans in Eighteenth Century Elmina" in *Brokers of Change: Atlantic Commerce and Cultures in Pre-colonial Western Africa*, ed. Toby Green, (Oxford: Published for the British Academy by Oxford University Press, 2012), 55–77.

59. Pernille Ipsen, *Daughters of the Trade: Atlantic Slavers and Interracial Marriage on the Gold Coast* (Philadelphia: University of Pennsylvania Press, 2015), 33–35.

60. On rape, see Sowande' M. Mustakeem, *Slavery at Sea: Terror, Sex, and Sickness in the Middle Passage* (Urbana: University of Illinois Press, 2016), 84–85.

61. Natalie Everts, "'Brought up well according to European standards': Helena van der Burgh and Whilhelmina van Naarssen: Two Christian Women from Elmina" in

Merchants, Missionaries and Migrants: 300 Years of Dutch-Ghanaian Relations, ed, I. an Kessel (Amsterdam: KIT Publishers, 2002),102.

62. Mark Meuwese, *Brothers in Arms, Partners in Trade: Dutch-Indigenous Alliances in the Atlantic World, 1595-1674* (Leiden: Brill, 2012), 65–66.

63. K Ratelband, ed. *Vijf Dagregisters van het kasteel sao gorge da Mina (Elmina) aan de Goudkust (1645–1647)* (S'Gravenhage: Martinus Nijhoff, 1953), 179.

64. Wim Klooster, *The Dutch Moment: War, Trade, and Settlement in the Seventeenth Century Atlantic World* (Ithaca: Cornell University Press, 2016), 80.

65. Mark Meuwese discusses this incident in "The Murder of Jacob Rabe: Contesting Dutch Colonial Authority in the Borderlands of Northeastern Brazil" in *New World Orders: Violence, Sanction, and Authority in the Colonial Americas, ed. John Smolenski and Thomas J. Humphrey* (Philadelphia: University of Pennsylvania Press, 2005), 133–156.

66. NL-HaNA, OWIC, 1.05.01.01, inv. nr. 76, April 19, 1646, *desselfs [Rabe's] huisvrouwe wesende een Brasilianinne sodanigh van haer mans naergelaeten middelen forcelijck berooft, dat de Brasiliannen dienaengaende mede geen genoegen konnen hebben.* See also NL-HaNA, OWIC, 1.05.01.01, inv. nr. 76, April 23, 1646. The aftermath of Rabe's murder is discussed in B.N. Teensma, "The Mission of Rudolph Baro in Search of Nhandui in the Macagua Mountains, 1647" in *Dutch Brazil Volume 1 Documents in the Leiden University Library*, ed. Cristina Ferrao and Jose Paulo Monteiro Soares (Rio de Janeiro: Editora Index, 1997), 15–30.

67. NL-HaNA, OWIC, 1.05.01.01, inv. nr. 69, August 28, 1642.

68. NL-HaNA, OWIC, 1.05.01.01, inv. nr. 74, November 28, 1650.

69. NL-HaNA, OWIC, 1.05.01.01, inv. nr. 74, December 6, 1650.

70. NL-HaNA, OWIC, 1.05.01.01, inv. nr. 75, March 24, 1651, *dat sij oock de vrouwen met dan tot hare slavinnen souden houden @ deselve weder mishandelt soude t'selve tusschen ons @ hare natie haet verwecken.*

71. NL-HaNA, OWIC, 1.05.01.01, inv. nr. 75, March 24, 1651.

72. NL-HaNA, OWIC, 1.05.01.01, inv. nr .75, March 24, 1651, *het een harde saecke is iemant van houwelycken te onthouden.*

73. NL-HaNA, OWIC, 1.05.01.01, inv. nr .75, March 24, 1651, *het een harde saecke is iemant van houwelycken te onthouden.* NL-HaNA, OWIC, 1.05.01.01, inv. nr. 75, March 24, 1651, *dat sij oock de vrouwen met dan tot hare slavinnen souden houden @ deselve weder mishandelt soude t'selve tusschen ons @ hare natie haet verwecken.*

74. Snow, Gehring, and Starna, *In Mohawk Country,* 43.

75. Everts, "'Brought up well,'" 101.

76. In the later seventeenth century, some of the free movement in the city would be constricted as the VOC mandated that many enslaved people live in a specific quarter of the city. In 1740, the extremely large Chinese population would also be forced to move outside the city walls. Marsley Kehoe, "Dutch Batavia: Exposing the Hierarchy of the Dutch Colonial City" *Journal of Historians of Netherlandish Art* 7 (2015), 21.

77. On the supposed improprieties of Gold Coast women, see Elizabeth Sutton, *Early Modern Dutch Prints of Africa* (New York: Routledge, 2012), 144.

78. Adam Jones, *German Sources for West African History, 1599–1669* (Wiesbaden: Franz Steiner Verlag, 1983), 32, 89; Pieter de Marees, *Description and historical account*

of the Gold Kingdom of Guinea (1602), eds. A van Dantzig and Adam Jones (New York: Published for the British Academy by Oxford University Press, 1987), 19–21.

79. Harvey M. Feinberg, Africans and Europeans in *West Africa: Elminans and Dutchmen on the Gold Coast during the Eighteenth Century* (Philadelphia: American Philosophical Society, 1989), 88–89.

80. Jones, *German Sources,* 214; De Marees, *Description,* 19–21

81. De Marees, *Description,* 38.

82. Deborah Hamer, "Marriage and the Construction of Colonial Order: Jurisdiction, Gender and Class in Seventeenth-century Dutch Batavia." *Gender & History* 29, no. 3 (Nov. 2017): 634.

83. Judith Brown, "Economic Organization and the Position of Women among the Iroquois," *Ethnohistory* 17, no. 3/4 (1970): 151–167. Jan Noel calculates that through their production of maize, women supplied two-thirds of the Iroquois diet. Jan Noel, "Revisiting Gender in Iroquoia" in *Gender and Sexuality in Indigenous North America, 1400–1850*, ed. Sandra Slater and Fay A. Yarbrough (Columbia: University of South Carolina Press, 2011). 48.

84. Gretchen Green, "Gender and the Longhouse: Iroquois Women in a Changing Culture" in *Women and Freedom in Early America*, ed. Larry D. Eldridge (New York: New York University Press, 1997), 9–10.

85. Green, "Gender and the Longhouse," 11–12; Jan Noel, "'Fertile with Fine Talk': Ungoverned Tongues among Haudenosaunee Women and Their Neighbors" *Ethnohistory* 57, no. 2 (2010): 210–15; Noel, "Revisiting Gender in Iroquoia," 53.

86. Romney, *New Netherland Connections,* 178–79.

87. Klooster, *The Dutch Moment,* 114–15.

88. Lotte Van de Pol, *The Burgher and the Whore: Prostitution in Early Modern Amsterdam* (Oxford: Oxford University Press, 2011), 160–65.

89. Alexandra Shepard, "From Anxious Patriarchs to Refined Gentlemen? Manhood in Britain, circa 1500–1700," *Journal of British Studies* 44 Issue 2 (April 2005), 291–93.

90. Charles T Gehring and Jacob Adriaan Schiltkamp, *Curacao Papers 1640–1665* (Interlaken, N.Y.: Heart of the Lakes Pub., 1987), 5.

91. On the virtue of the woman who stayed inside, see Wayne E. Franits, *Paragons of Virtue: Women and Domesticity in Seventeenth-Century Dutch Art* (New York: Cambridge University Press, 1995), 68–84.

92. On intermarriage and the fur trade, see Susan Sleeper-Smith, *Indian Women and French Men: Rethinking Cultural Encounter in the Western Great Lakes* (Amherst: University of Massachusetts Press, 2001), 19–20, 30, 38–40.

Las Casas de las Rabinas

This article appears in modified form as the second chapter in Michele Mericle, "Expanding the Realm of the Possible: Gender and Crypto-Judaism in Seventeenth-Century New Spain" (Ph.D. diss., Brown University, 2015).

1. Several scholars have investigated the events of this decade. See, for example: Solange Alberro, "Crypto-Jews and the Mexican Holy Office," in *The Jews and the*

Expansion of Europe to the West, 1450–1800, ed. Paolo Bernardini and Norman Fiering (New York: Berghahn Books, 2001); Solange Alberro and Henry Charles Lea Library, University of Pennsylvania, *Inquisición y Sociedad En México, 1571–1700,* ed. Sección de Obras de Historia (México: Fondo de Cultura Económica, 1988); Julio Caro Baroja, *Inquisicion, Brujeria, y Criptojudaismo,* 3rd ed. (Barcelona: Editorial Ariel, 1974); Michael Manuel Brescia, "The Cultural Politics of Episcopal Power: Juan de Palafox y Mendoza and Tridentine Catholicism in Seventeenth-Century Puebla de Los Angeles, Mexico" (Ph.D. diss., University of Arizona, 2002); David M. Gitlitz, *Secrecy and Deceit: The Religion of the Crypto-Jews,* 1st ed. (Philadelphia: Jewish Publication Society, 1996); Stanley M. Hordes, "The Inquisition and the Crypto-Jewish Community in Colonial New Spain and New Mexico," in *Cultural Encounters the Impact of the Inquisition in Spain and the New World,* ed. Mary Elizabeth Perry and Anne J. Cruz (Berkeley: University of California Press, 1991); Stanley M. Hordes, "The Crypto-Jewish Community of New Spain, 1620–1649: A Collective Biography" (Ph.D. diss., Tulane University, 1980); Jonathan Irvine Israel, *Race, Class, and Politics in Colonial Mexico, 1610–1670,* Oxford Historical Monographs (London: Oxford University Press, 1975); Jonathan I. Israel, *Diasporas within a Diaspora: Jews, Crypto-Jews, and the World Maritime Empires (1540–1740)* (Boston: Brill, 2002); Seymour B. Liebman, "The Great Conspiracy in New Spain," *The Americas* 30, no. 1 (1973); Seymour B. Liebman, trans. and ed., and Matías de Bocanegra, *Jews and the Inquisition of Mexico: The Great Auto de Fe of 1649, as Related by Mathias de Bocanegra, S.J.* (Lawrence, Kans.: Coronado Press, 1974); Ricardo Escobar Quevedo, *Inqusición y Judaizantes en América Española (Siglos Xvi–Xvii)* (Bogotá, Colombia: Editorial Universidad del Rosario, 2008); Jonathan Schorsch, *Swimming the Christian Atlantic: Judeoconversos, Afroiberians and Amerindians in the Seventeenth Century* (Boston: Brill, 2009); Daviken Studnicki-Gizbert, *A Nation upon the Ocean Sea: Portugal's Atlantic Diaspora and the Crisis of the Spanish Empire, 1492–1640* (New York: Oxford University Press, 2007); Eva Alexandra Uchmany, Daniel Carpi, and Shlomo Simonsohn, eds. *Simón Váez Sevilla,* vol. 8 (Jerusalem: "Daf-Chen" Press, Ltd., 1983); Eva Alexandra Uchmany, *La Vida entre el Judaísmo y el Cristianismo en La Nueva España, 1580–1606,* 1st ed., Sección de Obras de Historia (México: Archivo General de la Nación: Fondo de Cultura Económica, 1992); Nathan Wachtel, "Marrano Religiosity in Hispanic America in the Seventeenth Century," in *The Jews and the Expansion of Europe to the West, 1450–1800,* ed. Norman Fiering and Paolo Bernardini (New York: Berghahn Books, 2001); Arnold Wiznitzer, "Crypto-Jews in Seventeenth Century Mexico," in *The Jewish Experience in Latin America,* ed. Martin A. Cohen (Waltham, Mass.: American Jewish Historical Society, 1972).

2. Alberro, "Crypto-Jews and the Mexican Holy Office," 130.

3. See, for example: Ruth Behar, "Sexual Witchcraft, Colonialism, and Women's Powers: Views from the Mexican Inquisition," in *Sexuality and Marriage in Colonial Latin America,* ed. Asunción Lavrin (Lincoln: University of Nebraska Press, 1989); Kathryn Burns, *Colonial Habits: Convents and the Spiritual Economy of Cuzco, Peru* (Durham: Duke University Press, 1999); Martha Few, "Women, Religion, and Power: Gender and Resistance in Daily Life in Late-Seventeenth-Century Santiago De Guatemala," *Ethnohistory* 42, no. 4 (1995); Martha Few, *Women Who Live Evil Lives* (Austin: University of

Texas Press, 2002); Kimberly Gauderman, *Women's Lives in Colonial Quito: Gender, Law, and Economy in Spanish America* (Austin: University of Texas Press, 2003); Karen B. Graubart, *With Our Labor and Sweat: Indigenous Women and the Formation of Colonial Society in Peru, 1550–1700* (Stanford, Calif.: Stanford University Press, 2007); Nora E. Jaffary, *Gender, Race and Religion in the Colonization of the Americas* (Aldershot, England; Burlington, Vt.: Ashgate, 2007); Daniella Kostroun and Lisa Vollendorf, eds., *Women, Religion, and the Atlantic World (1600–1800)* (Toronto: University of Toronto Press, 2009); Asunción Lavrin, *Sexuality and Marriage in Colonial Latin America,* Latin American Studies Series (Lincoln: University of Nebraska Press, 1989); Asunción Lavrin, *Brides of Christ: Conventual Life in Colonial Mexico* (Stanford, Calif.: Stanford University Press, 2008); Stacey Schlau, "A Judaizing 'Old Christian' Woman and the Mexican Inquisition: The 'Unusual' Case of Maria De Zarate," in *Women, Religion, and the Atlantic World (1600–1800),* ed. Daniella Kostroun and Lisa Vollendorf (Toronto: University of Toronto Press, 2009); Patricia Seed, *To Love, Honor, and Obey in Colonial Mexico: Conflicts over Marriage Choice, 1574–1821* (Stanford, Calif.: Stanford University Press, 1988); Irene Silverblatt, "Lessons of Gender and Ethnohistory in Mesoamerica," *Ethnohistory* 42, no. 4 (1995); Irene Silverblatt, *Moon, Sun, and Witches: Gender Ideologies and Class in Inca and Colonial Peru* (Princeton, N.J.: Princeton University Press, 1987); Lisa Vollendorf, ed., *The Lives of Women: A New History of Inquisitorial Spain* (Nashville, Tenn.: Vanderbilt University Press, 2005).

4. Michele Mericle, "Expanding the Realm of the Possible: Gender and Crypto-Judaism in Seventeenth-Century New Spain" (Ph.D. diss., Brown University, 2015), 7–27.

5. Natalie Zemon Davis, *Fiction in the Archives: Pardon Tales and Their Tellers in Sixteenth-Century France*, Harry Camp Lectures at Stanford University (Stanford, Calif.: Stanford University Press, 1987), 3.

6. Davis, *Fiction in the Archives.*

7. Meredith B. McGuire, *Lived Religion: Faith and Practice in Everyday Life* (Oxford: Oxford University Press, 2008); Susan Starr Sered, "The Domestication of Religion: The Spiritual Guardianship of Elderly Jewish Women," *Man,* New Series 23, no. 3 (1988): 517–18. Sered observes that, in the then newly published fifteen-volume *Encyclopedia of Religion* (1987), a total of seventeen pages were devoted to the domestic observances of Jews, Christians, Muslims, Hindus, Chinese, and Japanese. See Sered, "The Domestication of Religion," 515.

8. Robert Redfield, *Peasant Society and Culture: An Anthropological Approach to Civilization* (Chicago: University of Chicago Press, 1956). Redfield distinguishes between the "great tradition," the official, generally male religion, and the "little tradition," the unofficial, generally female religion that coexisted with it.

9. Charles Stewart and Rosalind Shaw, *Syncretism/Anti-Syncretism: The Politics of Religious Synthesis* (London: Routledge, 1994).

10. According to Stewart and Shaw, "simply identifying a ritual or tradition as 'syncretic' tells us very little and gets us practically nowhere, since all religions have composite origins and are continually reconstructed through ongoing processes of synthesis and erasure." Stewart and Shaw, *Syncretism/Anti-Syncretism,* 7.

11. Much contemporary scholarship has addressed the question of how "Jewish" the crypto-Jews were. I maintain that this question is essentially unanswerable, for there is no true or static point of comparison, and the question has far more to do with current-day preoccupations with defining "Jewishness" than with questions of historical relevance.

12. McGuire, *Lived Religion,* 190.

13. Eliza F. Kent, "Secret Christians of Sivakasi: Gender, Syncretism, and Crypto-Religion in Early Twentieth-Century South India," *Journal of the American Academy of Religion* 79, no. 3 (2011): 680.

14. Several scholars have investigated crypto-religiosity and its potential for challenging prevailing norms. See, for example, Kent, "Secret Christians"; Maurus Reinkowski, "Hidden Believers, Hidden Apostates: The Phenomenon of Crypto-Jews and Crypto-Christians in the Middle East," in *Converting Cultures: Religion, Ideology and Transformations of Modernity,* ed. Dennis C. and A. Kevin Reinhart Washburn (Leiden, Netherlands: Brill, 2007); Joel Robbins, "Crypto-Religion and the Study of Cultural Mixes: Anthropology, Value and the Nature of Syncretism," *Journal of the American Academy of Religion* 79, no. 2 (2010).

15. Kent, "Secret Christians," 680.

16. Liebman, "The Great Conspiracy in New Spain"; Seymour B. Liebman, *New World Jewry, 1493–1825 : Requiem for the Forgotten* (New York: Ktav Publishing House, 1982); Irene Silverblatt, *Modern Inquisitions: Peru and the Colonial Origins of the Civilized World*; Israel, *Race, Class, and Politics in Colonial Mexico, 1610–1670*; Jonathan I. Israel, *Empires and Entrepots: The Dutch, the Spanish Monarchy, and the Jews, 1585–1713* (London; Roncevert, W. Va.: Hambledon Press, 1990); Israel, *Diasporas within a Diaspora*; Ana Schaposchnik, "Under the Eyes of the Inquisition: Crypto-Jews in the Ibero-American World (Peru, 1600s)" (Ph.D. diss., University of Wisconsin–Madison, 2007).

17. Alberro, "Crypto-Jews and the Mexican Holy Office," 180.

18. Interestingly, some the women who were reputed to have had flirtatious relations with Inquisition officials were members of the Váez-Enríquez family. Alberro, "Crypto-Jews and the Mexican Holy Office," 179.

19. Alberro and Henry Charles Lea Library, *Inquisición y Sociedad en* México, 1571–*1700,* 419–20.

20. The term "Old Christian" refers to those persons with individual and family histories that had no ties to Islam or Judaism. The term "New Christian" referred to those with individual and/or family histories that had ties to Islam or Judaism. In general, the terms "New Christian," "*converso,*" "Jew," and "Portuguese" were used interchangeably in New Spain at this time.

21. Irene Silverblatt, *Modern Inquisitions: Peru and the Colonial Origins of the Civilized World* (Durham: Duke University Press, 2004), 143–48.

22. Studnicki-Gizbert, *Nation upon the Ocean Sea,* 12.

23. Hordes, "The Crypto-Jewish Community of New Spain, 1620–1649"; Israel, *Diasporas,* 97–124.

24. Studnicki-Gizbert, *Nation upon the Ocean Sea,* 35.

25. Israel, *Diasporas,* 107.

26. Studnicki-Gizbert, *Nation upon the Ocean Sea,* 37.

27. Liebman and Bocanegra, *Jews and the Inquisition of Mexico,* 6.

28. Studnicki-Gizbert, *Nation upon the Ocean Sea,* 37.

29. The term "*converso*" applied to persons of Muslim or Jewish descent. For the purposes of this essay, however, it describes only persons of Jewish descent.

30. Israel, *Diasporas,* 97.

31. For more on this, see Renée Levine Melammed, *Heretics or Daughters of Israel?: The Crypto-Jewish Women of Castile* (New York: Oxford University Press, 1999).

32. Alberro and Henry Charles Lea Library, *Inquisición y Sociedad En* México, *1571–1700,* 442.

33. Israel, *Diasporas,* 110.

34. Liebman and Bocanegra, *Jews and the Inquisition of Mexico,* 113.

35. While no one at the time called the family "Váez-Enríquez," I have termed them in this way in order to describe the relationships created when Simon Váez and Juana Enríquez married.

36. Amos Megged, "Magic, Popular Medicine and Gender in Seventeenth-Century Mexico: The Case of Isabel De Montoya," *Social History* 19, no. 2 (1994): 190. Whether this preoccupation was merely coincident with or was in some way an outgrowth of these persecutions of the *conversos* requires further research. For more on semi-clandestine women's religion in colonial Spanish America, see Behar, "Sexual Witchcraft, Colonialism, and Women's Powers"; Few, "Women, Religion, and Power"; Schlau, "A Judaizing 'Old Christian' Woman and the Mexican Inquisition; Silverblatt, *Moon, Sun, and Witches.*

37. Megged, "Magic, Popular Medicine and Gender," 191.

38. Liebman and Bocanegra, *Jews and the Inquisition of Mexico,* 234–51. The three factions can be loosely described as headed by the Váez-Enríquez family, by Thomas Treviño de Sobremonte, and by Luis de Mezquita.

39. Gregorio Martín de Guijo, *Diario, 1648–1664,* Colección De Escritores Mexicanos, 64–65 (México: Editorial Porrúa, 1952), 40.

40. Liebman implies that, as a Jesuit, he was not eligible to be part of the Inquisition. See Liebman and Bocanegra, *Jews and the Inquisition of Mexico,* 5. However, Ken Ward pointed out in a personal conversation on January 18, 2012, that he has encountered in the documentary record of seventeenth-century Mexico several Jesuits who were part of the Inquisition.

41. Richard L. Kagan and Abigail Dyer, *Inquisitorial Inquiries: Brief Lives of Secret Jews and Other Heretics,* 2nd ed. (Baltimore: Johns Hopkins University Press, 2011), 163.

42. A vast amount of Inquisition documentation was also generated for Blanca Enríquez. See, for example, AGN, Mexico, Inquisición v. 399, exp. 3; AGN, Mexico, Inquisición 404, exp. 2, 3.

43. Liebman and Bocanegra, *Jews and the Inquisition of Mexico,* 192.

44. Helen Nader, *Power and Gender in Renaissance Spain: Eight Women of the Mendoza Family, 1450–1650,* Hispanisms (Urbana: University of Illinois Press, 2004); Eukene Lacarra Lanz, *Marriage and Sexuality in Medieval and Early Modern Iberia,* Hispanic Issues (New York: Routledge, 2002); Ronald E. Surtz, *Writing Women in Late Medieval*

and Early Modern Spain: The Mothers of Saint Teresa of Avila, Middle Ages Series (Philadelphia: University of Pennsylvania Press, 1995); Mary Elizabeth Perry, *Gender and Disorder in Early Modern Seville* (Princeton, N.J.: Princeton University Press, 1990).

45. AGN, Mexico, Inquisicion, v. 400, exp.1, 1a parte, 445. For evidence of the literacy of her sister, Beatriz Enríquez, see AGN México, Inquisición, exp.1, v. 393, not paginated, but found in her second audiencia, August 26, 1642. For another sister, Rafaela Enríquez, see AGN, México, Inquisición, exp. 1, v. 402, 248. Rafaela said that she knew how to read and write, but not very well. That literacy was widespread among this group of imprisoned crypto-Jews, men and women, is suggested by the method they used to communicate with one another in the prisons. They devised a system of knocks upon the walls, and it appears that a certain number of knocks represented certain letters. This method required sufficient literacy not only to know how to spell but also to be able to hold letters in mind as words were gradually spelled out. Such communication would be slow and painstaking, but the one thing the prisoners had was time, and the desire to interact with other prisoners was surely great. For a fascinating discussion of how these prison communications transpired and the slaves who facilitated them, see Jonathan Schorsch, *Swimming the Christian Atlantic: Judeoconversos, Afroiberians and Amerindians in the Seventeenth Century Atlantic World* (Boston: Brill, 2009), 245–82.

46. AGN, Mexico, Inquisición, v. 411, exp. 1, 141–43.

47. AGN, Mexico, Inquisición, v. 396, segunda parte, 554–55.

48. AGN, Mexico, Inquisición, v. 400, exp. 1, 1a parte, 434.

49. Liebman and Bocanegra, *Jews and the Inquisition of Mexico,* 106.

50. Lineage and status were intertwined in New Spain in complicated ways, and the *limpieza de sangre* statutes were, at least initially, directly related to the Crown's efforts to convert and/or expel Jews and Muslims from Spain. For more on this complicated issue, see Ilona Katzew, *Casta Painting: Images of Race in Eighteenth-Century Mexico* (New Haven: Yale University Press, 2004), 42–45; Maria Elena Martinez, *Genealogical Fictions: Limpieza de Sangre, Religion and Gender in Colonial Mexico* (Stanford, Calif.: Stanford University Press, 2008); David Niremberg, "Was There Race before Modernity? The Example of 'Jewish' Blood in Late Medieval Spain," in *The Origins of Racism in the West,* ed. Miriam Eliav-Feldon, Benjamin H. Isaac, and Joseph Ziegler (New York: Cambridge University Press, 2009).

51. For a similar phenomenon in Peru, see Charles F. Walker, *Shaky Colonialism: The 1746 Earthquake-Tsunami in Lima, Peru, and Its Long Aftermath* (Durham: Duke University Press, 2008).

52. William B. Taylor, *Drinking, Homicide, and Rebellion in Colonial Mexican Villages* (Stanford, Calif.: Stanford University Press, 1979); Nancy M. Farriss, *Maya Society under Colonial Rule: The Collective Enterprise of Survival* (Princeton, N.J.: Princeton University Press, 1984); Charles Gibson, *The Aztecs under Spanish Rule: A History of the Indians of the Valley of Mexico, 1519–1810* (Stanford, Calif.: Stanford University Press, 1964).

53. Solange Alberro, *El* Águila *y la Cruz: Orígenes Religiosos de la Conciencia Criolla. Mexico, Siglos Xvi–Xvii* (Mexico City: El Colegio de Mexico, 1999); Richard E. Greenleaf and James Denson Riley, *The Inquisition in Colonial Latin America: Selected*

Writings of Richard E. Greenleaf (Berkeley, Calif.: Academy of American Franciscan History, 2010).

54. AGN, Mexico, Inquisición, v. 381, exp. 7, passim; v. 390, exp. 11, passim; v. 400, exp. 1, 2a parte, passim; v. 488, exp. 5, passim.

55. Israel, *Diasporas,* 120–21.

56. Liebman and Bocanegra, *Jews and the Inquisition of Mexico,* 220.

57. See, for example, Gitlitz, *Secrecy and Deceit*; David L. Graizbord, *Souls in Dispute: Converso Identities in Iberia and the Jewish Diaspora, 1580–1700* (Philadelphia: University of Pennsylvania Press, 2004); Melammed, *Heretics or Daughters of Israel?*

58. Israel, *Diasporas,* 122.

59. Belinda Bozzoli, "Marxism, Feminism, and South African Studies," *Journal of South African Studies* 9, no. 2 (1983).

60. Gauderman, *Women's Lives in Colonial Quito,* especially Introduction and Conclusion.

"The Refuse of the whole Creation"

1. See, as a starting point, Jennifer L. Morgan, *Laboring Women: Reproduction and Gender in New World Slavery* (Philadelphia: University of Pennsylvania Press, 2004); Marisa Fuentes, *Dispossessed Lives: Enslaved Women, Violence, and the Archive* (Philadelphia: University of Pennsylvania Press, 2016); and Sasha Turner, *Contested Bodies: Pregnancy, Childrearing, and Slavery in Jamaica* (Philadelphia: University of Pennsylvania Press, 2017).

2. Some sources express confidence that Ward made the journey, such as Myra Jehlen and Michael Warner, eds., *The English Literatures of America, 1500–1800* (New York: Routledge, 1997), 299. Others are more circumspect, such as Jack P. Greene, *Evaluating Empire and Confronting Colonialism in Eighteenth-Century Britain* (New York: Cambridge University Press, 2013), 65–67.

3. The main work on Ward remains the biography and analysis by Howard William Troyer, *Ned Ward of Grub Street: A Study of Sub-Literary London in the Eighteenth Century* (London: Frank Cass & Co. Ltd., 1946). See also David S. Shields, *Civil Tongues & Polite Letters in British America* (Chapel Hill: University of North Carolina Press, 1997), 46–54, and Mona Narain, "Libertine Spaces and the Female Body in the Poetry of Rochester and Ned Ward," *English Literary History* 72, no. 3 (Fall 2005): 553–76. Beyond a few exceptions, usually relating to Ward's *The London Spy,* Ward primarily appears in historical and literary scholarship as a footnote, providing colorful and profane detail about everyday life for common people. For an analysis of Ward's work as "commercial satire," see Ashley Marshall, *The Practice of Satire in England, 1658–1770* (Baltimore: Johns Hopkins University Press, 2013), 136–39.

4. The Scriblerus Club was founded around 1712 and included Alexander Pope, Jonathan Swift, and John Gay, among others. Pope's *Dunciad,* published in four books between 1728 and 1743, mocked the dullest of poets, including Ned Ward.

5. See, for example, John Oldham, "Satyr upon a woman, who by her falshood and scorn was the Death of my Friend," in *Satyrs upon the Jesuits Written in the Year 1679 . . .*

(London, 1681), 145–54; Thomas Brown, *Love given o're, or, A Satyr against the pride, lust, and inconstancy &c. of woman* (1682); Richard Ames, *Sylvia's revenge, or, A satyr against man in answer to the Satyr against woman* (London, 1688); Robert Gould, *A satyrical epistle to the female author of a poem, call'd Silvia's revenge, &c. by the author of the satyr against woman* (London, 1691); Aphra Behn, *The Restor'd maiden-head a new satyr against woman: occasion'd by an infant who was the cause of the death of my friend* (London, 1691).

6. Edmund Hickeringill, *Jamaica viewed with all the ports, harbours, and their several soundings, towns, and settlements thereunto belonging together . . .* (London, 1661); Aphra Behn, *Oroonoko, or, The royal slave, A true history* (London, 1688); and Mary Pix, *The innocent mistress a comedy, as it was acted by His Majesty's servants at the theatre in Little-Lincolns-Inn-Fields* (London, 1697).

7. See *The satires of Decimus Junius Juvenalis translated into English verse by Mr. Dryden and several other eminent hands . . .* (London, 1693), 63.

8. *The satires of Decimus Junius Juvenalis,* 64–65.

9. *The satires of Decimus Junius Juvenalis,* 63.

10. For a broader view of the field, see Felicity A. Nussbaum, *The Brink of All We Hate: English Satires on Women 1660–1750* (Lexington: The University Press of Kentucky, 1984).

11. Howard William Troyer, "No Mean Talent: A Study of the Life and Writings of Edward Ward (1667–1731)" (University of Wisconsin-Madison Ph.D. diss., 1938), 2.

12. Edward Ward, *The poet's ramble after riches, or a night's transactions upon the road burlesqu'd* (London, 1691).

13. Edward Ward, *Female policy detected. Or, The arts of a designing woman laid open . . .* (London, 1695). Ward was not named as the author until the 1720 edition. See Troyer, *Ned Ward of Grub Street,* 12–13, 238, and James Sambrook, "Ward, Edward [Ned] (1667–1731)," in *Oxford Dictionary of National Biography,* online ed., ed. David Cannadine (Oxford: Oxford University Press, 2004), http://www.oxforddnb.com.proxy.libraries.uc.edu/view/article/28682.

14. Troyer, *Ned Ward of Grub Street,* 12–13.

15. Ward, *Female policy detected* (1695), 5–6.

16. Joseph Swetnam, *The araignment of leuud, idle, froward, and vnconstant women or the vanitie of them . . .* (London, 1615); Jacques Olivier, *A discourse of women, shewing their imperfections alphabetically newly translated out of the French into English* (London, 1662).

17. Ward, *Female policy detected* (1702), 44. The material originated in Swetnam, *Araignment,* 12.

18. Ward, *Female policy detected* (1702), 50, and Swetnam, *Arraignment,* 15–16.

19. Ward, *Female policy detected* (1702), 76, and Swetnam, *Arraignment,* 31.

20. Ward, *Female policy detected* (1702), 78, and Swetnam, *Arraignment,* 33.

21. See, for example, Trevor Burnard, *Mastery, Tyranny, and Desire: Thomas Thistlewood and His Slaves in the Anglo-Jamaican World* (Chapel Hill: University of North Carolina Press, 2004); Trevor Burnard, "'Impatient of Subordination' and 'Liable to Sudden Transports of Anger': White Masculinity and Homosocial Relations with Black

Men in Eighteenth-Century Jamaica," in Thomas A. Foster, ed., *New Men: Manliness in Early America* (New York: New York University Press, 2011), 134–49; and Carla Gardina Pestana, *The English Conquest of Jamaica: Oliver Cromwell's Bid for Empire* (Cambridge, Mass.: Belknap/Harvard University Press, 2017).

22. See, for example, Elizabeth Foyster, *Manhood in Early Modern England: Honour, Sex and Marriage* (New York: Routledge, 1999), and Alexandra Shepard, *Meanings of Manhood in Early Modern England* (Oxford: Oxford University Press, 2003).

23. Troyer, *Ned Ward of Grub Street,* 13–16, 247–52.

24. Ward, *A trip to Jamaica,* 4.

25. Ward, *A trip to Jamaica,* 6.

26. Ward, *A trip to Jamaica,* 9–10.

27. Ward, *A trip to Jamaica,* 13–14.

28. For more about the nautical elements of Ward's work, see Ruth Bourne, "The Wooden World Dissected," *Pacific Historical Review* 14, no. 3 (1945): 326–34.

29. Ward, *A trip to Jamaica,* 8–9.

30. Ward, *A trip to Jamaica,* 11.

31. Ward, *A trip to Jamaica,* 11.

32. Ward, *A trip to Jamaica,* 13.

33. Owen Felltham's travel narratives include *Three moneths obseruations of the Low-countries, especially Holland . . .* (London: 1648, 1652); *A true and exact true and exact character of the Low-Countreyes; especially Holland or, the Dutchman anatomized . . .* (London, 1652); *A brief character of the Low-Countreys under the States . . .* (London, 1652, 1659, 1660, 1662, 1671); *Batavia, or, The Hollander displayed . . .* (London, 1672, 1675, 1677, 1680, 1697).

34. Owen Felltham, *A trip to Holland, being a description of the country, people and manners . . .* (London, 1699). This narrative was attributed to Edward Ward at the time of publication, as well as by historians into the twentieth century.

35. Stephen Greenblatt, *Renaissance Self-Fashioning: From More to Shakespeare* (Chicago: University of Chicago Press, 1980).

36. Edward Ward, *A curry-comb for a cocks-comb: or, the Trip to Holland detected. By the Author of the Trip to Jamaica* (London: 1698/99).

37. Ward, *A curry-comb for a cocks-comb,* 1.

38. Ward, *A curry-comb for a cocks-comb,* 2.

39. Ward, *A curry-comb for a cocks-comb,* 2.

40. Anonymous, *The curry-comb turn'd to its right use; Or, the powder-monkey to a Jamaica ship, dress'd with it By the Author of the Trip to Holland* (London: 1698/99), 1.

41. Anonymous, *The curry-comb turn'd to its right use,* 1.

42. Anonymous, *The curry-comb turn'd to its right use,* 2.

43. For further evidence of Africans in early modern England, see Imtiaz Habib, *Black Lives in the English Archives, 1500–1677: Imprints of the Invisible* (Aldershot: Ashgate, 2008).

44. For a reflection on the overlap of this history and literature, see James Robertson, "Re-Writing the English Conquest of Jamaica in the Late Seventeenth Century," *English Historical Review* 117, no. 473 (2002): 813–39.

45. John Richardson, *Slavery and Augustan Literature: Swift, Pope, Gay,* Routledge Studies in Eighteenth-Century Literature (New York: Routledge, 2004), 4.

46. Richardson, *Slavery and Augustan Literature,* 6.

47. Edward Ward, *A trip to New-England with a character of the country and people, both English and Indians* (London, 1699); John Josselyn, *An account of two voyages to New-England . . .* (2nd ed., London, 1675); John Josselyn, *New England's rarities discovered* (London, 1672). For an account of Ward's borrowing, see Troyer, *Ned Ward of Grub Street,* 22.

48. Ward, *A trip to New-England,* 10.

49. For the ways that Ward's writings helped reveal the spatial London, see Cynthia Wall, *The Literary and Cultural Spaces of Restoration London* (Cambridge: Cambridge University Press, 1998).

50. Troyer, *Ned Ward of Grub Street,* 33.

"Inhabitant of Saint-Domingue, today refugee in this place"

1. *Testament de Jeanette Azulima,* February 27, 1811, Narcisse Broutin, vol. 24, 263, Notarial Archives Research Center, New Orleans, La. (hereafter cited as NARC); Nathalie Dessens, *From Saint-Domingue to New Orleans: Migration and Influences* (Gainesville: University Press of Florida, 2007), 27. The primary documents used for this paper are in French. All translations are by the author. The author would like to thank the American Society for Eighteenth-Century Studies and the American Studies Program, the Office of Graduate Studies and Research, and the Roy R. Charles Center at the College of William and Mary for their generous support of the research conducted for this article. For reading earlier drafts of this essay and providing helpful suggestions, the author would also like to thank Laura R. Prieto, Wendy Korwin, Frank Cha, Seth Feman, Brian Piper, and the attendees of the Carolina Lowcountry in the Atlantic World Conference, College of Charleston, March 2012.

2. Recent scholarship on Saint-Domingue free women of color refugees mostly focuses on their impact on New Orleans. Rebecca Scott and Jean Hébrard's study of the Tinchant family describes the migration experience of the former slave Rosalie and her daughter, Élisabeth, who traveled first to Cuba and then to New Orleans. See Scott and Hébrard, *Freedom Papers: An Atlantic Odyssey in the Age of Emancipation* (Cambridge, Mass.: Harvard University Press, 2012), especially chapters 2–4. Along with *Freedom Papers* and additional articles by Scott, work by Kenneth Aslakson illustrates the ways in which the refugees' arrival, coinciding with the Louisiana Purchase, challenged the black/white racial binary that Anglo-American settlers and government officials brought with them to the newly acquired territory. In their discussions of suits filed by refugees to regain their freedom in New Orleans, both Scott and Aslakson demonstrate how Saint-Domingue refugees of African descent utilized the court system to force local negotiations over the legal definitions of "free blacks" and "slaves." See Scott, "Paper Thin: Freedom and Re-Enslavement in the Diaspora of the Haitian Revolution," *Law and History Review* 29, no. 4 (2011): 1061–1082; Scott, "'She . . . Refuses to Deliver Up Herself as the Slave of Your Petitioner': Émigrés, Enslavement, and the 1808 Louisiana Digest

of the Civil Laws," *Tulane European and Civil Law Forum* 24 (2009): 115–36; Aslakson, "Making Race: The Role of Free Blacks in the Development of New Orleans' Three-Caste Society, 1791–1812" (Ph.D. diss., University of Texas, 2007). Anne Ulentin's dissertation examines free women of color slave owners in New Orleans, paying particular attention to Saint-Domingue refugees. See Ulentin, "Shades of Grey: Slaveholding Free Women of Color in Antebellum New Orleans, 1800–1840" (Ph.D. diss., Louisiana State University, 2012). The arrival of a large number of free women of color, in particular, had an important cultural impact as well. Aslakson and Emily Clark argue that the racial and sexual discourses surrounding mixed-race women and their supposedly institutionalized relationships with white men, known in New Orleans as *plaçage,* were a direct reaction to the presence of Saint-Domingue women. This "quadroon myth" has had a lasting effect on both popular and academic perceptions of New Orleans. See Aslakson, "The 'Quadroon-Plaçage Myth' of Antebellum New Orleans: Anglo-American (Mis)Interpretations of a French Caribbean Phenomenon," *Journal of Social History* 45, no. 3 (2012): 709–34; Clark, *The Strange History of the American Quadroon: Free Women of Color in the Revolutionary Atlantic* (Chapel Hill: University of North Carolina Press, 2013).

3. Dessens, *From Saint-Domingue to New Orleans,* 11–14. For a full narrative treatment of the Haitian Revolution, see Laurent Dubois, *Avengers of the New World: The Story of the Haitian Revolution* (Cambridge, Mass.: Harvard University Press, 2004).

4. Dessens, *From Saint-Domingue to New Orleans,* 15; R. Darrell Meadows, "Engineering Exile: Social Networks and the French Atlantic Community, 1789–1809," *French Historical Studies* 23 (2000): 70.

5. Dessens, *From Saint-Domingue to New Orleans,* 15, 68; Ashli White, *Encountering Revolution: Haiti and the Making of the Early Republic* (Baltimore: Johns Hopkins University Press, 2010), 2.

6. Dessens, *From Saint-Domingue to New Orleans,* 15; Jeremy Popkin, *You Are All Free: The Haitian Revolution and the Abolition of Slavery* (Cambridge, Mass.: Cambridge University Press, 2010), 2, 289–93, 295. Refugees landed in Norfolk, Baltimore, Philadelphia, New York, and Charleston.

7. Dessens, *From Saint-Domingue to New Orleans,* 13, 15; Paul Lachance, "Repercussions of the Haitian Revolution in Louisiana," in *The Impact of the Haitian Revolution in the Atlantic World,* ed. David Geggus (Columbia: University of South Carolina Press, 2001), 212; Gabriel Debien, "The Saint-Domingue Refugees in Cuba, 1793–1815," trans. David Cheramie, in *The Road to Louisiana: The Saint-Domingue Refugees, 1792–1809,* eds. Carl Brasseaux and Glenn Conrad (Lafayette: Center for Louisiana Studies, University of Southwestern Louisiana, 1992), 38. Besides Jamaica, some refugees went to Cuba and the United States at this point.

8. Dubois, *Avengers of the New World,* 293; Dessens, *From Saint-Domingue to New Orleans,* 13–15; Debien, "The Saint-Domingue Refugees in Cuba," 41; White, *Encountering Revolution,* 167, 170.

9. Lachance, "Repercussions," 212; Paul Lachance, "The 1809 Immigration of Saint-Domingue Refugees to New Orleans: Reception, Integration and Impact," in *The Road to Louisiana: The Saint-Domingue Refugees, 1792–1809,* eds. Carl Brasseaux and Glenn Conrad (Lafayette: Center for Louisiana Studies, University of Southwestern Louisiana,

1992), 246; Dessens, *From Saint-Domingue to New Orleans,* 15, 21–22. Some refugees did travel directly to New Orleans from Saint-Domingue, but most relocated there after first settling elsewhere. Gabriel Debien and René Le Gardeur, "The Saint-Domingue Refugees in Louisiana, 1792–1804," in *The Road to Louisiana: The Saint-Domingue Refugees, 1792–1809,* eds. Carl Brasseaux and Glenn Conrad (Lafayette: Center for Louisiana Studies, University of Southwestern Louisiana, 1992), 113–243.

10. Dessens, *From Saint-Domingue to New Orleans,* 1, 35; Lachance, "The 1809 Immigration," 248; Joseph Logsdon and Caryn Cossé Bell, "The Americanization of Black New Orleans, 1850–1900," in *Creole New Orleans: Race and Americanization,* eds. Arnold R. Hirsch and Joseph Logsdon (Baton Rouge: Louisiana State University Press, 1992), 205–6.

11. Dessens, *From Saint-Domingue to New Orleans,* 27; Lachance, "Repercussions," 213; Lachance, "The 1809 Immigration," 247–48; Scott, "Paper Thin," 1062.

12. Scott and Hébrard, *Freedom Papers,* 49, 66–71; Scott, "Paper Thin," 1063, 1065, 1073–1076, 1080–1085; Scott, "She . . . Refuses," 118, 121, 126–32; Aslakson, "Making Race," 57–58, 64–81.

13. Lachance, "The 1809 Immigration," 248; Lachance, "Repercussions," 213.

14. Jeremy Popkin, *A Concise History of the Haitian Revolution* (West Sussex: Wiley-Blackwell, 2012), 131; Popkin, *You Are All Free,* 291; Debien, "The Saint-Domingue Refugees in Cuba," 45.

15. Dessens, *From Saint-Domingue to New Orleans,* 43; Scott and Hébrard, *Freedom Papers,* 65.

16. Dessens, *From Saint-Domingue to New Orleans,* 43; White, *Encountering Revolution,* 185. Sacramental and notary records in New Orleans indicate that free men of color from Saint-Domingue did settle in New Orleans. Some men entered New Orleans through Barataria, the wetlands south of the city. Caryn Cossé Bell, "Haitian Immigration to Louisiana in the Eighteenth and Nineteenth Centuries," in *In Motion: The African-American Migration Experience* (New York: Schomburg Center for Research in Black Culture, 2005), http://www.inmotionaame.org /texts/viewer.cfm?id=5_000T&page=1. Free black men played an important role in the Battle of New Orleans against the British in 1815. One battalion was composed of 250 former Saint-Dominguans. Caryn Cossé Bell, *Revolution, Romanticism, and the Afro-Creole Protest in Louisiana* (Baton Rouge: Louisiana State University Press, 1997), 55–56.

17. Dessens, *From Saint-Domingue to New Orleans,* 20, 47. Dessens mentions "the few memoirs written by people of African descent" but cites only one: *Memoir of Pierre Toussaint.* Dessens, *From Saint-Domingue to New Orleans,* 47, 193 note 1. For examples of letters written by free women of color refugees see Ulentin, "Shades of Grey," 59, 66–67, 127–30. For white refugee eyewitness accounts see Jeremy Popkin, *Facing Racial Revolution: Eyewitness Accounts of the Haitian Revolution* (Chicago: University of Chicago Press, 2007). For his study of white refugees, R. Darrell Meadows uses "memoirs and correspondence." Meadows, "Engineering Exile," 74.

18. For this essay, I mainly draw from two archival sources: The Consulats Américains collection at the Archives Nationales d'Outre Mer in Aix-en-Provence, France, and New Orleans notarial records at the Notarial Archives Research Center in New Orleans,

La. The Consulats Américains records are documents recorded by refugees in Santiago de Cuba and Baracoa, Cuba; Philadelphia; Baltimore; New York City; and Charleston by French government officials in each place. In the 1820s, when the French government sought proof for indemnity claims by former property owners in Saint-Domingue, it requested that all documents relating to former inhabitants of the colony be returned to the metropole. As a French and then Spanish colonial center, New Orleans had a notary system in place when the United States took control of the Louisiana territory in 1803. With the authority to make legally binding contracts, notaries recorded various types of documents, including slave and land transactions, business partnerships, marriage contracts, and wills and estate inventories, as well as registrations of previously written documents and declarations of assorted natures. The notarial system in New Orleans remains today, and the city's notary ledgers have been archived together since the late nineteenth century.

19. Scott and Hébrard, *Freedom Papers,* 3, 44–46, 48–50, 54–55, 57, 63–64.

20. Bernard Bailyn, *Atlantic History: Concept and Contours* (Cambridge, Mass.: Harvard University Press, 2005), 95.

21. White, *Encountering Revolution,* 26.

22. Meadows, "Engineering Exile," 72–73, 78–79, 82, 87, 102. Focusing on elites, Meadows also includes exiles of the French Revolution in his study. He defines "weak" ties as "distant kin, acquaintances, 'vaguely known compatriots.'" Meadows, "Engineering Exile," 72.

23. Bernard Bailyn described the history of the Atlantic as "a story of a world in motion." Bailyn, *Atlantic History,* 61.

24. *Testament de Rosalie Chesneau, fcl,* January 25, 1810, Narcisse Broutin, vol. 21, 226, NARC; *Rosalie Chaineau Sa procuration,* September 12, 1821, Marc Lafitte, vol. 19, 288, NARC; État *Général des Habitations de la Paroisse de Jean Rabel,* 1 Florèal, An 3 [April 20, 1795], État Général et Particulier du Nord, 5SUPSDOM-1, Archives Nationales d'Outre Mer, Aix-en-Provence, France (hereafter cited as ANOM).

25. David Geggus, *Slavery, War, and Revolution: The British Occupation of Saint Domingue, 1793–1798* (Oxford: Clarendon Press, 1982), 108, 115, 232, 337.

26. *Testament de Rosalie Chesneau*; *Inventaire des biens dependant de la Succession de feu Rosalie Chesneau,* September 9, 1833, L. T. Caire, vol. 32, Act 957, NARC; *Rosalie Chaineau Enregt de pièce,* May 26, 1821, Marc Lafitte, vol. 19, 195, NARC; *Vente d'esclave par Rosalie Chesneau à Marie Zilia neg.sse lib.,* April 10, 1832, Theodore Seghers, vol. 5, Act 161, NARC.

27. *Contrat de Mariage entre le Sieur Jean-Baptiste Augebert Delaunay & la nommée Margueritte Guitonne Reine, négresse libre,* April 30, 1806, Consulats Américains (1794–1826), 6SUPSDOM-4, ANOM.

28. *Contrat de Mariage.* Spanish colonial officials did not allow a French consulate in Cuba, but the Captain General of Guadeloupe authorized his clerks working in the privateering regulation agency set up in Cuba to record copies or accept deposits of papers by Saint-Dominguans. Scott and Hébrard, *Freedom Papers,* 55.

29. Charles Nolan, ed., *Sacramental Records of the Roman Catholic Church of the Archdiocese of New Orleans,* vol. 10, 1810–1812 (New Orleans: Archdiocese of New

Orleans, 1995), 110. The eighth child, Adelaide Josephine, was born in Baracoa on June 3, 1809.

30. Debien, "The Saint-Domingue Refugees in Cuba," 33–34, 40–41, 44–45. In 1808 there were 7,449 refugees in Santiago de Cuba. Matt Childs, "'A Black French General Arrived to Conquer the Island': Images of the Haitian Revolution in Cuba's 1812 Aponte Rebellion," in *The Impact of the Haitian Revolution in the Atlantic World,* ed. David Geggus (Columbia: University of South Carolina Press, 2001), 139.

31. *Déclaration La Liberté de Marguerite Caillou,* 5 Brumaire, An 13 [October 27, 1804], Consulats Américains, 6SUPSDOM-1, ANOM.

32. For other references to the French army's evacuation, see *Enrégistrement de la liberté de Fanchette,* September 24, 1806, Consulats Américains, 6SUPSDOM-3; *Déclaration de la Citoyenne Zaire,* September 26, 1806, Consulats Américains, 6SUPSDOM-3, ANOM.

33. *Déclaration sur les droits de propriété de la nommée* Cécile *Charlesteguy sur le nègre Jean Baptiste dit La Guerre,* 15 Nivôse, An 13 [January 5, 1805], Consulats Américains, 6SUPSDOM-1.

34. Meadows, "Engineering Exile," 93; Dessens, *From Saint-Domingue to New Orleans,* 46–47, 54, 62–63.

35. For examples of documents with this phrase, see *Déclaration sur les droits de propriété de la nommée* Cécile *Charlesteguy; Déclaration de Marie Louise Didier Vve. Renaud,* 14 Frimaire, An 13 [December 5, 1804], Consulats Américains, 6SUPSDOM-3; *Enrégistrement du testament de Marie Louise Dubourg,* 25 Brumaire, An 13 [November 16, 1804], Consulats Américains, 6SUPSDOM-3, ANOM.

36. Scott and Hébrard, *Freedom Papers,* 43, 46–50. For an example of free people of color imprisoned after arriving in Charleston, see *Déclaration de Hen.tte Dessources,* March 23, 1810, Consulats Américains, 6SUPSDOM-10, ANOM.

37. *Contrat de Mariage.*

38. Debien, "The Saint-Domingue Refugees in Cuba," 41–42. Other women procured documentation of their free status before leaving Saint-Domingue, although not all individuals were able to access a notary. See, for example, Scott and Hébrard's discussion of the "improvised document" written by Michel Vincent for his partner, Rosalie, in *Freedom Papers,* 44–47.

39. *Enregistrement de la liberté de Fanchette,* September 24, 1806, Consulats Américains, 6SUPSDOM-3, ANOM. In the Francophone Atlantic, "Arada" often served as a general term to describe enslaved people exported from the Bight of Benin. See Gwendolyn Midlo Hall, *Slavery and African Ethnicities in the Americas: Restoring the Links* (Chapel Hill: University of North Carolina Press, 2005), 17, 111–12; Dubois, *Avengers of the New World,* 40.

40. *Enregistrement de la liberté de Fanchette.*

41. Jacques Nicolas Léger, *Haiti: Her History and Her Detractors* (New York: Neale Publishing Company, 1907), 145.

42. *Déclaration de la Citoyenne Zaire;* Dubois, *Avengers of the New World,* 269–70.

43. Scott and Hébrard, *Freedom Papers,* quote on 57, 58.

44. *Déclaration La Liberté de Marguerite Caillou.*

45. *Déclaration La Liberté de Marguerite Caillou.*

46. *Déclaration La Liberté de Marguerite Caillou.*

47. Dubois, *Avengers of the New World,* 270.

48. *Déclaration La Liberté de Marguerite Caillou.*

49. Dubois, *Avengers of the New World,* 270–71.

50. "*Dit/e*" names (*dit/e* meaning "called") were nicknames. They could be self-appointed, bestowed by friends or family, and/or given to mark significant moments such as baptism or gaining freedom.

51. *Hervey dit Romain (fmoc), Louis v. Rodriguez, John,* case no. 1893, October 16, 1809, New Orleans City Court, New Orleans Public Library, New Orleans, La. (hereafter cited as *Hervey v. Rodriguez*).

52. *Enquête pour constater l'etat civil du nommé Romain dit Hervé actuellement à la N.lle Orléans,* November 23, 1808, Consulats Américains, 6SUPSDOM-2, ANOM.

53. *Procuration par Marie Françoise Lambert Veuve Bastard,* November 24, 1808, Consulats Américains, 6SUPSDOM-2, ANOM. Antoine Rocheville de Menard was a native of Port-au-Prince. In New Orleans, he had several children with a free woman of color named Marie Louise Bremard, a native of Saint-Marc. Nolan, *Sacramental Records,* 8:231; 9:252, 315; 11:377; 13:295.

54. *Hervey v. Rodriguez.* All quotes are from the case documents. The judge was Louis Elisabeth Casimir Moreau-Lislet, a white Saint-Domingue refugee. For more on Moreau-Lislet and the freedom suits in New Orleans City Court, see Aslakson, "Making Race," Chapter 2, especially 63–89, and Scott, "She . . . Refuses," especially 117–22.

55. *Déclaration sur les droits de propriété de la nommée* Cécile *Charlesteguy.*

56. White, *Encountering Revolution,* 26–27; Dessens, *From Saint-Domingue to New Orleans,* 52, 59–60.

57. *Testament de Barbe,* May 11, 1811, Narcisse Broutin, vol. 24, 278, NARC.

58. *Déclaration de Hen.tte Dessources.*

59. White, *Encountering Revolution,* 26.

60. Scott and Hébrard, *Freedom Papers,* 51.

61. *Inventaire des biens*; *Testament de Rosalie Chesneau; Vente d'esclave par Rosalie Chesneau.*

62. Chesneau recorded multiple wills between 1810 and 1833. Each will included the emancipation of the enslaved women she brought with her, but this did not go into effect until she died. In the interim years, Chesneau freed Marie Zilia and Marie Madeleine. Chesneau also sold Marie Zilia's daughter, Toussine, to her in 1832. The other three women did not receive their freedom until after Chesneau's death. In 1835, her executor emancipated Octavie, Marie Joseph, Beatrix, and Beatrix's three children. *Testament de Rosalie Chesneau* (1810); *Acte de liberté Rosalie Chesneau f.l.en faveur de Marie Madelaine,* February 12, 1821, Michel de Armas, vol. 20, Act 29, NARC; *Vente d'esclave par Rosalie Chesneau; Testament de Rosalie Chesneau,* June 29, 1833, L. T. Caire, vol. 30, Act 797, NARC; *Affranchissement par Jean Rousseau exécuteur testamentaire de feu Rosalie Chesneau des esclaves Marie Joseph, Octavie, Aimée, Béatrice, Silvérie & Orestille,* December 8, 1835, L. T. Caire, vol. 48A, Act 907, NARC.

63. Scott and Hébrard, *Freedom Papers,* 43, 50, 70; Scott, "Paper Thin," 1063, 1073, 1077–1078.

64. Scott and Hébrard, *Freedom Papers,* 48; Scott, "Paper Thin," especially 1075–1007, 1080–1081, 1086; Scott, "She . . . Refuses," especially 133–34.

65. *Déclaration de la nommée M.ie J.ne Thomas mulâtresse libre & acte de notoriété sur le fait de cette déclaration,* 5 Germinal, An 13 [March 26, 1805], Consulats Américains, 6SUPSDOM-3, ANOM. Evidence from New Orleans sacramental records suggests that Duthil was the father of Marie Jeanne Thomas's granddaughter. Nolan, *Sacramental Records,* 11:160.

66. *Déclaration sur les droits de propriété de la nommée* Cécile *Charlesteguy.*

67. *Procuration de la nommée* Cécile *Charlesteguy au Sieur Marc Lafitte,* 15 Nivôse, An 13 [January 5, 1805], Consulats Américains, 6SUPSDOM-1.

68. Dessens, *From Saint-Domingue to New Orleans,* 50; "Notaries 1731–1970," New Orleans Notarial Archives, http://www.notarialarchives.org/Notaries/listl.htm. Lafitte served as a notary from 1810 to 1826.

69. *Déclaration de Marie Louise Didier.*

70. Gwendolyn Midlo Hall, *Databases for the Study of Afro-Louisiana History and Genealogy 1699–1860,* http://www.ibiblio.org/laslave/individ.php?sid=34450.

71. Quoted in Debien and Le Gardeur, "The Saint-Domingue Refugees in Louisiana," 199.

72. Debien and Le Gardeur, "The Saint-Domingue Refugees in Louisiana," 175.

73. Quoted in Debien, "The Saint-Domingue Refugees in Cuba," 86.

74. *Procuration par Dlle Me Gve Fortunat à M Gillet,* April 21, 1808, Consulats Américains, 6SUPSDOM-4, ANOM.

75. Meadows, "Engineering Exile," 81–83; Dessens, *From Saint-Domingue to New Orleans,* 46–47, 50; White, *Encountering Revolution,* 30; *Testament de Barbe.*

76. *Testament de Barbe.* Evidence from New Orleans sacramental records suggests that Barbe could have known Lavigne in Saint-Domingue. Nolan, *Sacramental Records,* 10:273.

77. *Déclaration La Liberté de Marguerite Caillou.*

78. See, for example, *Notoriété pour le n.e Pre Gilles,* September 9, 1788, Grimperel, SDOM-870, ANOM.

79. Quoted in Scott, "She . . . Refuses," 120–21.

80. John Garrigus, *Before Haiti: Race and Citizenship in French Saint-Domingue* (New York: Palgrave Macmillan, 2006), 26.

81. *Enquête pour constater l'etat civil du nommé Romain.*

82. John Adems Paxton, comp., *The New Orleans Directory and Register* (New Orleans, 1822), microform, Historic New Orleans Collection, New Orleans, La.; Nolan, *Sacramental Records,* 10:260; *Enquête pour constater l'etat civil du nommé Romain.*

83. *Testament de François Verdry,* July 21, 1820, Christoval de Armas, vol. 3, Act 165, 271, NARC.

84. Nolan, *Sacramental Records,* 11:218.

85. Rosalie Chesneau was from Jean-Rabel, in the north, whereas Marie Genevieve Zelime Fortunat lived in Jérémie, in the south. *Testament de Rosalie Chesneau* (1810); *Procuration par Dlle Me Gve Fortunat à M Gillet.*

86. *Rosalie Chaineau Enregt de pièce.*

87. *Dépôt de pièce par Rosalie Chesneau,* May 12, 1814, Michel de Armas, vol. 8, Act 231, 123, NARC.

88. *Quittance Jn. Bte. Braud à Rosalie Chesneau,* June 13, 1814, Michel de Armas, vol. 8, Act 325, 171, NARC.

Intimate Entanglement in the Early Republic

1. For the Colbert family's history, see Draper Manuscript Collection, Series U, vol. 10, Frontier War Papers; Ronald Eugene Craig, "The Colberts in Chickasaw History, 1783–1818: A Study in Internal Tribal Dynamics" (Ph.D. diss., University of New Mexico, 1998), 112–33; Natalie Inman, "Networks in Negotiation: The Role of Family and Kinship in Intercultural Diplomacy on the Trans-Appalachian Frontier, 1680–1840" (Ph.D. diss., Vanderbilt University, 2010), 23–26; Arrell Gibson, *The Chickasaw* (Norman: University of Oklahoma Press, 1972), 65–66; James Atkinson, *Splendid Land, Splendid People: The Chickasaw Indians to Removal* (Tuscaloosa: University of Alabama Press, 2004).

2. The Juzan family's history has been pieced together from the following sources: Orphan Court Records Washington County, Alabama, Minute Book A; Washington County Alabama Probate Records, Deed Book I, 168; George S. Gaines, *The Reminiscences of George Strother Gaines: Pioneer and Statesman of Early Alabama and Mississippi, 1805–1843,* ed. James P. Pate (Tuscaloosa: University of Alabama Press, 1998), 162; Albert James Pickett, *History of Alabama* (Sheffield, Ala.: Robert C. Randolph, publisher, 1896), 290; H. S. Halbert, "Bernard Roman's Map of 1772," *Publications of the Mississippi Historical Society,* vol. 6, ed. Franklin L. Riley (Oxford: Published by the Mississippi Historical Society, 1902), 417.

3. For a description of Colbert's wealth, see "Declaration of Silbestre Labadie, July 5, 1782," in Lawrence Kinnaird, *Spain and the Mississippi Valley, 1765–1794, Vol. 2* (Washington, D.C.: Government Printing Office, 1946), 21–34, and "Deposition of Dona Anicanora Ramos," in Louis Houck, *The Spanish Regime in Missouri, Vol. 1* (San Bernadino, Calif.: Ulan Press, 2011), 214–31.

4. For an overview of Chickasaw and Choctaw kinship practices, see James Taylor Carson, "Choctaw and Chickasaw Women, 1690–1834," in *Mississippi Women: Their Histories, Their Lives,* vol. 2, eds. Elizabeth Ann Payne, Martha H. Swain, and Marjorie Julian Spruill (Athens: University of Georgia Press, 2010), 7–11; Patricia Galloway, *Choctaw Genesis: 1500–1700* (Lincoln: University of Nebraska Press, 1995), 121–23, 320–22; Michelene Pesantubbee, *Choctaw Women in a Chaotic World* (Albuquerque: University of New Mexico Press, 2005), 46–47.

5. John Lawson, *New Voyage to Carolina* (London, 1709), 46, 190 ("Winchester Weddings"); "Affidavit of James Maxwell, June 12, 1751," in *Documents Relating to Indian Affairs,* vol. 1, ed. William McDowell (Columbia: South Carolina Archives Department, 1958), 70; Randy Sparks, *Where the Negroes Are Masters: An African Port in the Era of the Slave Trade* (Cambridge, Mass.: Harvard University Press, 2014), 22–23, 80; David Northup, *Africa's Discovery of Europe: 1450–1850* (Oxford: Oxford University Press, 2009), 72; George Brooks, "The Signares of Saint-Louis and Goree: Women Entrepreneurs

in Eighteenth-Century Senegal," in *Women in Africa: Studies in Social and Economic Change,* eds. Nancy J. Hafkin and Edna G. Bay (Stanford, Calif.: Stanford University Press, 1976), 19–44; Durba Ghosh, *Sex and the Family in Colonial India: The Making of Empire* (Cambridge: Cambridge University Press, 2006), 35.

6. Quoted in Ibram Kendi, *Stamped from the Beginning: The Definitive History of Racist Ideas in America* (New York: Nation Books, 2016), 80–82.

7. Kendi, *Stamped from the Beginning,* 79–103; Reginald Horsman, *Race and Manifest Destiny: The Origins of American Racial Anglo-Saxonism* (Cambridge, Mass.: Harvard University Press, 1981), 43–61; Claudio Saunt, *Black, White, and Indian: Race and the Unmaking of American Family* (Oxford: Oxford University Press, 2006), 66–83; Winthrop Jordan, *Black over White: American Attitudes toward the Negro, 1550–1812* (Chapel Hill: University of North Carolina Press, 1968), 216–68.

8. Henry Knox to George Washington, July 7, 1789, Founders Online, National Archives, https://founders.archives.gov/documents/Washington/05-3-2-067.

9. Francis Paul Prucha, *Documents of United States Indian Policy* (Lincoln: University of Nebraska Press, 2000), 51; Thomas Jefferson to Hendrick Aupaumut, December 21, 1808, Founders Online, National Archives.

10. Quoted in Greg O'Brien, *Choctaws in a Revolutionary Age, 1750–1830* (Lincoln: University of Nebraska Press, 2005), 100, 103.

11. Theda Perdue, *Cherokee Women: Gender and Culture Change, 1700–1835* (Lincoln: University of Nebraska Press, 1998), 115–34; Carson, "Choctaw and Chickasaw Women," 7–22; James Taylor Carson, "Horses and the Economy and Culture of the Choctaw Indians, 1690–1840," *Ethnohistory* 42 (1995): 498–502; James Taylor Carson, "Native Americans, the Market Revolution, and Culture Change: The Choctaw Cattle Economy, 1690–1830," *Agricultural History* 71 (1997): 1–18.

12. Hugh Montgomery to William Raburn, July 3, 1817, Southeastern Native American Documents, 1730–1842, http://neptune3.galib.uga.edu/ssp/cgi-bin/tei-natamer-idx.pl?sessionid=7f000001&type=doc&tei2id=TCC453.

13. Quoted in Saunt, *Black, White, and Indian,* 35.

14. James Atkinson, *Splendid Land, Splendid People: The Chickasaw Indians to Removal* (Tuscaloosa: University of Alabama Press, 2004), 228–30; Arthur De Rosier, *The Removal of the Choctaw Indians* (Knoxville: University of Tennessee Press, 1970), 116–29.

15. Ishtehotopa et al. to Andrew Jackson, December 24, 1835, National Archives Microfilm, M234, Roll 236.

16. Ishtehotopa et al. to Andrew Jackson, December 24, 1835.

17. Ishtehotopa et al. to Andrew Jackson, December 24, 1835.

18. Ishtehotopa et al. to Andrew Jackson, December 24, 1835.

19. Ishtehotopa et al. to Andrew Jackson, December 24, 1835.

20. Interview of Elizabeth Kemp Mead, Indian Pioneer Collection, Western History Collection, University of Oklahoma, http://digital.libraries.ou.edu/cdm/ref/collection/indianpp/id/7836; George Leftwich, "Cotton Gin Port and Gaines' Trace," in *Publications of the Mississippi Historical Quarterly* 7 (1903): 269–71; Dennis J. Mitchell, *A New History of Mississippi* (Oxford: University of Mississippi Press, 2014), 100–101.

21. *Wall vs. Williamson,* Supreme Court of Alabama, 8 Ala. 48, 1845 (hereafter cited

as Wall I), and *Wall vs, Williams,* Supreme Court of Alabama, 11 Ala. 826, 1847 (hereafter cited as Wall II).

22. *Brashear vs. Williams,* Supreme Court of Alabama, 10 Ala. 630, 1846.

23. Wall II.

24. Wall I.

25. Wall II.

26. Marcia Haag and Henry Willis, *A Gathering of Statesmen: Records of the Choctaw Council Meetings, 1826–1828* (Norman: University of Oklahoma Press, 2013), 83–99.

27. Wall II.

28. Delila Wall to Sebelle Wall, Sumter County Probate Court, Deed Book B, 587.

29. *Morgan vs. McGhee,* Supreme Court of Tennessee, 24 Tenn. 13, 1844; Laurel Shire Clark, *The Threshold of Manifest Destiny: Gender and National Expansion in Florida* (Philadelphia: University of Pennsylvania Press, 2016); Laurel Shire Clark, "The Rights of a Florida Wife: Slavery, U.S. Expansion, and Married Women's Property Law," *Journal of Women's History* 22 (2010): 39–63; Bethany Ruth Berger, "After Pocahontas: Indian Women and the Law, 1830–1934," *American Indian Law Review* 21 (1997): 1–62.

30. *Wells and Wells vs. Thompson, Reports of Cases Argued and Determined in the Supreme Court of Alabama,* 2nd ed. (St. Paul, Minn.: West Publishing Company, 1907), 308–13.

31. *Wells and Wells vs. Thompson,* 312.

32. *Rhoda Gunn vs. Samuel Colbert,* Mississippi Superior Court of Chancery, October Term 1835. I would like to thank Natalie Inman for providing me with information on Rhoda Gunn.

33. Theda Perdue convincingly argues that the term "half-breed" was meaningless to most Native tribes, since persons with white fathers and Native mothers were accorded the rights and privileges given to "full blood" Natives. See Theda Perdue, *"Mixed Blood" Indians: Racial Construction in the Early South* (Athens: University of Georgia Press, 2003), 39.

34. Many excellent studies have been done detailing the impact of racial slavery on Native society. For a recent account, see Christina Snyder, *Slavery in Indian Country* (Cambridge, Mass.: Harvard University Press, 2010); see also Theda Perdue, *Slavery and the Evolution of Cherokee Society, 1540–1866* (Knoxville: University of Tennessee Press, 1987).

35. *Rhoda Gunn vs. Samuel Colbert.*

36. Charles Francis Eastmond was a white man married to Elizabeth Colbert, the daughter of Major James Colbert and therefore a Chickasaw "half breed." Deed Book J, Marshall County, MS. See also R. Bell and Gordon to Jackson, February 10, 1832, Office of Indian Affairs, Chickasaw Agency.

37. De Soto County, MS Probate Court, Deed Book B, 179.

38. Perdue, *Cherokee Women,* 98–99. For Bullen's comments, see "Extracts from the Journal of the Rev. Mr. Bullen, Missionary to the Chickasaw," *New York Missionary Magazine, and Repository of Religious Intelligence,* January 4, 1800.

39. Peter Wood, "The Changing Population of the Colonial South: An Overview by Race and Region, 1685–1790," in *Powhatan's Mantle: Indians in the Colonial South,*

eds. Gregory Waselkov, Peter Wood, and M. Thomas Hatley (Lincoln: University of Nebraska Press, 2006), 57–131.

40. Kirsten McKenzie, "'My Own Mind Dying within Me': Eliza Fairbarin and the Reinvention of Colonial Middle-Class Domesticity in Cape Town," *South African Historical Journal* 36 (1997): 22–23; Catherine Hall, "Of Gender and Empire," *Gender and Empire,* ed. Philippa Levine (Oxford: Oxford University Press, 2007), 46–76.

41. The historiography on mixed-race families throughout the Atlantic world has expanded significantly in recent years. See especially Kit Candlin, *Enterprising Women: Gender, Race, and Power in the Revolutionary Atlantic* (Athens: University of Georgia Press, 2015), 179; Pernille Ipsen, *Daughters of the Trade: Atlantic Slavers and Interracial Marriage on the Gold Coast* (Philadelphia: University of Philadelphia Press, 2015); Brooke Newman, "Gender, Sexuality, and the Formation of Racial Identities in the Eighteenth-Century Anglo-Caribbean World," *Gender and History* 22 (2010): 585–602; Jennifer Spear, *Race, Sex, and Social Order in Early New Orleans* (Baltimore: Johns Hopkins University Press, 2014); Andrew Frank, *Creeks and Southerners: Biculturalism on the Early American Frontier* (Lincoln: University of Nebraska Press, 2005).

Building Black Civic Manhood

1. José Correia Leite, "Valor da raça," *O Clarim*, April 6, 1924. In subsequent years, the newspaper also went under the name *O Clarim d'Alvorada* (The Clarion of Dawn).

2. Leite, "Valor da Raça."

3. Arquivo do Estado de São Paulo, Sociedades Civis, Estatuas/Compromissos, Sociedade Maçônica Loja Capitular Luiz Gama, 10/4/1897, C10389; Club 13 de Maio de Homens Pretos, 07/10/1902, C10393; Sociedade Beneficente dos Homens de Cor, 8/1/1909, C10401; and Centro da Federacão dos Homens de Côr de São Paulo, 28/08/1914, C10414. I have maintained the original Portuguese orthography utilized in each organizational charter. The dates listed as part of the archival identifier indicate when the provincial government approved the group's organizational statutes, not the association's date of establishment. Hereafter, the Arquivo do Estado de São Paulo is cited as AESP.

4. The term *Paulistano* refers to residents of the city of São Paulo. For scholarship that chronicles the proliferation of black social organizations, especially after the 1920s, see Florestan Fernandes, *Integração do negro na sociedade de classes: No limiar de uma nova era,* vol. 2 (São Paulo: Dominus, 1965), 33–95; George Reid Andrews, *Blacks and Whites in São Paulo, Brazil, 1888–1988* (Madison: University of Wisconsin Press, 1991), 139–56, 181–224; Kim Butler, *Freedoms Given, Freedoms Won: Afro-Brazilians in Post-Abolition São Paulo and Salvador* (New Brunswick, N.J.: Rutgers University Press, 1998),78–128; and Paulina Alberto, *Terms of Inclusion: Black Intellectuals in Twentieth-Century Brazil* (Chapel Hill: University of North Carolina Press, 2011), 33–56.

5. For critical works on black voluntary associations in Cuba, see Philip Howard, *Changing History: Afro-Cuban Cabildos and Societies of Color in the Nineteenth Century* (Baton Rouge: Louisiana State University Press, 1998); Aline Helg, *Our Rightful Share: The Afro-Cuban Struggle for Equality, 1886–1912* (Chapel Hill: University of North

Carolina Press, 1995), 30–32, 131–32; Oilda Hevia Lanier, *El directorio central de las sociedades negras de Cuba, 1886–1894* (Havana: Editorial de Ciencias Sociales, 1996); and Carmen V. Montejo Arrechea, *Sociedades de instruccíon y recreo de pardos y morenos que existieron en Cuba colonial* (Veracruz, México: Instituto Veracruzano de Cultura, 1993). For critical works on black secular associations in the United States, see Theda Skocpol, Ariane Liazos, and Marshall Ganz, eds., *What a Mighty Power We Can Be: African American Fraternal Groups and the Struggle for Racial Equality* (Princeton: Princeton University Press, 2006); Jacqueline M. Moore, *Leading the Race: The Transformation of the Black Elite in the Nation's Capital, 1880–1920* (Charlottesville: University Press of Virginia, 1999), chapter 8; Stephen Kantrowitz, "'Intended for the Better Government of Man': The Political History of African American Freemasonry in the Era of Emancipation," *Journal of American History* 96, no. 4 (March 2010): 1002–1026; and Peter P. Hinks and Stephen Kantrowitz, eds., *All Men Free and Brethren: Essays on the History of African American Freemasonry* (Ithaca, N.Y.: Cornell University Press, 2013).

6. Diana Paton and Pamela Scully, "Introduction: Gender and Slave Emancipation in Comparative Perspective," in *Gender and Slave Emancipation in the Atlantic World*, eds. Pamela Scully and Diana Paton (Durham: Duke University Press, 2005), 17–18.

7. For critical discussion of the terms "manhood" and "manliness" in Brazil and in Latin America, see Peter Beattie, *Tribute of Blood: Army, Honor, Race and Nation in Brazil, 1864–1945* (Durham: Duke University Press, 2001); Peter Beattie, "Measures of Manhood: Honor, Enlisted Army Service, and Slavery's Decline in Brazil, 1850–1890," in *Changing Men and Masculinities in Latin America*, ed. Matthew C. Gutmann (Durham: Duke University Press, 2003), 234–51; Peter Beattie, "The House, the Street, and Barracks: Reform and Honorable Masculine Space in Brazil," *Hispanic American Historical Review* 76, no. 3 (August 1996): 439–73; Martha S. Santos, *Cleansing Honor with Blood: Masculinity, Violence, and Power in the Backlands of Northeast Brazil, 1845–1889* (Stanford, Calif.: Stanford University Press, 2012); Matthew C. Gutmann, "Introduction," in *Changing Men and Masculinities in Latin America*, ed. Matthew C. Gutmann (Durham: Duke University Press, 2003), 1–4; Matthew C. Gutmann, *The Meanings of Macho: Being a Man in Mexico City* (Berkeley: University of California Press, 1996). For an excellent recent anthology on masculinity and manhood in Anglo Atlantic contexts, see Thomas A. Foster, ed., *New Man: Manliness in Early America* (New York: New York University Press, 2011).

8. For discussion of the popularity of the concept of fraternity with regard to Afro-Brazilians in the mainstream press and Afro-Brazilian press, see Alberto, *Terms of Inclusion*, 40–41.

9. For more on the idea of Brazil as a "racial democracy" and the reality of widespread discrimination in the country in the nineteenth and twentieth centuries, see Andrews, *Blacks and Whites*, 129–32; Thomas E. Skidmore, *Black into White: Race and Nationality in Brazilian Thought*, 2nd ed. (Durham: Duke University Press, 1993), 22–24, 38–77. Scholarship has indicated that nonwhites of African descent faced severe disadvantages in terms of wages, educational attainment, and even choice of potential marital partners. For discussion of these findings, see Stanley R. Bailey, *Legacies of Race: Identities, Attitudes, and Politics in Brazil* (Stanford, Calif.: Stanford University Press, 2009);

Michael Hanchard, ed., *Racial Politics in Contemporary Brazil* (Durham: Duke University Press, 1999); Nelson Do Valle Silva, "Updating the Cost of Not Being White," in *Race, Class, and Power in Brazil,* ed. Pierre-Michel Fontaine (Los Angeles: University of California, 1985), 42–55; and John Burdick, *Blessed Anastácia: Women, Race, and Popular Christianity in Brazil* (New York: Routledge, 1998), chapter 1.

10. Joaquim Nabuco, *O abolicionismo* (London: 1883), 22–23, cited in Skidmore, *Black into White*, 23.

11. Skidmore, *Black into White,* 38–77; Celia Maria Azevedo, *Onda negra, medo branco: O negro no imaginário das elites-século XIX* (Rio de Janeiro: Paz e Terra, 1987), especially 251–58; Lilia Moritz Schwarcz, *Retrato em branco e negro: Jornais, escravos, e cidadãos em* São Paulo no final do *século XIX* (São Paulo: Círculo de Livros, 1987); and Marc A. Hertzman, "Making Music and Masculinity in Vagrancy's Shadow: Race, Wealth, and *Malandragem* in Post-Abolition Rio de Janeiro," *Hispanic American Historical Review* 90, no. 4 (2010): 591–92.

12. Louis Agassiz, *A Journey in Brazil* (Boston: Ticknor and Fields, 1868), 293.

13. Dain Borges, "'Puffy, Ugly, Slothful, and Inert': Degeneration in Brazilian Social Thought, 1880–1940," *Journal of Latin American Studies* 25, no. 2 (May 1993): 235–56.

14. For discussion of masculinity in reference to men of color and lower-sector men in Brazil in the late nineteenth and early twentieth centuries, see Beattie, "Measures of Manhood," 234–51; Beattie, "The House, the Street, and Barracks," 439–73; Sandra Lauderdale Graham, "Honor among Slaves," in *Faces of Honor: Sex, Shame, and Violence in Colonial Latin America,* ed. Lyman Johnson and Sonya Lipsett-Rivera (Albuquerque: University of New Mexico Press, 1998), 201–29; Santos, *Cleansing Honor with Blood;* and Hertzman, "Making Music and Masculinity," 591–625.

15. Lauderdale Graham, "Honor among Slaves," 208–23.

16. Lauderdale Graham, "Honor among Slaves," 208–23.

17. Alexandre Mansur Barata, *Luz e sombras: A* ação da maçonaria brasileira, 1870–*1910* (Campinas: Editora da Unicamp, 1999), 175–88.

18. AESP, Sociedades Civis, Estatuas/Compromissos, Sociedade Maçônica Loja Capitular Luiz Gama, 10/4/1897, C10389.

19. Barata, *Luz e sombras,*185. The Guilherme Dias Lodge of the Masons was founded in 1897 in the provincial capital.

20. For an introduction to Masonic organizing in Europe, see James Melton, *The Rise of the Public in Enlightenment Europe* (New York: Cambridge University Press, 2001), chapter 8; and for the classic work on the topic, see Margaret C. Jacob, *Living the Enlightenment: Freemasonry and Politics in Eighteenth-Century Europe* (New York: Oxford University Press, 1991). For analysis of Masons in the United States, see Jessica Harland Jacobs, *Builders of Empire: Freemasons and British Imperialism, 1717–1927* (Chapel Hill: University of North Carolina Press, 2007); Mark Tabbert, *American Freemasons: Three Centuries of Building Communities* (New York: New York University Press, 2005); Joy Porter, *Native American Freemasonry: Associationalism and Performance in America* (Lincoln: University of Nebraska Press, 2011); Kantrowitz, "'Intended for the Better Government of Man,'" 1005–1011; Maurice Wallace, "'Are We Men?': Prince Hall, Martin Delany, and the Masculine Ideal in Black Freemasonry, 1775–1865," *American Literary*

History 9, no. 3 (Autumn 1997): 397–424; and Hinks and Kantrowitz, *All Men Free and Brethren.*

21. Celia Maria Mariho de Azevedo, *Maçonaria, anti-racismo e cidadania: Uma história de lutas e debates transnacionais* (São Paulo: Annablume, 2010), 37–45, especially 41.

22. Barata, *Luz e sombras,* 175–80.

23. Azevedo, *Maçonaria,* 38.

24. AESP, Sociedades Civis, Estatuas/Compromissos, Sociedade Maçônica Loja Capitular Luiz Gama, 10/4/1897, C10389.

25. Hendrik Kraay, "'Shelter of the Uniform': The Brazilian Army and Runaway Slaves, 1800–1888," *Journal of Social History* 29, no. 3 (Spring 1996): 646–47; Andrews, *Blacks and Whites,* 35, 274; Conrad, *Destruction of Brazilian Slavery,* 110–11, 117; and Alberto, *Terms of Inclusion,* 9. For more on the interprovincial slave trade in Brazil to the southeast region, see Richard Graham, "Another Middle Passage? Internal Slave Trade in Brazil," in *The Chattel Principle: Internal Slave Trades in the Americas,* ed. Walter Hawthorne (New Haven: Yale University Press, 2004), 291–324; Mary Karasch, *Slave Life in Rio de Janeiro, 1808–1850* (Princeton: Princeton University Press, 1987), 50–54; Francisco Vidal Luna and Herbert Klein, *Slavery and the Economy of São Paulo, 1750–1850* (Stanford, Calif.: Stanford University Press, 2003), 17.

26. Kraay, "'Shelter of the Uniform,'" 646–47; Andrews, *Blacks and Whites,* 35, 274; Robert Conrad, *Destruction of Brazilian Slavery, 1850–1888,* 2nd ed. (Malabar, Fla.: Krieger Publishing Company, 1993), 110–11, 117; and Alberto, *Terms of Inclusion,* 9.

27. Kraay, "'Shelter of the Uniform,'" 646–47; Andrews, *Blacks and Whites,* 35, 274; Conrad, *Destruction of Brazilian Slavery,* 110–11, 117; Alberto, *Terms of Inclusion,* 9; and Elciene Azevedo, *O direito dos escravos: Lutas jurídicas e abolicionismo na província de São Paulo* (Campinas: Editora Unicamp, 2010), 78, 83, 100–103.

28. "Noticario," *A Provincia de São Paulo,* January 12, 1875; and "Luiz Gama," *A Provincia de São Paulo,* November 24, 1889.

29. Ernani Silva Bruno, *História e tradições da cidade de São Paulo* (Rio de Janeiro: José Olympio, 1953), vol. 2, unpaged appendix; and AESP, Sociedades Civis, Estatuas/Compromissos, Sociedade Maçônica Loja Capitular Luiz Gama, 10/4/1897, C10389.

30. See AESP, Sociedades Civis, Estatuas/Compromissos, Sociedade Maçônica Loja Capitular Luiz Gama, 10/4/1897, C10389; Raul Joviano de Amaral, *Os pretos do Rosário de São Paulo: Subsidios históricos,* 2nd ed. (São Paulo: João Scortecci Editora, 1991), 124, 157–68, and *Os pretos do Rosário de São Paulo: Subsidios históricos* (São Paulo: Alarico, 1953) (unpaged back matter, member index). The members of both the Rosary brotherhood and the Luiz Gama Masonic Lodge were Theophilo Dias de Castro, Rufino José de Almeida, and Benedito Esteves do Nascimento. Two other officers of the Luiz Gama Masonic Lodge, João Baptista dos Santos and Bento Candido Nogueira, were officers of the Thirteenth of May Club of Black Men of São Paulo. See AESP, Sociedades Civis, Estatuas/Compromissos, Club13 de Maio de Homens Pretos, 17/10/1902, C10393. While I expected the overlap for the Rosary Brotherhood to be greater, literacy restrictions may have limited broader participation, since, in 1890, at least three Rosary executive council members could not write their names. For examples, see Arquivo da Cúria Metropolitana de São Paulo, Uncatalogued Folder, Irmandades XXVI, Nossa Senhora do Rosário

dos Homens Pretos. Hereafter, the Arquivo da Cúria Metropolitana de São Paulo is cited as ACMSP.

31. Amaral, *Os pretos do Rosário,* 2nd ed., 124, 157–68.

32. Butler, *Freedoms Given, Freedom Won,* 82; Andrews, *Blacks and Whites,* 142; and June Hahner, *Poverty and Politics: The Urban Poor in Brazil, 1870–1920* (Albuquerque: University of New Mexico Press, 1986), 218.

33. Azevedo, *Maçonaria,* 159–218.

34. AESP, Sociedades Civis, Estatuas/Compromissos, Sociedade Maçônica Loja Capitular Luiz Gama, 10/4/1897, C10389, Titulo 1, Art. 1 (A sociedade maçonica Loja Capitular Luiz Gama . . . compõe-se de cidadãos brasileiras e extrangeiros de qualquer profissão ou classe social uma vez que saibam ler e escrever que sejam dotados de bons costumes e estejam no gozo dos direitos civis e adoptem uma confissão religiosa qualquer).

35. AESP, Sociedades Civis, Estatuas/Compromissos, Sociedade Maçônica Loja Capitular Luiz Gama, 10/4/1897, C10389, Título 1, Art. 1 (. . . adoptem uma confissão religiosa qualquer . . .).

36. For discussion of changing citizenship criteria and qualification for suffrage in the nineteenth century, see Richard Graham, *Patronage and Politics in Nineteenth-Century Brazil* (Stanford, Calif.: Stanford University Press, 1990), 103–7, 191–92, 198–202; and Sueann Caulfield, *In Defense of Honor: Sexual Morality, Modernity, and Nation in Early Twentieth Century Brazil* (Durham: Duke University Press, 2000), 26.

37. AESP, Sociedades Civis, Estatuas/Compromissos, Sociedade Maçônica Loja Capitular Luiz Gama, 10/4/1897, C10389, Título 1, Art. 1 (. . . estejam no gozo dos direitos civis . . .) and Caulfield, *In Defense of Honor,* 26.

38. Barata, *Luzes e sombras,* 42 (. . . ser maçom era sinônimo de ser cidadão).

39. AESP, Sociedades Civis, Estatuas/Compromissos, Sociedade Maçônica Loja Capitular Luiz Gama, 10/4/1897, C10389, Título 1, Art. 1 (. . . *uma vez* que saibam ler e escrever . . .). Emphasis added.

40. AESP, Sociedades Civis, Estatuas/Compromissos, Sociedade Maçônica Loja Capitular Luiz Gama, 10/4/1897, C10389.

41. Lay Catholic brotherhoods, also called confraternities and sodalities, are devotional societies organized to celebrate the lives and virtues of selected saints. For evidence of women's participation in sodalities in Brazil, see Elizabeth Kiddy, *Blacks of the Rosary: Memory and History in Minas Gerais Brazil* (University Park: Pennsylvania State University Press, 2005), 96–98, 154; João José Reis, *Death Is a Festival: Funeral Rites and Rebellion in Nineteenth Century Brazil,* trans. H. Sabrina Gledhill (Chapel Hill: University of North Carolina Press, 2003), 45–48, 50–51; Mariza de Carvalho Soares, "Can Women Guide and Govern Men? Gendering Politics among African Catholics in Colonial Brazil," in *Women and Slavery: The Modern Atlantic,* ed. Gwyn Campbell, Suzanne Miers, and Joseph C. Miller (Athens: Ohio University Press, 2008); and Alicia Monroe, "Brotherhoods of Their Own: Black Confraternities and Civic Leadership in São Paulo, Brazil, 1850–1930" (Ph.D. diss., Emory University, 2014), chapter 3.

42. The Seventh of September Lodge was established in 1863. For evidence of the Seventh of September Lodge as the oldest Masonic association in the city of São Paulo,

see Barata, *Luzes e sombras,* 175. The Lodge took its name from the day commemorating Brazilian independence. For more on the proclamation of September 7, 1822 declaring Brazil an independent empire separate from Portugal, see Roderick J. Barman, *Citizen Emperor: Pedro II and the Making of Brazil, 1825–91* (Stanford, Calif.: Stanford University Press, 1999), 4, and Emilia Viotti da Costa, *The Brazilian Empire: Myths and Histories,* rev. ed. (Chapel Hill: University of North Carolina Press, 2000), 17–20.

43. For evidence of the female lodge and its affiliation with the Seventh of September Lodge, see Antonio José Baptista de Luné, *Almanak da Provincia de São Paulo para 1873 organizado e publicado por Antonio Jose Baptista de Luné e Paulo Delfino da Fonseca* (1873; repr., São Paulo: Imprensa Oficial do Estado; Arquivo do Estado, 1985), 112–13. For more on women's auxiliary lodges in African American Masonry, see Skocpol, Liazos, and Ganz, *What a Mighty Power We Can Be,* 69–79; and Brittney C. Cooper, "'They are Nevertheless Our Brethren': The Order of the Eastern Star and the Battle for Women's Leadership, 1874–1925," in Peter P. Hinks and Stephen Kantrowitz, ed., *All Men Free and Brethren: Essays on the History of African American Freemasonry* (Ithaca, N.Y.: Cornell University Press, 2013), 114–30. For evidence of women's participation and exclusion in Masonic associations in early modern Europe, see Jacob, *Living the Enlightenment,* 4–5, 124–26.

44. The other organization that permitted female restriction, but which is not analyzed in this essay, was the Federated Center of Men of Color (1914). AESP, Sociedades Civis, Estatuas/Compromissos, Centro da Federação dos Homens de Côr de São Paulo, 28/08/1914, C10414, Capítulo 1, Art. 1 and Art. 2 (O Centro admittirá como socio todas as pessoas de maior edade e de boa conducta, sem distinção de crenças, nacionalidade, and *sexo*).

45. AESP, Sociedades Civis, Estatuas/Compromissos, Sociedade Beneficente dos Homens de Cor, 8/1/1909, C10401, Capítulo 2, Art. 4 (Do admissão . . . 4.0. Para alguma sera admittido a fazer parte da socidade um que seja previamente proposto por um socio . . . com declaração de nome, estado, naturalidade estado, profissão, e residenica do proposto . . .).

46. AESP, Sociedades Civis, Estatuas/Compromissos, Sociedade Beneficente dos Homens de Cor, 8/1/1909, C10401, Capítulo 2, Art. 4.1–4.3 (Do admissão . . . 4.1. Ser de bons costumes; 4.2. Acharem-se em estado de perfeita saúde; 4.3. Ser maior de 14 annos e menor de 50). Exactly what founders meant in terms of the requirement of a "perfect state of health" is unclear. No further detail was given.

47. AESP, Sociedades Civis, Estatuas/Compromissos, Sociedade Beneficente dos Homens de Cor, 8/1/1909, C10401, Capítulo 2, Art. 5 (Só podem fazer parte da sociedade, as senhoras dos socios, filhos dos socios e irmãs dos socios . . .).

48. AESP, Sociedades Civis, Estatuas/Compromissos, Sociedade Beneficente dos Homens de Cor, 8/1/1909, C10401, Capítulo 2, Art. 5 (Só podem fazer parte da sociedade, as senhoras dos socios, filhos dos socios e irmãs dos socios . . . e não serem maior de quarenta annos e menos de quinze annos).

49. See AESP, Sociedades Civis, Estatuas/Compromissos, Sociedade Beneficente dos Homens de Cor, 8/1/1909, C10401, Capítulo 2, Art. 5 and Art. 9–Art. 15. Member categories included "effectivos," "remitidos," "benefeitores," and "honorarios." Effective

members paid minimal entrance fees and had minimal responsibilities in the association.

50. AESP, Sociedades Civis, Estatuas/Compromissos, Sociedade Beneficente dos Homens de Cor, 8/1/1909, C10401, Capítulo 2, Art. 5 (Único-Deveram tambem apresentar attestado de medico do quadro, provando achar-se de perfeita saude . . .).

51. Borges, "Ugly, Puffy, Slothful," 238, 240; and Nancy Leys Stephen, *The Hour of Eugenics: Race, Gender, and Nation in Latin America* (Ithaca, N.Y.: Cornell University Press, 1991), 44–45.

52. Sandra Lauderdale Graham, *House and Street: The Domestic World of Servants and Masters in Nineteenth-Century Rio de Janeiro* (Austin: University of Texas Press, 1992), 4; Karasch, *Slave Life in Rio,* 191, 206–10; Beattie, *Tribute of Blood,* 8.

53. Beattie, *Tribute of Blood,* 8; Andrews, *Blacks and Whites,* 33; Butler, *Freedoms Given, Freedoms Won,* 69; and Ian Read, *Hierarchies of Slavery in Santos, Brazil, 1822–1888* (Stanford: Stanford University Press, 2012), 112, 133. For discussion of women's bodies and state control see Lauderdale Graham, *House and Street,* 112-136; Stephan, *Hour of Eugenics,* 43-44 and 110; Caulfield, *In Defense of Honor,* 54–78; Alberto Heráclito Ferreira Filho, *Quem pariu e bateu, que balance! Mundos femininos, maternidade e pobreza Salvador–1890–1940* (Salvador: Centro de Estudos Baianos da UFBA, 2003), 63–65, 70–72, 94–113; and Okezi T. Otovo, "From Mãe Preta to Mãe Desamparada: Maternity and Public Health in Post-Abolition Bahia," *Luso-Brazilian Review* 48, no. 2 (2011): 161–91.

54. Lauderdale Graham, *House and Street,* 116–17.

55. Robin L. Anderson, "Public Health and Public Healthiness, São Paulo, Brazil, 1876–1893," *Journal of the History of Medicine and Allied Sciences* 41 (July 1986): 297.

56. Otovo, "From Mãe Preta," 172–73.

57. Otovo, "From Mãe Preta," 172–73; Anderson, "Public Health," 297; Lauderdale Graham, *House and Street,* 116–35; and Caulfield, *In Defense of Honor,* 55–61.

58. AESP, Sociedades Civis, Estatuas/Compromissos, Sociedade Maçônica Loja Capitular Luiz Gama, 10/4/1897, C10389, Título 1, Art. 2.1 (Ministar subsidios pecunarios, soccoros medicos e pharaceuticos aos associados que, por motivo de molestia ficarem temporariamente impossibilitidados de exercer o seu trabalho).

59. AESP, Sociedades Civis, Estatuas/Compromissos, Sociedade Maçônica Loja Capitular Luiz Gama, 10/4/1897, C10389, Título 1, Art. 2.1 (Ministar subsidios pecunarios, soccoros medicos e pharaceuticos aos associados que, por motivo de molestia ficarem temporariamente impossibilitidados de exercer o seu trabalho).

60. Hahner, *Poverty and Politics,* 210.

61. Luné, *Almanak de Provincia,* 116.

62. Luís Soares de Camargo, "Viver e morrer em São Paulo: A vida, as doenças, e morte da cidade no século XIX" (Ph.D. diss., Pontifíca Universidade Católica de São Paulo, 2007), 42 (. . . Em 1878, o número de médicos subiria para 19 (dezenove) mas, do mesmo modo, todos eles encontravam-se atuando na área urbana entre a Sé a Santa Ifigênia).

63. Read, *Hierarchies of Slavery,* 133; Anderson, "Public Health," 296, 303; Hahner, *Poverty and Politics,* 210; Richard Morse, *From Community to Metropolis: a Biography of*

São Paulo, Brazil (Gainesville: University of Florida Press, 1958), 72; and Karasch, *Slave Life in Rio*, 135.

64. Read, *Hierarchies of Slavery*, 133; Anderson, "Public Health," 296, 303; Hahner, *Poverty and Politics*, 210; Morse, 72; and Karasch, *Slave Life in Rio*, 135.

65. Morse, *From Community to Metropolis*, 180.

66. AESP, Sociedades Civis, Estatuas/Compromissos, Sociedade Maçônica Loja Capitular Luiz Gama, 10/4/1897, C10389, Título 1, Art. 2.2 (Auxiliar com uma pensão mensal pelo tempo que fôr necessario aos socios, que por molestia chronica ou defeito physico cahirem em estado de invalidez).

67. AESP, Sociedades Civis, Estatuas/Compromissos, Sociedade Maçônica Loja Capitular Luiz Gama, 10/4/1897, C10389, Título 1, Art. 2.2 (Auxiliar com uma pensão mensal pelo tempo que fôr necessario aos socios, que por molestia chronica ou defeito physico cahirem em estado de invalidez.) and Titulo 1, Art. 2.3 (Fazer o funeral dos socios que fallecerem sem recurso para isso).

68. See Reis, *Death Is a Festival*; ACMSP, Compromisso da Irmandade de Nossa Senhora do Rosário dos Homens Pretos de São Paulo, 1778, 01–3–8; AESP, Sociedades Civis, Estatuas/Compromissos, Irmandade de São Benedicto da Cidade de São Paulo, 1/02/1896, C10388.

69. AESP, Sociedades Civis, Estatuas/Compromissos, Sociedade Beneficente dos Homens de Cor, 8/1/1909, C10401, Capítulo 1, Art. 3.1 (Soccorrer os seus socios com medico e pharmacia e uma diaria de um mil-réis). The amount of assistance, while undoubtedly welcome, represented a meager replacement for a regular salary, since daily wages alone averaged between five and seven *mil-réis* for textile workers of the period. Hahner, *Poverty and Politics*, 197–99.

70. *Suffragios* refer to prayer, almsgiving, or any other act of piety performed for the salvation of a deceased person's soul. AESP, Sociedades Civis, Estatuas/Compromissos, Sociedade Beneficente dos Homens de Cor, 8/1/1909, C10401, Capítulo 1, Art. 3.2 (No caso do fallecimento do qualquer socio, dar-lhe um auxilio de cento e vinte mil-réis para o funeral e os suffragios devidos).

71. AESP, Sociedades Civis, Estatuas/Compromissos, Sociedade Maçônica Loja Capitular Luiz Gama, 10/4/1897, C10389, Título 1, Art. 2.6 (Conceder, por tempo determinado, uma pensão mensal ás viúvas ou orphãos dos socios que della necessitarem, enquanto se mostrarem merecedores). Also see AESP, Sociedades Civis, Estatuas/Compromissos, Sociedade Beneficente dos Homens de Cor, 8/1/1909, C10401, Capítulo 1, Art. 3.4 (Soccorrer por tempo indeterminado, com uma pensão mensual, as viúvas dos socios, quando necessitadas e que dellas forem merecedoras).

72. See Muriel Nazzari, *Disappearance of the Dowry: Women, Families, and Social Change in São Paulo, Brazil (1600–1900)* (Stanford, Calif.: Stanford University Press, 1991), 168, for evidence of increasing reliance on the nuclear family in São Paulo in the nineteenth century.

73. Beattie, "The House, the Street, and Barracks," 441. For similar arguments see Susan Besse, *Restructuring Patriarchy: The Modernization of Gender Inequality in Brazil, 1914–1940* (Chapel Hill: University of North Carolina Press, 1996), 48; Lauderdale Graham, *House and Street*, 77; and Caulfield, *In Defense of Honor*, 6.

74. Beattie, "The House, the Street, and Barracks," 441; Besse, *Restructuring Patriarchy,* 48; Lauderdale Graham, *House and Street,* 77; and Caulfield, *In Defense of Honor,* 6. See Beattie, *Tribute of Blood,* 8, 84, and Joan Meznar, "The Ranks of the Poor: Military Service and Social Differentiation in Northeast Brazil,1830–1875," *Hispanic American Historical Review* 72, no. 3 (August 1992): 337, 342–43.

75. Graham, *Patronage and Politics,* 20–31 and 251–63; AESP, Sociedades Civis, Estatuas/Compromissos, Sociedade Maçônica Loja Capitular Luiz Gama, 10/4/1897, C10389, Título 1, Art. 2.4 (Promover a collacação dos associados quando privados de trabalho).

76. AESP, Sociedades Civis, Estatuas/Compromissos, Sociedade Beneficente dos Homens de Cor, 8/1/1909, C10401, Capítulo 1, Art. 3.6 (Procurar trabalho honesto aos associados na medida de suas forças).

77. AESP, Sociedades Civis, Estatuas/Compromissos, Sociedade Beneficente dos Homens de Cor, 8/1/1909, C104, Capítulo 1, Art. 2.5 (Proteger pelos meios regulares ao seu alcance aos associados que se acharem presos ou processados por motivos injustos ou illegães).

78. Boris Fausto, *Crime e cotidiano: A criminalidade em* São Paulo (1880–*1924),* 2nd ed. (São Paulo: Editora da Universidade de São Paulo, 2001), 45–52; Beattie, *Tribute of Blood,* xx–xxi, 129, 140; and Graham, *Patronage and Politics,* 31.

79. AESP, Sociedades Civis, Estatuas/Compromissos, Sociedade Beneficente dos Homens de Cor, 8/1/1909, C10401, Capítulo 1, Art. 3.7 (Proteger seus associados, quando presos ou processados, uma vez que a causa desses factos não seja deshonesto ao infamante).

80. AESP, Sociedades Civis, Estatuas/Compromissos, Loja Capitular Luiz Gama, 10/4/1897, C10389, Título 1, Art. 8 (Promover conferencias ou prelecçöes sobre assumptos do ordem scientifica, philosophica ou artistica que possam concorrer para o progresso intellectual, ethico e effectivo dos socios em particular e da humanidade em geral).

81. AESP, Sociedades Civis, Estatuas/Compromissos, Sociedade Beneficente dos Homens de Cor, 08/01/1909, C10401, Capítulo 1, Art. 3.5 (Fundar escolas primarias de ambos sexos para os filhos dos associados).

82. Butler, *Freedoms Won, Freedoms Given,* 77.

Great Circle Sailing

I'd like to thank the Massachusetts Historical Society for supporting this project through the Ruth R. and Alyson R. Miller Fellowship for research in women's history. I'm especially grateful to Anna Clutterbuck-Cook, who brought the Alice Bache Gould papers to my attention, and to Amanda Strauss, who read an earlier version of this essay.

1. "Education: Alice in Seville," *Time,* July 7 1952. I derived the note on birds from K. N. Chaudhuri, *Asia before Europe: Economy and Civilisation of the Indian Ocean from the Rise of Islam to 1750* (Cambridge: Cambridge University Press, 1991), 14.

2. Mary Rolland Newcomer McKinney, "Alice Bache Gould and Her Columbian Writings: A New Insight into Hispanic Historiography" (Ph.D. diss., University of Texas at Arlington, 1984), 233–36.

3. The construction of both these archives buildings was completed under Felipe II (Braudel's focus). Braudel began his doctoral research in Salamanca in 1927.

4. McKinney, "Alice Bache Gould and Her Columbian Writings," 74.

5. See Darcy R. Fryer, "Creative Disorientation: The Challenges of Studying, and Teaching, Atlantic World History," *Common-Place* 13, no. 4 (Summer 2013); other books that take this approach include Lisa Lindsay and John Wood Sweet, eds., *Biography and the Black Atlantic* (Philadelphia: University of Pennsylvania Press, 2013); John Wood Sweet and Gary Nash, eds., *Struggle and Survival in Colonial* America (Berkeley: University of California Press, 1981); and Karen Racine and Beatriz G. Mamigonian, *The Human Tradition in the Atlantic World, 1500–1850* (Lanham, Md.: Rowman & Littlefield, 2009).

6. See Natalie Zemon Davis, *Women on the Margins: Three Seventeenth-Century Lives* (New York: Belknap Press, 1995); Jon Sensbach, *Rebecca's Revival* (Cambridge, Mass.: Harvard University Press, 2006); Camilla Townsend, *Malintzin's Choices: An Indian Woman in the Conquest of Mexico* (Albuquerque: University of New Mexico Press, 2006); Catherine A. Brekus, *Sarah Osborn's World: The Rise of Evangelical Christianity in Early America* (New Haven: Yale University Press, 2013); and, in world history, Linda Colley, *The Ordeal of Elizabeth Marsh* (New York: Pantheon, 2007).

7. Karen Racine and Beatriz G. Mamigonian, for instance, argue that "the advent of steam travel and industrialization dramatically altered the nature and speed of life throughout the Atlantic world." Introduction, *The Human Tradition in the Atlantic World* (Lanham, Md.: Rowman & Littlefield, 2010), xi. Amanda Warnock does not include U.S. imperialism in her consideration of gender and colonialism within her essay "Gender and Identity in the Twentieth-Century Atlantic World," in *The Atlantic World, 1450–2000,* eds. Toyin Falola and Kevin D. Roberts (Bloomington: Indiana University Press, 2008), 315–37.

8. George C. Comstock, *Biographical Memoir [of] Benjamin Apthorp Gould* (Washington DC: National Academy of Sciences, 1924), 164.

9. Comstock, *Biographical Memoir,* 165.

10. Deborah Kent, "Alice Bache Gould, Brocardian Geometry and Spanish Archives," *Revista de la Sociedad Espanola de Historia de las Ciencias* 34, no. 74 (December 2011): 189. Tragedy disrupted the family idyll when her two older sisters, Susan and Lucretia, drowned in the Rio Primero in 1874.

11. It is unclear how old Gould was when she returned permanently to the United States. Ramón Carande claims she was twelve, while other secondary sources give an even younger age. The family's periodic trips back to Cambridge complicate the matter, but Gould's vivid memories of Argentina and her facility with the Spanish language suggest that she lived there for an extended period. What is definite is that after Mary Gould died, Benjamin left his children in Massachusetts and returned to Argentina alone. In 1884 Benjamin referred to his "dreary separation from my children and home," which may have been a recent change in the family dynamic. Ramón Carande, "Alicia Bache Gould," in Alicia B. Gould, *Nueva lista documentada de los tripulantes de Colon en 1492* (Madrid: Real Academia de la Historia, 1984), 4; Comstock, *Biographical Memoir,* 167.

12. Benjamin Apthorp Gould to Alice Bache Gould, October 8, 1883, Alice Bache Gould Papers, N-1309, Massachusetts Historical Society, Boston, Mass. (hereafter ABG-MHS). Alice's mother had died on June 22.

13. Mercedes Moritz Randall, *Improper Bostonian: Emily Greene Balch, Nobel Peace Laureate, 1946* (Ardent Media, 1964), 54–55. Alice's friend Emily Greene Balch, for example, considered the University of Wisconsin and Radcliffe before deciding on Bryn Mawr. Kristen E. Gwinn, "'Peace is too Small a Word': The Life and Ideas of Emily Greene Balch" (Ph.D. diss., George Washington University, 2008), 38, citing EGB to ABG, 19 July 1885, ABG Papers, ABG-MHS.

14. Randall, *Improper Bostonian,* 50–51. Kenney reports that Alice's father forbade her to study at Radcliffe because it would harm his reputation among his fellow Harvard professors. But, according to Deborah Kent, Gould did study mathematics for one year at Radcliffe. Kent, "Alice Bache Gould, Brocardian Geometry and Spanish Archives," 189. Kent includes a brief bibliography on Brocardian geometry at the end of her article.

15. Bryn Mawr College Calendar, 1903.

16. MIT began accepting women students in 1883, largely thanks to the efforts of Ellen Swallow Richards, who ran a Women's Laboratory there from 1876.

17. Ruth Gentry received a Ph.D. in mathematics from Bryn Mawr, ABG's undergraduate alma mater, in 1894; in 1908, Mary Emily Sinclair became the first woman Ph.D. to graduate from the University of Chicago.

18. ABG to Miss Palmie, February 8, 1898, ABG-MHS, cited in McKinney, "Alice Bache Gould and Her Columbian Writings," 23. This may have differed by discipline; Gould's friend the economist Emily Greene Balch taught at Wellesley and won the Nobel Prize. Then again, Balch's Nobel was for peace, not for economics.

19. There were no women on the Harvard faculty until Alice Hamilton in 1919.

20. "Confounded and everlasting larynx. . . . If I breathe hard, or laugh gently, I choke, just as if I had a cold in the head, and all the time I haven't any." ABG to [Cousin Emily],November 23, 1905, Box 19, Folder 5 (Oct 28, 1905–May 15, 1906); also see Kent, "Alice Bache Gould, Brocardian Geometry and Spanish Archives," 190. The ABG-MHS finding aid claims she went to PR to "recover from the flu."

21. See Jean Strouse, *Alice James: A Biography* (Boston: Houghton Mifflin, 1980).

22. McKinney, "Alice Bache Gould and Her Columbian Writings," 19.

23. For instance, Henrietta commented approvingly on Alice Freeman Palmer, at whose funeral "all testified to her usefulness in the cause of education, both before and after her marriage." Henrietta to ABG, [February 6, 1903], Box 14, Folder 14, ABG-MHS.

24. Fanny to ABG, January 28 [1903], Box 14, Folder 13, ABG-MHS.

25. Alice Bache Gould, *Louis Agassiz* (Boston: Small, Maynard & Co., 1900).

26. Gould, *Louis Agassiz,* 26, 101. Agassiz's subsequent biographers have widely noted this also.

27. Charles D. Howell, "An Unforgettable Scientist: The Life of Louis Agassiz," *Fortnightly Club* Meeting #1407 (March 13, 1986).

28. Gould, *Louis Agassiz,* 100.

29. Gould, *Louis Agassiz,* 30; for example, Gould, *Louis Agassiz,* 138.

30. Elizabeth Agassiz, *Louis Agassiz: Life and Correspondence,* 2 vols. (Boston: Houghton, Mifflin and Co., 1885).

31. William B. Hall, review of "*Louis Agassiz.* By Alice Bache Gould," *Sewanee Review* 9, no. 4 (October 1901): 505.

32. McKinney, "Alice Bache Gould and Her Columbian Writings," 155.

33. Alice Bache Gould Diary, 1902, Box 1, ABG Papers (N-1309), ABG-MHS.

34. See Diane Price Herndl, *Invalid Women: Figuring Feminine Illness in American Fiction and Culture, 1840–1940* (Durham: University of North Carolina Press, 1993); Francis George Gosling, *Before Freud: Neurasthenia and the American Medical Community, 1870–1910* (Champaign: University of Illinois Press, 1987).

35. Gould, *Louis Agassiz,* 106.

36. Gould, *Louis Agassiz,* 109.

37. Duncan Macdowall, *Another World: Bermuda and the Rise of Modern Tourism* (London: Macmillan Caribbean, 1999).

38. Alice Bache Gould, Diary, 1900, Box 1, ABG-MHS.

39. Albert Thorndike [her brother-in-law] to ABG, September 16, 1902, and DeLisle Stewart to ABG, September 23, 1902, Box 14, Folder 5, ABG Papers (N-1309), ABG-MHS.

40. Massachusetts Historical Society, *Proceedings* II (October 1886), 132, 135.

41. Gilbert Ballet, *Neurasthenia* (London: Kimpton, 1911), 191. In his study of Gould's contemporary the minister and entrepreneur Wallace Nutting, the scholar Thomas Andrew Denenberg refers to this as the "camera cure." Denenberg, *Wallace Nutting and the Invention of Old America* (New Haven: Yale University Press, 2003), 27–29.

42. Henrietta Child to ABG, undated [1903], Box 14, Folder 11, ABG-MHS: "I wonder how you both are, Miss Preble & you, well I hope, & book work advancing steadily." This may have been her mathematics dissertation, a plan of intense reading and research on a new topic, perhaps even the manuscript on Great Circle Sailing that she completed but left undated.

43. Along with Puerto Rico, the other favored "tropical attractions" for the early twentieth-century elite were Cuba, Haiti, Jamaica, and the Dominican Republic. Dennis Merrill, *Negotiating Paradise: U.S. Tourism and Empire in Twentieth-Century Latin America* (Chapel Hill: University of North Carolina Press, 2009), 180–81. Merrill describes tourism on the island as a "colonial project," modeled after Cuba. ("Early U.S. tourism in Puerto Rico in fact took on some of the exploitative characteristics that came to define Cuban tourism. Imposed on the island by outsiders and reliant on foreign capital for hotels and infrastructure, tourism was a colonial project, pure and simple.") But that transformation postdated Gould's trip. Puerto Rico did not emphasize tourism as part of its economic development plans until the 1930s. James L. Dietz, *Economic History of Puerto Rico: Institutional Change and Capitalist Development* (Princeton: Princeton University Press, 1986), 144, 151.

44. Merrill, *Negotiating Paradise,* 180.

45. "Representations of Puerto Rico also depicted a colonial oasis on the cusp of modernity, both an exotic, frontier destination and a safe, familiar part of an expanding American empire. Thus, tourists could relish the sense of masculine adventure and

reconnect with U.S. pioneer myths . . . U.S. tourists, moreover, might imagine themselves as agents of civilization." Merrill, *Negotiating Paradise,* 182.

46. See Aida Negron de Montilla, *Americanization in Puerto Rico and the Public School System, 1900–1930* (Rio Piedras, Puerto Rico: Editorial Universitaria, 1975); Ellen Walsh, "'Advancing the Kingdom': Missionaries and Americanization in Puerto Rico, 1898–1930s" (Ph.D. diss., University of Pittsburgh, 2008).

47. ABG to Mrs. Luce, n.d. [November 1905], Box 19, Folder 5 (October 28, 1905–May 15, 1906).

48. ABG to Aunt Fanny, April 26, 1903, Box 14, Folder 20, ABG-MHS.

49. ABG to Fanny, December 15, 1902, ABG-MHS.

50. ABC to Fanny, San Juan, December 22, 1902, Box 14, Folder 8, ABG-MHS.

51. Fanny to ABG, January 28 [1903], Box 14, Folder 13, ABG-MHS.

52. "I have become devoted to alligator pears, which are not at all what I thought they were. . . . There is a sort of artistic pleasure in the way the thing is its own dish, like an egg in its shell." ABG to Fanny, November 23, 1902, ABG-MHS; ABG to Fanny, February 7, 1903, Box 14, Folder 15, ABG-MHS.

53. ABG to Fanny, February 7, 1903, Box 14, Folder 15, ABG-MHS.

54. ABG to Fanny, February 7, 1903, Box 14, Folder 15, ABG-MHS.

55. ABG to Fanny, November 23, 1902, ABG-MHS. Years earlier, Gould had remarked that the weather in Bermuda, too, "felt like childhood."

56. ABG to Fanny, November 23, 1902, ABG-MHS.

57. "San Juan is said to have 'a depressing effect' and it certainly affects Miss Preble that way—I believe the chief trouble with me is lack of exercise." ABG to Aunt Fanny, January 13, 1903, Box 14, Folder 12, ABG-MHS.

58. ABG to Fanny, February 20, 1903, Box 14, Folder 14, ABG-MHS. Merrill notes how contemporary guidebooks specifically promoted the "beautiful girls from Aguadilla at Columbus Park." Merrill, *Negotiating Paradise,* 182.

59. ABG to Fanny, April 26, 1903, Box 14, Folder 20, ABG-MHS.

60. ABG to Fanny, February 7, 1903, Box 14, Folder 15, ABG-MHS.

61. "Taken looking out our door at the Olimpo. . . ." Photo 166.178, Box 2, Alice Bache Gould Photographs (Photo Coll 166), ABG-MHS. "The sea ought to show in the very [furthest?] distance but the plate doesn't give it." ABG to Aunty Fanny, March 30, 1903 (mistakenly attributed to February 16, 1903), Box 14, Folder 15, ABG-MHS.

62. "My kodak is now actually working successfully and it is the most delightful possession I have had." ABG to Aunty Fanny, March 30, 1903 (mistakenly attributed to February 16, 1903), Box 14, Folder 15, ABG-MHS.

63. ABG to Aunt Fanny, April 26, 1903, Box 14, Folder 20, ABG-MHS.

64. See Curtis M. Hinsley Jr., *Savages and Scientists: The Smithsonian Institution and the Development of American Anthropology, 1846–1910* (Washington, D.C.: Smithsonian Institution Press, 1981).

65. Jesse Walter Fewkes, *The Aborigines of Puerto Rico and Neighboring Islands* (Tuscaloosa: University of Alabama Press, 2009), 3. Fewkes's study was originally published as the *Twenty-Fifth Annual Report of the Bureau of American Ethnology to the Secretary of the Smithsonian Institution,* 1907.

66. Fewkes, *Aborigines of Puerto Rico,* 87–89. See J. Alden Mason and Irving Rouse, *A Large Archaeological Site at Capa, Utuado: Scientific Survey of Puerto Rico and the Virgin Islands*, vol. 13, part 2 (orig. 1914–1915); Peter E. Siegel, ed., *Ancient Borinquen: Archaeology and Ethnohistory of Native Puerto Rico* (Tuscaloosa: University of Alabama Press, 2005).

67. ABG to Aunt Fanny, January 13, 1903, Box 14, Folder 12, ABG-MHS.

68. ABG to Aunt Fanny, February 7, 1903, Box 14, Folder 15, ABG-MHS.

69. Fewkes, *Aborigines of Puerto Rico,* 89.

70. ABG to Aunt Fanny, February 16, 1903, Box 14, Folder 15, ABG-MHS.

71. ABG to Aunt Fanny, February 16, 1903, Box 14, Folder 15, ABG-MHS.

72. ABG to Aunt Fanny, February 16, 1903, Box 14, Folder 15, ABG-MHS.

73. ABG to Aunt Melia, February 16, 1903, Box 14, Folder 15, ABG-MHS.

74. ABG to Fanny, April 21 [1903], Box 14, Folder 20, ABG-MHS.

75. ABG to Aunt Fanny, April 26, 1903, Box 14, Folder 20, ABG-MHS.

76. Jonathan E. Reyman, "Women in Southwest Archaeology, 1895–1945," in *Assembling the Past: Studies in the Professionalization of Archaeology,* ed. Alice Beck Kehoe and Mary Beth Emmerichs (Albuquerque: University of New Mexico Press, 1999), 218.

77. Reyman, "Women in Southwest Archaeology," 214, 215.

78. Hilary Lynn Chester, "Frances Eliza Babbitt and the Growth of Professionalism of Women in Archaeology" in David L. Browman and Stephen Williams, eds., New Perspectives on the Origins of Americanist Archaeology (Tuscaloosa: University of Alabama Press, 2002), 165.

79. See Cheryl Claassen, ed., *Women in Archaeology* (Philadelphia: University of Pennsylvania Press, 1994).

80. Mary Ann Levine, "Uncovering a Buried Past: Women in Americanist Archaeology before the First World War," in *Assembling the Past: Studies in the Professionalization of Archaeology,* eds. Alice Beck Kehoe and Mary Beth Emmerichs (Albuquerque: University of New Mexico Press, 1999), 144–45.

81. Nancy Parezo, ed., *Hidden Scholars* (Albuquerque: University of New Mexico Press, 1993), 180.

82. Reyman, "Women in Southwest Archaeology," 214, 215.

83. Fewkes, *Aborigines of Puerto Rico,* 156.

84. Reyman,"Women in Southwest Archaeology," 22; Alice B. Kehoe, "Professionals May Not Be Women," in *Assembling the Past: Studies in the Professionalization of Archaeology,* eds. Alice Beck Kehoe and Mary Beth Emmerichs (Albuquerque: University of New Mexico Press, 1999), 117.

85. "According to one account, Columbus brought their ancestors from the Canary islands; according to another every aboriginal Indian who came to meet Columbus carried a little white dog round his neck as a sort of throat muffler." ABG to Aunt Fanny, April 26, 1903, Box 14, Folder 20, ABG-MHS.

86. "Columbus might have seen him looking just like that." ABG to Aunt Fanny, February 7, 1903, Box 14, Folder 15, ABG-MHS.

87. Katharine R. Crowell, *Star-49? A Story of Happenings in Port Rico* (New York: Woman's Board of Home Missions, 1910), 12.

88. Kent, "Alice Bache Gould, Brocardian Geometry and Spanish Archives," 190. The Tamiment Library finding aid claims that, while in Puerto Rico, Gould discovered an important document about Barbados.

89. ABG to Aunt Fanny, April 26, 1903, Box 14, Folder 20, ABG-MHS.

90. M. Carey Thomas to ABG, May 21, 1906, Box 15, Folder 21, ABG-MHS.

91. Fewkes to ABG, October 22, 1907, Box 16, Folder 3, and Fewkes to ABG, n.d. [1908], Box 16, Folder 4, ABG-MHS.

92. Justo Formentin Ibanez y Maria Jose Villegas Sanz, "Miss Alice B. Gould," *Boletin de la Real Academia de la Historia* 194, no. 3 (1997).

93. See Henrietta Child to ABG, October 27, 1903, and November 3, 1903, Box 14, Folder 27a, ABG-MHS.

94. Gould also favored suffrage for women and sent generous donations to the *Woman's Journal.*

95. See for example Warwick Anderson, *Colonial Pathologies* (Durham: Duke University Press, 2006); Mariola Espinosa, *Epidemic Invasions: Yellow Fever and the Limits of Cuban Independence, 1878–1930* (Chicago: University of Chicago Press, 2009); Winifred Connerton, "Have Cap Will Travel: U.S. Nurses Abroad, 1898–1917" (Ph.D. diss., University of Pennsylvania, 2010).

96. Walsh, "'Advancing the Kingdom.'"

97. Gould included this in a draft of a fundraising letter, then crossed it out (but saved the entire draft). ABG to "Gardy," August 6, 1905, Box 15, Folder 14, ABG-MHS.

98. Helen Butler to ABG, May 11, 1906, Box 15, Folder 20, ABG-MHS.

99. Augusta M. Brown to ABG, August 8, 1906, Box 15, Folder 24, ABG-MHS.

100. Typescript about nursing and hospital, undated [1906?], Box 15, Folder 17, ABG-MHS.

101. Grace De W. Lugo-Viña (hereafter GLV) to ABG, July 19, 1903, Box 14, Folder 21, ABG-MHS.

102. GLV to ABG, January 26, 1904, Box 15, Folder 3, ABG-MHS; GLV to ABG, October 6, 1903, Box 14, Folder 25, ABG-MHS.

103. The initial moneys she raised were mistakenly taken for "general uses" of the affiliated hospital. Beekman Winthrop to ABG, May 16, 1906, Box 15, Folder 20, ABG-MHS. Another gift of $2,000 went toward "paying the salary of a *very* much needed assistant nurse." Jessie Grahame to ABG, [August 1905,] Box 15, Folder 14, ABG-MHS.

104. Gould learned from a U.S. military surgeon that, despite her efforts, the women's hospital in San Juan was in "desperate" financial straits. Major W. F. Lippitt to ABG, November 6, 1905, Box 15, Folder 16, ABG-MHS. Lippitt was surgeon at the hospital.

105. Louisa C. Lippitt to ABG, November 18, 1905, Box 15, Folder 16, ABG-MHS.

106. Eileen J. Suárez-Finlay, *Imposing Decency: The Politics of Sexuality and Race in Puerto Rico, 1870–1920* (Durham: Duke University Press, 1999), 118–20.

107. Lippitt to ABG, November 26, 1906, Box 15, Folder 26.

108. Lippitt to ABG, November 18, 1905, Box 15, Folder 16, ABG-MHS. For a fuller analysis of how American racism and racial perceptions shaped nursing in early twentieth-century Puerto Rico, see Walsh, "'Advancing the Kingdom.'"

109. See Melza Winthrop to ABG, June 13, 1906, and Louisa Lippitt to ABG, June

24, 1906, Box 15, Folder 22; Beekman Winthrop to ABG, July 2, 1906, Box 15, Folder 23, ABG-MHS.

110. ABG to "Gardy," August 6, 1905, Box 15, Folder 14, ABG-MHS.

111. GLV to ABG, February 10, 1906, Box 15, Folder 18, ABG-MHS.

112. Beekman Winthrop to ABG, May 16, 1906, Box 15, Folder 20, ABG-MHS.

113. Melza Winthrop to ABG, June 13, 1906, Box 15, Folder 22, ABG-MHS.

114. See letter from John W. Colbert to ABG, November 14, 1905, Box 15, Folder 16, ABG-MHS, in reply to ABG's request for a report on nursing and nurse education there; GLV to ABG, January 26, 1904, Box 15, Folder 3, ABG-MHS.

115. ABG, June 13, 1906, ABG-MHS.

116. Beekman Winthrop to ABG, February 25, 1907, Box 15, Folder 30, ABG-MHS. Winthrop told Gould that the hospital closed because it was unsafe during hurricanes, but this seems a disingenuous explanation. According to the historian Ellen Walsh, the island's first nursing school, directed by a U.S. nurse and established in 1902 "failed in just four years, graduating only a few nurses." Walsh, "'Advancing the Kingdom,'" 165; Melza Riggs Winthrop to ABG, January 28, 1907, Box 15, Folder 29, ABG-MHS.

117. M. Adelaide Nutting and Lavinia L. Dock, *A History of Nursing* (NY: Putnam, 1912), 307; Lyndia Flanagan, *One Strong Voice: The Story of the American Nurses' Association* (Kansas City, Mo.: American Nurses' Association, 1976).

118. National Tuberculosis Association, *A Tuberculosis Directory* (National Association for the Study and Prevention of Tuberculosis, 1911). According to Philip P. Jacobs, "Tuberculosis," *Survey* 21 (January 16, 1909), 687, "the membership of the league includes most of the American residents of the island and many prominent Porto Ricans."

119. "The exhibit followed the model of two others already touring Florida and Kansas. Spanish language and accompanied by "numerous public meetings." Jacobs, "Tuberculosis," 687.

120. At the end of her life, Gould donated these materials to the Library of Congress, where they form the core of the Puerto Rican Memorial Collection.

121. Bailey K. Ashford to ABG, April 17, 1907, Box 16 Folder 1, ABG-MHS.

122. Fernando Picó, "Historiography of Puerto Rico," in *General History of the Caribbean: Methodology and Historiography of the Caribbean*, vol. VI, eds. B. W. Higman and Franklin W. Knight (London: UNESCO Publishing, 1999), 424.

123. Hispanic Society of America to ABG, January 17, 1910, Box 16, Folder 13, ABG-MHS. The HSA's original trustees were mostly railroad magnates.

124. Kent, "Alice Bache Gould, Brocardian Geometry and Spanish Archives," 46, claims that Gould began her "Great Circle Sailing" book during World War I, inspired by "swelling interest in navigational instruction," as evidenced by the courses she offered to naval officers via the University of Chicago in 1918. But her correspondence from 1908 indicates she was already thinking about the project then. See Gould Papers, ABG-MHS, Box 16, Folder 8. Gould never finished or published the manuscript; her historical research overtook it.

125. McKinney, "Alice Bache Gould and Her Columbian Writings," 35; Kent, "Alice Bache Gould, Brocardian Geometry and Spanish Archives,"45.

126. Justo Formamentia Íbañez and María José Villegas Sanz, "Miss Alice B. Gould,"

Boletín de la Real Academia de la Historia 194, no. 3 (1997): 511. This and other secondary sources state that the cause of Gould's delay was that her companion fell ill in Gibraltar. Ursula Lamb, who knew Gould personally in Gould's later years, relates that Gould's "ship was laid up" in Seville on the way to Rome. Ursula Lamb, "Pioneers of Discovery History in the Spanish Archives: Alice Gould and Irene Wright: A Memoir," *Primary Sources and Original Works* 2, no. 3–4 (1993): 481.

127. Alice Bache Gould, "Nueva Lista Documentada de Los Tripulantes de Colón en 1492," *Boletín de la Real Academia de la Historia* 85 (1924).

128. McKinney, "Alice Bache Gould and Her Columbian Writings"; Lamb, "Pioneers of Discovery History," 481.

129. Íbañez and Villegas Sanz, "Miss Alice B. Gould," 511.

130. Miles H. Davidson, *Columbus Then and Now: A Life Reexamined* (Norman: University of Oklahoma Press, 1997), 235–36.

131. Davidson, *Columbus Then and Now,* 192.

132. Gould, *Nueva Lista Documentada de los Tripulantes de Colón en 1492.*

133. For the promulgation of this view of the "sorry crew," see, for example, Jakob Wassermann, *Columbus: Don Quixote of the Seas* (New York: Little, Brown, 1930), 174.

134. Reprinted in Ellery Sedgwick, ed., *Atlantic Harvest: Memoirs of the Atlantic* (New York: Little, Brown, 1947).

135. Alice Bache Gould, "The Adventure of the Missing Fortnight," *Atlantic Monthly,* July 1919, 36.

136. "I was at least free from all prejudice about Charles's doings in 1538," she noted mischievously.

137. Gould, " . . . Missing Fortnight," 43.

138. Gould, " . . . Missing Fortnight," 34. The exact quotation is: "A really careful itinerary is an instrument of precision, like any other gauge, and it means much arduous laboring over facts in themselves as unimportant as any scratch upon a vernier scale."

139. See Bonnie Smith, *The Gender of History: Men, Women, and Historical Practice* (Cambridge, Mass.: Harvard University Press, 1998).

140. Íbañez and Villegas Sanz, "Miss Alice B. Gould," 512–15, detail the accusations that Gould was stealing archival documents rather than doing legitimate research of her own.

141. "Education: Alice in Seville," *Time,* July7, 1952.

142. Not only perfectionism but wars delayed her progress: "He perdido un tiempo irrecuperable," she mourned after the Spanish Civil War interrupted her work and resulted in the destruction of key sources. Íbañez and Villegas Sanz, "Miss Alice B. Gould," 511.

143. These experts, one should note, were no more academically trained as historians than she was; the three previous compilers of the *tripulantes* lists, as well as Don Manuel Foronda, scholar of Emperor Charles V, were all "self-made" historians like Gould. Though she did not name him, Gould did corrected the conclusions of another self-made American historian of Columbus, John Boyd Thacher.

144. Manuel de Foronda y Aguilera, *Discursos leídos ante la Real Academia de la historia en la recepción pública del Excmo,* June 11, 1916 (Madrid: s.n., 1916), 23.

145. McKinney, "Alice Bache Gould and Her Columbian Writings," 47; Samuel Eliot Morison, *Admiral of the Ocean Sea: A Life of Christopher Columbus* (Boston: Little Brown & Co, 1949).

146. Lamb, "Pioneers of Discovery History," 485.

147. "Mi vida se ha deslizado placidamente": Íbañez and Villegas Sanz, "Miss Alice B. Gould," 512.

148. Reuters, "Expert on Columbus Voyage Devoted 40 Years to Study," *Reading Eagle* (September 7, 1953).

White Noise?

1. Toni Morrison, *Desdemona* (London: Oberon Books, 2012).

2. Peter Sellars, postperformance conversation, Barbican Theatre, London, July 19, 2012.

3. William Shakespeare, *Othello* (Walton on Thames: Thomas Nelson: 1998), IV.iii.24.

4. "Disenfranchised Voices of Women, Africans, Ring out in Morrison's Revision of *Othello*," *Washington Post* Lifestyle, October 14, 2011. http://www.washingtonpost.com/lifestyle/disenfranchised-voices-of-women,-Africans.

5. Brent Hayes Edwards, *The Practice of Diaspora: Literature, Translation, and the Rise of Black Internationalism* (Cambridge, Mass.: Harvard University Press, 2003), 7, 11, 13.

6. Jason Zindman, "Othello's Wife Gives Her Side of the Story," *New York Times*, November 3, 2011. http://theater.nytimes.com/2011/11/04/theater/reviews/desdemona-at-lincoln-center-white-light-festival-review.html.

7. Morrison, *Desdemona*, 39.

8. Morrison, *Desdemona*, 54.

9. Parallel but by no means irrelevant to this critique of *Desdemona* is a cautionary skepticism about the apparently unambivalent celebration and promotion of "global" and "globalized" Shakespeare that is itself a feature of these early decades of the twenty-first century.

10. Simon Lewis, panel discussion at Carolina Lowcountry and the Atlantic World Conference, College of Charleston, Charleston, S.C., March 2012.

11. Jonathan Bate and Dora Thornton, *Shakespeare: Staging the World* (London: British Museum Press, 2012), 35,53; Morrison, *Desdemona*, 25.

12. In the Nanterre production, the chorus singers were Fatim Kouyaté, Bintou Soumbounou, and Mamah Diabaté. The *n'goni* player was Mamah Diabaté and the *kora* player, Mamadyba Camara. The performers were identical in London except that Kadiatou Sangaré was not present.

13. Shakespeare, *Othello*, IV.iii.24.

14. Morrison, *Desdemona*, 47, 49.

15. Kim Hall, *Things of Darkness: Economies of Race and Gender in Early Modern England* (Ithaca, N.Y.: Cornell University Press, 1995), 17.

16. Edwards, *Practice of Diaspora*, 5.

17. Daniel Fischlin and Mark Fortier, eds., *Adaptations of Shakespeare: A Critical*

Anthology of Plays from the Seventeenth Century to the Present (London and New York: Routledge, 2000), 5.

18. Pascal James Imperato, *Mali: A Search for Direction* (Dartmouth and London: Westview Press, 1989), 91.

19. Edwards, *Practice of Diaspora,* 6–7.

20. A recent overview of the situation in Mali that informs this essay is Joshua Hammer, "When the Jihad Came to Mali," *New York Review of Books,* March 21, 2013, 12–14.

21. Imperato, *Mali: A Search for Direction,* 94, 81.

22. Hammer, "When the Jihad Came to Mali," 12–13.

23. Hammer, "When the Jihad Came to Mali,"14; Morrison, *Desdemona,* 31.

24. Peter Sellars, Foreword, in Morrison, *Desdemona,* 7–11

25. Sellars, Foreword, 7.

26. Sellars, Foreword. 8.

27. Shakespeare, *Othello,* IV.iii.24–28.

28. I am grateful to my colleague Tiffany Sterne for this insight.

29. Shakespeare, *Othello,* I.i.110.

30. E. A. Honigmann in Shakespeare, *Othello,* 290 n. 24.

31. Ania Loomba, *Shakespeare, Race and Colonialism* (Oxford: Oxford University Press, 2002), 4; Bate and Thornton, *Staging,* 34.

32. For a review of the exhibition and discussion of Giluia de Medici, see Miranda Kauffmann, "The Black Face of Renaissance Europe," http://www.historytoday.com/blog/2013/05/black-face-renaissance-europe.

33. Sellars, Foreword, 9

34. Sellars, Foreword, 8.

35. Morrison, *Desdemona,* 23.

36. Morrison, *Desdemona,* 23.

37. These words are in French in the Nanterre program; the translation back into English is my own.

38. Sellars, *Foreword,* 7.

39. On the Moroccan ambassadorial visit to London in 1600–1601, see Bate and Thornton, *Staging,* 34–35; E. A. Honigmann, Introduction, in Shakespeare, *Othello,* 1–111, 2; Virginia Mason Vaughan, *Othello: A Contextual History* (Cambridge: Cambridge University Press, 1994), 58.

40. Bate and Thornton, *Staging,* 34; Vaughan, *Contextual History,* 58.

41. Emily C. Bartels, *Speaking of the Moor: From* Alcazar *to* Othello (Philadelphia: University of Pennsylvania Press, 2008), 22.

42. Bate and Thornton, *Staging,* 144.

43. Hall, *Things of Darkness,* 28.

44. Bate and Thornton, *Staging,* 35.

45. Richard Hakluyt, "A Generall Description of All Africa," in Johannes Leo (Leo Africanus), *A Geographical Historie of Africa,* translated by John Pory (1600; New York: Da Capo Press, 1969), 1–8, 4.

46. Hakyluyt, "Generall Description," 4.

47. Johannes Leo (Leo Africanus), *A Geographical Historie of Africa,* translated by John Pory (1600; New York: Da Capo Press, 1969), 2, 3, 5.

48. Leo, *Geographical Historie,* 6.

49. Sellars, Foreword, 8.

50. See Morrison, *Desdemona,* 45, 53.

51. Ross Velton, *Mali* (Chalfont St Peters: Bradt, 2009), 14.

52. Sellars, Foreword, 7.

53. Toni Morrison, "On *The Radiance of the King* by Camara Laye," in Morrison, *What Moves at the Margin: Selected Nonfiction,* ed. Carolyn C. Denard (Jackson: University of Mississippi Press, 2008), 118–32.

54. Toni Morrison, *Playing in the Dark: Whiteness and the Literary Imagination* (1992; London: Picador, 1993), 5–6.

55. Morrison, *Desdemona,* 53.

56. Morrison, *Desdemona,* 18.

57. Shakespeare, *Othello,* IV.iii.25.

58. Morrison, *Desdemona,* 18.

59. Program notes to the Nanterre production, in French; my translation into English, my emphasis.

60. Sellars, Foreword, 9.

61. See http://www.whitelightfestival.org/archive/2011/index.php/white-light-2011-desdemona.

62. Morrison, *Desdemona,* 15.

63. Morrison, *Desdemona,* 17, 22.

64. Morrison, *Desdemona,* 36.

65. Morrison, *Desdemona,* 37.

66. Ann-Marie MacDonald, *Goodnight Desdemona (Good Morning Juliet)* (1990; New York: Grove Press, 1998), 52–53.

67. MacDonald, *Goodnight Desdemona,* 52.

68. Djanet Sears, *Harlem Duet,* in Daniel Fischlin and Mark Fortier, eds., *Adaptations of Shakespeare: A Critical Anthology of Plays from the Seventeenth Century to the Present* (London and New York: Routledge, 2000), 285–31, 304.

69. Sears, *Harlem Duet,* 304.

70. Toni Morrison, "What the Black Woman Thinks about Women's Lib," in Morrison, *What Moves at the Margin: Selected Nonfiction,* ed. Carolyn C. Denard (Jackson: University of Mississippi Press, 2008), 18–30, 20.

71. Morrison, *Desdemona,* 27.

72. Morrison, *Desdemona,* 45.

73. Morrison, *Desdemona,* 13.

74. Morrison, *Desdemona,* 45.

75. Morrison, *Desdemona,* 48.

76. Jennifer Morgan made this salient point during a panel discussion at the Carolina Lowcountry and the Atlantic World Conference, College of Charleston, Charleston, S.C., March 2012.

77. Toni Morrison, *Beloved* (1987; New York and London: Vintage, 2005) 235; Morrison, *Desdemona,* 38.

78. Edwards, *Practice of Diaspora,* 15.

79. Lucy Durán, "Mali: Gold Dust by the River," in *The Rough Guide to World Music: Africa and Middle East,* 3rd ed., eds. Simon Broughton, Mark Ellingham, and Jon Lusk (London: Penguin, 2006), 219–38, 219.

80. Durán, "Mali: Gold Dust by the River," 220.

81. See www.rokiatraore.net/bio-english/.

82. Interview with Robert Ambrose. *The Beat* 20, no. 1 (2001): 36–37, 65, 37; see www.rokiatraore.net/bio-english/.

83. On *Wati,* see http://www.guardian.co.U.K./music/2007/jul/06/worldmusic.classicalmusicandopera.

84. Imperato, *Mali: A Search for Direction,* 9, 88.

85. Durán, "Mali: Gold Dust by the River," 220–21.

86. Sellars, Foreword, 10; Morrison, *Desdemona,* 29.

87. For example, she told Robert Ambrose in 2001, "My life is for women, in favour of women, of justice." Interview with Ambrose, *The Beat,* 37.

88. Nigel Williamson, "From Mali to Mississippi . . . and Back," in *The Rough Guide to World Music: Africa and Middle East,* 3rd ed., eds. Simon Broughton, Mark Ellingham, and Jon Lusk (London: Penguin, 2006), 225.

89. Williamson, "From Mali to Mississippi," 225.

90. Interview with Robert Ambrose, *The Beat,* 36.

91. John Michael Vlach, *The Afro-American Tradition in Decorative Arts* (Athens: University of Georgia Press, 1990), 139, 143.

92. Vlach, *Afro-American Tradition,* 143.

93. Imperato, *Mali: A Search for Direction,* 11.

94. Email from Mohamedoun Ag Mohamed to the author, June 13, 2013. I am grateful to Mohamedoun Ag Mohamed for his help in translating the Bambara titles of the songs in *Desdemona* and for answering my questions about Mali.

95. Shakespeare, *Othello* I.ii.21–22.

96. Hammer, "When the Jihad Came to Mali," 14.

97. Hammer, "When the Jihad Came to Mali," 14.

98. Hammer, "When the Jihad Came to Mali," 12.

99. Sellars, postperformance conversation, Barbican Theatre, July 19, 2012.

100. Morrison, *Beloved,* 324.

Bibliography

Alberro, Solange. "Crypto-Jews and the Mexican Holy Office." In *The Jews and the Expansion of Europe to the West, 1450–1800,* edited by Paolo Bernardini and Norman Fiering. New York: Berghahn Books, 2001.

Andrews, George Reid. *Blacks and Whites in São Paulo, Brazil, 1888–1988.* Madison: University of Wisconsin Press, 1991.

Armitage, David. "Three Concepts of Atlantic History." In *The British Atlantic World, 1500–1800,* edited by David Armitage and Michael J. Braddick. New York: Palgrave Macmillan, 2002.

Atkinson, James. *Splendid Land, Splendid People: The Chickasaw Indians to Removal.* Tuscaloosa: University of Alabama Press, 2004.

Bailyn, Bernard. *Atlantic History: Concept and Contours.* Cambridge, Mass.: Harvard University Press, 2005.

Beattie, Peter. *Tribute of Blood: Army, Honor, Race and Nation in Brazil, 1864–1945.* Durham: Duke University Press, 2001.

Burnard, Trevor. "'Impatient of Subordination' and 'Liable to Sudden Transports of Anger': White Masculinity and Homosocial Relations with Black Men in Eighteenth-Century Jamaica." In *New Men: Manliness in Early America,* edited by Thomas A. Foster. New York: New York University Press, 2011.

Butler, Kim. *Freedoms Given, Freedoms Won: Afro-Brazilians in Post-Abolition São Paulo and Salvador.* New Brunswick, N.J.: Rutgers University Press, 1998.

Calloway, Colin G. *New Worlds for All: Indians, Europeans, and the Remaking of Early America.* Baltimore: Johns Hopkins University Press, 1997.

Candlin, Kit. *Enterprising Women: Gender, Race, and Power in the Revolutionary Atlantic.* Athens: University of Georgia Press, 2015.

Cevallos-Candau, Francisco Javier, ed. *Coded Encounters: Writing, Gender, and Ethnicity in Colonial Latin America.* Amherst: University of Massachusetts Press, 1995.

Chaplin, Joyce E. "The Atlantic Ocean and Its Contemporary Meanings, 1492–1808." In *Atlantic History: A Critical Appraisal,* edited by Jack P. Greene and Philip D. Morgan. New York: Oxford University Press, 2009.

Clark, Emily. *The Strange History of the American Quadroon: Free Women of Color in the Revolutionary Atlantic.* Chapel Hill: University of North Carolina Press, 2013.

Coclanis, Peter. "Atlantic World or Atlantic/World?" *William and Mary Quarterly* 63, no. 4 (2006): 725–742.

Cronon, William. *Changes in the Land: Indians, Colonists, and the Ecology of New England.* New York: Hill and Wang, 1983.

Crosby, Alfred. *The Columbian Exchange: Biological and Cultural Consequences of 1492.* Westport, Conn.: Greenwood, 1972.

Davis, Natalie Zemon. "Decentering History: Local Stories and Cultural Crossings in a Global World." *History and Theory* 50, no. 2 (2011): 188–202.

Davis, Natalie Zemon. *Women on the Margins: Three Seventeenth-Century Lives.* New York: Belknap Press, 1995.

Dessens, Natalie. *From Saint-Domingue to New Orleans: Migration and Influences.* Gainesville: University Press of Florida, 2007.

Edwards, Brent Hayes. *The Practice of Diaspora: Literature, Translation, and the Rise of Black Internationalism.* Cambridge, Mass.: Harvard University Press, 2003.

Frank, Andrew. *Creeks and Southerners: Biculturalism on the Early American Frontier.* Lincoln: University of Nebraska Press, 2005.

Fryer, Darcy R. "Creative Disorientation: The Challenges of Studying, and Teaching, Atlantic World History." *Common-Place* 13, no. 4 (Summer 2013).

Fuentes, Marisa. *Dispossessed Lives: Enslaved Women, Violence, and the Archive.* Philadelphia: University of Pennsylvania Press, 2016.

Games, Alison. "Beyond the Atlantic: English Globetrotters and Transoceanic Connections." *William and Mary Quarterly* 63, no. 4 (2006): 675–692.

Greene, Jack P. *Evaluating Empire and Confronting Colonialism in Eighteenth-Century Britain.* New York: Cambridge University Press, 2013.

Habib, Imtiaz. *Black Lives in the English Archives, 1500–1677: Imprints of the Invisible.* Aldershot: Ashgate, 2008.

Hall, Catherine. "Of Gender and Empire." In *Gender and Empire,* edited by Philippa Levine. Oxford: Oxford University Press, 2007.

Hall, Kim. *Things of Darkness: Economies of Race and Gender in Early Modern England.* Ithaca, N.Y., and London: Cornell University Press, 1995.

Helg, Aline. *Our Rightful Share: The Afro-Cuban Struggle for Equality, 1886–1912.* Chapel Hill: University of North Carolina Press, 1995.

Hodes, Martha. "The Mercurial Nature and Abiding Power of Race: A Transnational Family Story." *American Historical Review* 108, no. 1 (February 2003): 84–85.

Horsman, Reginald. *Race and Manifest Destiny: The Origins of American Racial Anglo-Saxonism.* Cambridge, Mass.: Harvard University Press, 1981.

Ipsen, Pernille. *Daughters of the Trade: Atlantic Slavers and Interracial Marriage on the Gold Coast.* Philadelphia: University of Pennsylvania Press, 2015.

Israel, Jonathan I. *Diasporas within a Diaspora: Jews, Crypto-Jews and the World Maritime Empires (1540–1740).* Boston: Brill, 2002.

Jaffary, Nora E., ed. *Gender, Race, and Religion in the Colonization of the Americas.* Burlington, Vt.: Ashgate, 2007.

Kendi, Ibram. *Stamped from the Beginning: The Definitive History of Racist Ideas in America.* New York: Nation Books, 2016.

Klooster, Wim. *The Dutch Moment: War, Trade, and Settlement in the Seventeenth Century Atlantic World.* Ithaca, N.Y.: Cornell University Press, 2016.

Kostroun, Daniella, and Lisa Vollendorf, eds. *Women, Religion, and the Atlantic World (1600–1800).* Toronto: University of Toronto Press, 2009.

Lachance, Paul. "Repercussions of the Haitian Revolution in Louisiana." In *The Impact of the Haitian Revolution in the Atlantic World,* edited by David Geggus. Columbia: University of South Carolina Press, 2001.

Lindsay, Lisa, and John Wood Sweet, eds. *Biography and the Black Atlantic.* Philadelphia: University of Pennsylvania Press, 2013.

Livesay, Daniel. "Emerging from the Shadows: New Developments in the History of Interracial Sex and Intermarriage in Colonial North America and the Caribbean." *History Compass* 13, no. 3 (2015): 122–133.

Loomba, Ania. *Shakespeare, Race and Colonialism.* Oxford: Oxford University Press, 2002.

Martinez, Maria Elena. *Genealogical Fictions: Limpieza De Sangre, Religion and Gender in Colonial Mexico.* Stanford, Calif.: Stanford University Press, 2008.

Meadows, Darrell. "Engineering Exile: Social Networks and the French Atlantic Community, 1789–1809." *French Historical Studies* 23 (2000): 70.

Merrill, Dennis. *Negotiating Paradise: U.S. Tourism and Empire in Twentieth-Century Latin America.* Chapel Hill: University of North Carolina Press, 2009.

Montrose, Louis. "The Work of Gender in the Discourse of Discovery." *Representations,* no. 33, "Special Issue: The New World" (Winter 1991): 1–41.

Morgan, Jennifer L. *Laboring Women: Reproduction and Gender in New World Slavery.* Philadelphia: University of Pennsylvania Press, 2004.

Nash, Gary, and John Wood Sweet, eds. *Struggle and Survival in Colonial America.* Berkeley: University of California Press, 1981.

Newman, Brooke. "Gender, Sexuality, and the Formation of Racial Identities in the Eighteenth-Century Anglo-Caribbean World." *Gender and History* 22 (2010): 585–602.

Paton, Diana, and Pamela Scully. "Introduction: Gender and Slave Emancipation in Comparative Perspective." In *Gender and Slave Emancipation in the Atlantic World,* edited by Pamela Scully and Diana Paton. Durham: Duke University Press, 2005.

Racine, Karen and Beatrice G. Mamigonian. *The Human Tradition in the Atlantic World, 1500–1850.* Lanham, Md.: Rowman & Littlefield, 2009.

Robertson, James. "Re-Writing the English Conquest of Jamaica in the Late Seventeenth Century." *English Historical Review* 117, no. 473 (2002): 813–839.

Romney, Susanah Shaw. *New Netherland Connections: Intimate Networks and Atlantic Ties in Seventeenth-Century America.* Chapel Hill: University of North Carolina Press for the Omohundro Institute of Early American History and Culture, 2014.

Scott, Rebecca J. "Paper Thin: Freedom and Re-Enslavement in the Diaspora of the Haitian Revolution." *Law and History Review* 29, no. 4 (2011): 1061–1082.

Shaw, Rosalind, and Charles Stewart. *Syncretism/Anti-Syncretism: The Politics of Religious Synthesis.* London: Routledge, 1994.

Shepard, Alexandra. *Meanings of Manhood in Early Modern England.* Oxford: Oxford University Press, 2003.

Sidbury, James and Jorge Cañizares-Esguerra. "Mapping Ethnogenesis in the Early Modern Atlantic." *William and Mary Quarterly* 68, no. 2 (April 2011): 181–208.

Smith, Bonnie. *The Gender of History: Men, Women, and Historical Practice.* Cambridge, Mass.: Harvard University Press, 1998.

Soares, Mariza de Carvalho. "Can Women Guide and Govern Men? Gendering Politics among African Catholics in Colonial Brazil." In *Women and Slavery: The Modern Atlantic,* edited by Gwyn Campbell, Suzanne Miers, and Joseph C. Miller. Athens: Ohio University Press, 2008.

Stoler, Ann Laura. "Tense and Tender Ties: The Politics of Comparison in North American History and (Post)Colonial Studies," *Journal of American History* 88, no. 3 (2001): 829–865.

Studnicki-Gizbert, Daviken. *A Nation upon the Ocean Sea: Portugal's Atlantic Diaspora and the Crisis of the Spanish Empire, 1492–1640.* Oxford: Oxford University Press, 2007.

Suárez-Finlay, Eileen J. *Imposing Decency: The Politics of Sexuality and Race in Puerto Rico, 1870–1920.* Durham: Duke University Press, 1999.

Turner, Sasha. *Contested Bodies: Pregnancy, Childrearing, and Slavery in Jamaica.* Philadelphia: University of Pennsylvania Press, 2017.

Warnock, Amanda. "Gender and Identity in the Twentieth-Century Atlantic World." In *The Atlantic World, 1450–2000,* edited by Toyin Falola and Kevin D. Roberts. Bloomington: Indiana University Press, 2008, 315–337.

Contributors

JOSHUA L. BEARDEN is assistant professor of history at Los Medanos College. He has a Ph.D. in history from the University of Maryland, and his areas of research interest include race, gender, and power in the early American republic.

STEPHEN R. BERRY is associate professor of history at Simmons University, where he teaches courses in early American, Atlantic world, and American religious history. His first book, *A Path in the Mighty Waters: Shipboard Life and Atlantic Crossings,* was published by Yale University Press in 2015.

ERIKA GASSER is associate professor of history at the University of Cincinnati, where she researches and teaches the history of gender in colonial New England, early modern England, and the Anglo-Atlantic world. Her book, *Vexed with Devils: Manhood and Witchcraft in Old and New England* (2017), analyzes the role of manhood in writings about demonic possession, witchcraft, and religion from the late sixteenth century to the mid-eighteenth century. She is currently pursuing two projects, one related to the history of possession through the lens of the senses and one that examines competitive languages of manhood across the long eighteenth century.

DEBORAH HAMER is a research associate at the Omohundro Institute of Early American History and Culture in Williamsburg, Virginia. From 2015 to 2018, she was the National Endowment for the Humanities–Omohundro Institute postdoctoral fellow. She received her Ph.D. in early modern European history from Columbia University in 2014, and her dissertation was awarded the 2016 Hendricks Prize from the New Netherland Institute for best dissertation on the subject of New Netherland and the Dutch Atlantic world. Her work has received support from the New Netherland Institute, the American Jewish Historical Society, and the American Association of Netherlandic Studies. She is currently completing a book titled *Uniting Nations: Marriage, Sex, and the Foundations of the Dutch Global Empire.*

MICHELE MERICLE is a visiting scholar at the Center for Latin American and Caribbean Studies at Brown University. She earned her doctorate in Latin American history from Brown University in 2015, where her dissertation examined the religious and familial authority of crypto-Jewish women in seventeenth-century Mexico, as well as some of the social dynamics of crypto-religiosity more generally. Her current project is a new reading of Miguel Sanchez's book *Imagen de la Virgen Maria de Guadalupe.*

ALICIA L. MONROE is teaching assistant professor in African, African-American, and Diaspora Studies at the University of North Carolina at Chapel Hill. She earned a doctorate in Latin American history at Emory University. Her research, which has received support from the J. William Fulbright Fellowship and the Lapidus Center for the Historical Analysis of Transatlantic Slavery, focuses on African diaspora religious experiences in black confraternities and on the development of postemancipation Afro-Brazilian civic societies in late nineteenth- and twentieth-century Brazil.

After graduating from Tulane University, ELIZABETH C. NEIDENBACH earned her M.A. and Ph.D. in American Studies from the College of William and Mary. She has worked as a public historian for the National Park Service in Richmond, Virginia, and New Orleans, Louisiana, and currently works for The Historic New Orleans Collection. Elizabeth is completing a book to be titled *The Life and Legacy of Marie Couvent: Social Networks, Property Ownership, and the Making of a Free People of Color Community in New Orleans.* Her scholarship has been published in *Transatlantica* and the *Journal of Urban History.*

LAURA R. PRIETO is the Alumni Professor in Public Humanities and professor of history and of women's and gender studies at Simmons University. Her first book was *At Home in the Studio: The Professionalization of Women Artists in the United States* (2001). Other publications include contributions to *Competing Kingdoms: Women, Nation, Mission and American Empire* (2010) and *Women in Transnational History* (2016). Her most recent research concerns women and American imperialism in the early twentieth-century Caribbean and Pacific.

TESSA ROYNON is a senior research fellow at the Rothermere American Institute, University of Oxford, where she teaches literatures in English. She is the author of *The Cambridge Introduction to Toni Morrison* (2012); *Toni Morrison and the Classical Tradition* (2013); and *The Classical Tradition in Modern American Fiction* (2020). She is coeditor of *African Athena: New* Agendas (2011), "Ovid and Identity in the Twenty-First Century" (special issue of the *IJCT,* 2019), and *Global Ralph Ellison* (2020).

Index